"The Negro a Beast"

...or...

"In the Image of God"

...BY...

CHAS. CARROLL,

ISBN: 978-1-63923-787-6

Printed: March 2023

Published and Distributed By:
Lushena Books
607 Country Club Drive, Unit E
Bensenville, IL 60106
www.lushenabks.com

ISBN: 978-1-63923-787-6

PUBLISHER'S ANNOUNCEMENT.

In placing this book entitled "The Negro a Beast" or "In the Image of God" upon the American market, we do so knowing that there will be many learned men who will take issue with us, but while we are fully convinced of this, we are also convinced that when this book is read and its contents duly weighed and considered in an intelligent and prayerful manner, that it will be to the minds of the American people like unto the voice of God from the clouds appealing unto Paul on his way to Damascus. We have not brought out this book hurriedly and without due thought and consideration, but on the other hand we have had the manuscript under advisement for considerable time, and we have read and reread it until the ponderous, sledge hammer blows of Prof. Carroll rang in our ears until the clang and din of his arguments convinced us that it would be a sin before God and man to withhold from the reading public such an array of biblical, scientific and common sense arguments. We are placing this book before the reading public as a witness to be questioned and cross-examined by the world, and if its pages will not stand the righteous attack of criticism, then we are willing for its arguments to be trailed in the dust of oblivion. We ask the reading public to carefully peruse its pages, and if in any particular there can be produced evidence that this book is not founded upon the bible *in toto*, and scientifically digested, then we are ready to close our doors, and place over its portals in burning letters of fire, "Deluded and Misguided by an Array of Biblical Truths Scientifically Discussed."

THE PUBLISHERS.

LIST OF ILLUSTRATIONS.

TABLE OF CONTENTS.

Morning of the Creation of Man.

Heaven.

Direct Line Of Kinship With God.

ADAM AND EVE
IN THE GARDEN OF EDEN.

Where does the line of kinship between
God and Adam and Eve connect with
the Negro?

Chapter I.

The Formation of the Negro and other Beasts—then Man on the Sixth Day.

There are just two schools of learning in the world to-day, which propose to explain the existence of the heavens and the earth, with all the phenomena which characterize each. These are (1) The Scriptural School of Divine Creation, (2) The Atheistic School of Natural Development.

In discussing this subject Mr. Haeckel says: "As is now very generally acknowledged, both by the adherents of and the opponents of the theory of descent, the choice in the matter of the origin of the human race, lies between two radically different assumptions: We must either accustom ourselves to the idea that the various species of animals and plants, man

included, originated independently of each other, by
the supernatural process of a divine 'creation,' which
as such is entirely removed from the sphere of scientific
observation—or we are compelled to accept the theory
of descent in its entirety, and trace the human race,
equally with the various animals and plant species,
from an entirely simple primeval parent form. Between these two assumptions there is no third course.''
—*The Evolution of Man,* ·Vol· II·, pp, 36, 37.

The School of Creation teaches that the heaven and
the earth, with all the phenomena which characterize
each, is the product of divine creation. In direct
opposition to this scriptural school, the School of
Atheism teaches that the heaven and the earth, with
all the phenomena which characterize each, is the result of natural causes working without design to accomplish their formation.

In our investigations, with a view to decide intelligently whether the phenomena of the universe is
the product of divine creation, or whether it is the
result of natural causes, we have three reliable guides
to a correct decision. These are Science, Reason and
Revelation.

Science teaches that the lowest element of which
it has any knowledge is matter. Science also teaches
that matter exists in the material universe in just three
forms, the solid, liquid and gaseous. And inasmuch
as all bodies, celestial and terrestial, are resolvable into
matter in its gaseous state, science very properly

decides that matter in its gaseous state was the primitive condition of all bodies. Science also teaches that "matter is not self-existent."—*Guyot*. "Creation," appendix.

But to the question, from whence came matter? Science, which deals alone with second causes, gives no answer. But just at this point in our investigations, to which science leads us, and beyond which Science is powerless to guide us, reason comes to our assistance, with the assurance that, inasmuch as matter, is not self-existent, it must have been created. Hence, the very presence of matter, even in its primitive state, the gaseous, clearly demonstrates the existence of a Creator while its combination in all the varied forms, celestial and terrestrial, in which we find it to-day, bespeaks the most infinite design; and reason assures us that design can alone be formed and expressed by intelligence.

But to the question: "When and by whom was matter created?" Reason gives no answer. But just at this point in our investigation, to which Reason leads us, and beyond which Reason is powerless to guide us, and it would seem that any further advance that we may attempt must be merely speculative, Revelation generously comes to our assistance with that sublime assurance that, "In the beginning God created the heaven and the earth."

Thus Revelation, in harmony with Science, and with Reason, emphatically confirms the teachings of each, that there is a God; a personal God; a Creator, distinct from his creation; that there was a creation, and as clearly stated in the Mosaic Record, there was a definite plan of the creation; a creation successive—extending through "six days."

The initial step was the creation "in the beginning" of the lowest element—matter—as stated in the first verse; this is followed in the second verse by a correct description of matter in its primitive, or gaseous state, and this by the production of light—cosmic light—on the first day; continuing by the formation of the heavens on the second day; the separation of the "dry land" from the "waters" and the introduction of plant life on the third day; the formation of the luminaries on the fourth day; the introduction of animal life in the fish, followed by the fowl on the fifth day; the bringing fourth of the cattle, creeping things, and beasts; the whole terminating in the creation of Man "in the image of God," on the sixth day.

We are thus enabled to realize "the necessity of a direct revelation of these great fundamental truths, to which human wisdom could not attain in any other way, which without the sanction of God's word were doomed to remain simple hypotheses, incapable of proof."—*Guyot*

"In the first verse we are taught that this universe had a beginning; that it was created—and that God was its Creator. The central idea is creation. The Hebrew word is bara, translated by create. It has been doubted whether the word meant a creation, in the sense that the

world was not derived from any pre-existing material,
nor from the substance of God Himself; but the manner
in which it is here used does not seem to justify such a
doubt. For whatever be the use of the word in other
parts of the Bible, it is employed in this chapter in a
discriminating way, which is very remarkable, and
cannot but be intentional. Elsewhere, when only
transformations are meant, as in the second and fourth
days, or a continuation of the same kind of creation;
as in the land animals of the fifth day, the word asah
(make) is used. Again, it is a significant fact that in
the whole Bible where the simple form of bara is used
it is always with reference to a work made by God, but
never by man."—*Ibid.* pp. 29, 30, 31.

The Mosaic Record teaches that there is just three
creations. The first of these is described in connection
with "the heaven and the earth, in the beginning."
The second creation is described in connection with the
introduction of animal life on the fifth day; and the
third creation is described in connection with the first
appearance of Man on the sixth day.

In order that we may properly appreciate the value
of this scriptural teaching, we must first understand
what constitutes a creation, as described in the Mosaic
Record. This we understand to be the introduction
into the material universe of some element, that had no
prior existence there. This leads us to decide that,
in the remote past—in the beginning—what is now the
material universe was empty space. This condition

gave place to the creations, and formations described in the Record.

First, the creation of "the heaven and the earth," "in the beginning;" that is, the creation of matter, the material out of which "the heaven and the earth," with most of the phenomena which characterize each, were formed.

That matter was the creation described in the first verse of the Mosaic Record, is clearly proven by the correct description of matter in its primitive or gaseous state, as given in the second verse of the Record, as follows:

"And the earth was without form and void; and darkness was upon the face of the deep. And the Spirit of God moved upon the face of the waters."

Mr. Guyot says: "The matter just created was gaseous; it was without form, for the property of gas is to expand indefinitely. It was void, or empty, because, apparently, homogeneous and invisible. It was dark, because as yet inactive, light being the result of the action of physical and chemical forces not yet awakened. It was a deep, for its expansion in space, though indefinite, was not infinite, and it had dimensions. And the Spirit of God moved upon the face of that vast, inert, gaseous mass, ready to impart to it motion, and to direct all its subsequent activity, according to a plan gradually revealed by the works of the great cosmic days."—*Ibid*, p. 38.

. We are thus enabled to recognize the broad distinction which the inspired author draws between creation and formation. A creation is the first introduction into the material universe of some element that had no prior existence there. A formation is something made out of some pre-existing material; the result of a mere change wrought in the form of the original element.

"The era of progress opens with the first day's work. At God's command, movement begins, and the first result is the production of light. This was no creation, but a simple manifestation of the activity of matter; for, according to modern physics, heat and light are but different intensities of the vibratory motions of matter."—*Guyot.*

The production of the heavens on the second day, was not a creation, and is not described as such; they were simply formations out of the original creation, matter. The introduction of plant life on the third day was not a creation, and is not described as such. God simply commanded the earth to bring it forth. The luminaries which made their appearance on the fourth day, were not creations and are not so described; they were mere formations out of the original creation—matter.

From the creation of matter "in the beginning," throughout the first four days, the work of God was confined to the handling of matter. But the fifth day is distinguished from its predecessors by the introduction, on that day, of a new element, which made its first appearance in the material universe in combination with matter, as presented in the physical organism of the fish, which is described as follows: "And God created the great stretched out sea monsters; and all living creatures that creep, which the waters breed abundantly after their kind."

It is the universal opinion of theologians, and of such scientists as accept the Bible as true, that this creation was that of animal life. To this view, which is at once opposed to the teachings of scripture and of science, we are compelled to dissent. Animal life is not a creation. Life itself is not a creation; neither plant life nor animal life; and it is not so described in the Mosaic Record.

Aside from the teachings of scripture and of science our personal observation teaches us that there is not such difference between plant life and animal life as would justify us in deciding that plant life was merely a combination of the elements inherent in matter, and that animal life was a creation distinct from matter. Each has its germ, "containing the same elements in the same proportions." (Dana.) Each has its circulating fluid; each its forminative period; each its youth; each its maturity; each its decline and final dissolution. Mr. Dana says: "The vegetable and animal kingdoms are the opposite, but mutually dependent sides or parts of one system of life." (See Manual of Geology, p. 115). Hence, if life was a new element in the material universe, it would have been described as a creation, when plant life, which is merely "one side or part" of the "system," made its first appearance on the globe. But inasmuch as plant life, the first "side or part" of the "system," to make its appearance is not described as a creation it would be at once irrational, unscientific, and unscriptural, to decide that animal life the other "side or part" of "the system," which afterwards made its appearance, was a creation. In other words, if the "system of life" was a creation distinct from matter, it would have been so described at its first appearance in the plant.

The strength of our position is clearly demonstrated by the more detailed description of the subject given in the fourth and fifth verses of the second chapter of Genesis, as follows:

"These are the generations of the heavens and the earth, when they were created, in the day that the Lord God made the earth and the heavens; and every plant of the field before it was in the earth, and every herb of the field before it grew."

We are thus plainly taught, that the elements of plant life are simply parts of the original creation—matter. Hence, they existed in matter prior to the formation of matter into the earth. Thus by creating in matter the elements of life, "the Lord God" made "every plant of the field before it was in the earth, and every herb of the field before it grew."

Inasmuch as plant life and animal life are "mutually dependent sides or parts of one system of life,"

whose elements are identical, it follows, that the elements of animal life, like those of plant life, were a part
of the original creation—matter.   And that they existed
in matter prior to the formation of matter into the earth.
Hence the combination of these original elements into
plants and animals, and the first appearance of these on
the globe in obedience to God's command, were not
creations, and are not described as such in the Mosaic
Record.

That the elements of life—both plant and animal
life—were parts of the original creation—matter and
that they existed in matter prior to the formation of
matter into the earth, is further shown by the identity
of language used by God in commanding the earth and
the waters to bring forth plant and animal life, as
follows:

"And God said, Let the earth bring forth grass, the
herb yielding seed, and the fruit tree yielding fruit
after his kind, whose seed is in itself, upon the earth;
and it was so.

"And God said, Let the waters bring forth abnud-
antly the moving creatures that hath life."

"And God said, Let the earth bring forth the living
creature after his kind; cattle, and creeping things, and
beasts of the earth after his kind; and it was so.   (See
Gen. ii, 11, 20, 24).

What "was so"? Why, just as in deference to
Divine will, the waters of the Red Sea parted, and stood
mountain high on either side, while Israel passed over

"dry shod," so, in obedience to divine command did the earth and the waters combine the elements of plant and animal life, and "bring forth" plants" and animals "after his kind."

Since the "system of life" is not a creation, what new element described as a creation made its appearance on the fifth day, in combination with matter as presented in the physical organism of the fish? To answer this question intelligently we must first ascertain what character pre-eminently distinguishes not only the highest but the lowest order of animals from the plant.

Mr. Dana says; "Plants have no consciousness of self, or of other existences; animals are conscious of an outer world, and even the lowest show it by avoiding obstacles."—*Ibid*, p. 116.

The physical organism of the fish was simply a combination of elements of matter. But consciousness, which made its first appearance in the material universe on the fifth day, was an element distinct from matter. It was not present in light, nor in the heavens, nor in the plants, nor in the luminaries. It was a new element. Hence it is properly described as a creation.

What is consciousness? Mr. Webster defines it as "The knowledge of sensations, or of what passes in one's own mind." In support of this, he refers to Locke, Reid, and the encyclopedias. (See Unabridged Dictionary.) A moment's reflection should convince us that mind is an element distinct from matter.

Since consciousness is always associated with mind, and is never found in separation from it, we must decide that it is one of its attributes; and that its presence clearly demonstrates the existence of mind. Hence this new element, described as a creation which made its appearance in the material universe on the fifth day, in combination with matter as presented in the physical structure of the lowest order of animal—the fish —was mind, in its simplest form.

From the introduction of the fish, God handles this combination of matter and mind on up through the different grades of animals until the creation of man. The evidence of this is found in the fact that, though the higher orders of fowls and beasts possess more highly developed physical and mental structures than the fish, the difference between them is merely one of degree. They present no new element, but, like the fish, are simply a combination of matter and mind. Hence, they are not described as creations.

The belief is widely disseminated that mind is peculiar to man. Hence, man alone possesses the faculty of reason; and that the lower animals possess mere instinct. The fallacy of this belief has long since been demonstrated. Mr. Darwin says: "Of all the faculties of the human mind, it will, I presume, be admitted that reason stands at the summit. Only a few persons now dispute that animals possess some power of reasoning. Animals may constantly be seen to pause, deliberate, and resolve. It is a significant fact that the more the habits of any animal are studied by a naturalist, the more he attributes to reason and the less to unlearned instincts.'' For futher information of the existence of mind, and the display of its various attributes in the fish and fowl and beast, see the works of Curvier, Darwin, Quatrefages, Hartman and others.

When the fish and fowl and beast were all made after their kind, God then said, "Let us make man in our own image after our likness. * * * So God created man in his own image, in the image of God created he him; male and female created he them.''—Gen. i, 26-27.

In the more detailed description of the creation of man given in the 2d chapter of Genesis, verse 7, we are taught that "The Lord God formed man out of the dust of the ground, and breathed into his nostrils the breath of life; and man became a living soul.'' "The dust of the ground,'' "out'' of which "The Lord God formed man.'' was a part of the original creation—matter. We are thus plainly taught that the physical structure of man was simply a formation out of matter; and like the fish and fowl and beast, man received his animal life from matter. Hence, when his physical and mental organisms were completed, man, like the lower animals, was simply a combination of matter and mind.

Geological research demonstrates that death—physical death—entered the world almost simultaneously with life plant life. And that it followed closely upon the intro- duction of animal life. Since man, like the lower animals derived his animal life from matter, it follows that his physical and mental organisms, like theirs, must be subject to accident, disease, decay, and final dissolution. Hence, the idea that Adam would have lived on indefinitely, and perhaps never have experienced physical death, had he not violated Divine law, is too absurd for serious consideration. Man like the lower orders of animal life. and like the plants has his germ, his formative period, his youth, his maturity, his decline, and his physical dissolution.

" The breath of life" which God "breathed into" man's "nostrils" was spiritual, immortal life; life which, like God's life, never dies; " and man became a living soul." This spiritual, immortal life—this living soul— was a new element in the material universe. Hence, man, with whose physical and mental structure it was combined, is properly described as a creation.

Thus, the three creations—matter, mind and spiritual life—were combined in man; that sublime creature whom God honored in the creation by the bestowal of his likeness and his image, and to whom he confided dominion over the works of his hands. Well might David exclaim in describing God's creation of man: "Thou mad'st him a little lower than the angels, and has crowned him with glory and honor."

In obedience to Divine command, the waters and the earth brought forth the fish and fowl and beast after their kind. But God created man in his own image, upon a plan carefully matured and as carefully preserved in his "book." Well may we exclaim in the language of the Psalmist: "I will praise thee, for I am fearfully and wonderfully made; marvelous are thy works; and that my soul knoweth right well. My substance was not hid from thee when I was made in secret and curiously wrought in the lowest parts of the earth. Thine eyes did see my substance, yet being imperfect; and in thy book all my members were written, which in continuance were fashioned, when as yet there was none of them."—Ps. cxxxix.

Prior to the creation of man, there was no connecting link, no tie of kinship between the creator and his creation. But when "the Lord God formed man out of the dust of the ground," this "dust of the ground" being a part of the original creation—matter—and "breathed into his nostrils the breath of life"—spiritual, immortal life—man became "a living soul." This spiritual, immortal life, this living soul, was a part of the substance of God. Hence its combination with matter and with mind, as presented in Adam, formed the connecting link, the link of kinship between the creator and his creature. Thus, Adam became, literally and truly, as he is described in scripture, the son of God. (Luke iii, 38.) Adam was as literally and truly the son of God as was Isaac the son of Abraham. And the descendants of Adam, of pure Adamic stock, are sons and daughters of God, throughout all time, just as the descendants, of Abraham of pure Abrahamic stock are sons and daughters of Abraham throughout all time. But in drawing this comparison we should be careful not to confound processes with results. The combination of spiritual, immortal life—a living soul—itself a part of the substance of God, with matter and with mind as presented in Adam's physical, mental and spiritual organisms, was the result of a creative act of the creator; while the presence of these characteristic in Isaac, himself a descendant of Adam, was the result of a generaative act of the creature.

Further evidence that Adam was the son of God is found in the fact that when our Saviour was on earth he recognized the pure-blooded descendants of Adam as his brethren and sisters. (See Matt. xii. 49; also Mark iii, 35.)

The completion of the life system of man, by the creation of the female, did not immediately follow that of the male. We are taught that "the Lord God planted a garden eastward in Eden; and there he put the man whom he had formed." (See Gen. ii.:8.) What period of time intervened between the creation of man and that of woman we have no means of ascertaining. However, we are led to decide that it was one of considerable length; for it was in this interval that "Adam gave names to all cattle, and to the fowl of the air, and to every beast of the field." (See Gen. ii.:20). The successful accomplishment of this great task, requiring the highest intelligence and the finest discriminating power, would have been creditable to a Cuvier or a Darwin. Hence, Adam's successful accomplishment of it clearly demonstrates his towering intellectuality.

In this early dawn of Adamic history, the great Architect of the universe looked out upon his yet unfinished creation and said : "It is not good that man should be alone; I will make him a helpmeet for him. * * * And the Lord God caused a deep sleep to fall upon Adam, and he slept; and he took one of his ribs, and closed up the flesh instead thereof. And the rib, which the Lord God had taken from man, made he a woman, and brought her unto the man."

We of modern times are wont to boast our greater enlightenment as compared with that of preceding ages; and as an evidence of it we proudly point to the sacredness of marriage, woman's honorable position, and her higher education. But a glimpse of very ancient history suffices to convince us that this is but a reformatory movement, indicating a disposition to return to primitive conditions. Among the Toltecs, who developed one of the great civilizations of America in ancient times, "the position of woman was honorable." Among the Aryans, who thousands of years ago developed the splendid civilization of ancient India, "woman was held in respect, and marriage was sacred." And there are beautiful hymns in existence to-day which were composed and written by the ladies and queens of Aryans.

When we trace to its fountain source this elevated, ennobling character in man, his respectful devotion to woman, it leads us to the creation. This noble character found its first expression in the first recorded utterance of Adam, upon his reception of that lovely helpmeet whom God had made for him. "This is now bone of my bones, and flesh of my flesh; she shall be called woman, because she was taken out of man. Therefore shall a man leave his father and his mother and cleave unto his wife; and they shall be one flesh."

We would vainly search the annals of the world for a sentiment more chaste, more elevated, and more devotional than this, to the fair sex of our mother; not one of the gallant knights who wielded a lance in the age of chivalry ever gave expression to a sentiment more chivalrous toward the lady of his choice, whose feelings and whose honor he stood pledged to defend with his life.

Man, the male, and woman, the female, are "the opposite but mutually dependent sides or parts" of the spiritual life system of the globe; and the presence of each is essential to the existence and perpetuation of the system. Hence, "it is not good that man should be alone."

In addition to this, the presence of woman has exerted a beneficial influence upon the man throughout the ages that have passed. All history, sacred and profane, and all tradition, ancient and modern, and all observation and experience combine to teach us:

"That man is the cloud of coming storm,
    Dark as the raven's murky plume,
Save where the sunbeams light and warm
Of woman's soul and woman's form
    Gleams brightly o'er the gath'ring gloom."

While in all that is angelic, woman stands peerless in the realm of created things. And when we'd seek some symbol of her, even in the floral kingdom, that wondrous exhibition of the most exquisite taste, displayed by the great Artist of the universe, we find perhaps her fittest symbol in that matchless combination of beauty and fragrance, the night-blooming cereus, which, while generously contributing its odors to enrich the world's wealth of fragrance, modestly conceals its beauties 'neath the veil of night.

Thus it is shown that man is a creation as separate and distinct from the fish and fowl and beast as he is from the plant or the planet. Hence, we might with just as much propriety consider man a member of the sidereal kingdom as to consider him simply a member of the animal kingdom. It would be no more irrational, no more unscientific, if you please, and certainly no more unscriptural, to consider man an undeveloped planet than to consider him merely "a highly developed animal."

In harmony with the teachings of the Mosaic Record, St. Paul says: "All flesh is not the same flesh ; but there is one kind of flesh of men, another flesh of beasts, another of fishes, and another of birds." (See I. Cor. xv. 39,) Since there are four different kinds of flesh, each separate and distinct from the others, it follows that even the flesh of man is a "kind of flesh" distinct from that of the fish or

fowl or beast. Hence we are emphatically taught
that there is no kinship between man and the animals;
but that the kinship is between God and man.

We should also note the broad distinction in point
of numbers and variety which God made in the creation between the representatives of the spiritual life
of the globe, as presented in man, and the representatives of mere animal life, and those of plant
life. The plants and the fish and fowl and beast
were all made in great numbers and in great variety.
While there are such resemblances between certain
plants, and between certain animals, as justifies the
naturalist in deciding that they are of the same
family or species, there are such differences between
certain members of these families or species as justifies the naturalist in deciding that they are different
races. These, whether of plant or fish or fowl or
beast, were all made after their kind. But not so
with man. Man was not made after any kind, but
was created "in the image of God." Neither was
man made in great numbers and varieties, but was
created a single pair. Hence, unlike the plants and
fish and fowl and beast, man was not made in species
and races, but is a distinct creation. Had God desired man, like the plants and animals, to be a
species, divisible into races, no good reason could be
advanced as to why he did not so create them.
Had there been a plurality of gods, man would
have been created a species, comprising a greater or

less number of men; and this species of man would
have been divided into different races of men, each of
whose racial characters would have corresponded with
the characters of the god in whose image they were
made. But, inasmuch as there is only one God, so
was there created in his image just one man, whom
he called "Adam, the son of God." And not only is
man distinguished from the mere animals by his
possession of spiritual, immortal life—a living soul,
itself a part of the substance of God—but even his
flesh is a different kind of flesh from that of the fish
or fowl or beast. (See I. Cor. xv, 39.) And when,
in order that the Adamic creation should be enabled
to perpetuate its existence, and increase its numbers
on earth, God decided to "make a helpmeet" for
Adam, it is significant that he made the female man
out of the male man. Thus completed and perfected
by the presence of woman, it was possible for man to
beget offspring, to whom he would transmit his physical, mental and spiritual characters, and be thus
enabled to execute those divine laws: "Be fruitful
and multiply, and replenish the earth and subdue it;
and have dominion over the fish of the sea, and over
the fowl of the air, and over every living thing that
moveth upon the earth." (Gen. i, 28.)

Inasmuch as man was created the son of God,
was made "a little lower than the angels," and was
assigned to dominion over the works of God's hands,
it follows that he is not a development from a lower

form ; and it also follows that he could never develop into a higher or more perfect form while he lived on the earth.

In this professedly Christian age we hear much of a "human species" which is divisible into "races of men." In view of the plain teaching of the Bible that man is a distinct creation, it is pertinent to inquire where the modern world obtained this absurd idea that man is a "species" which is divisible into "races of men"—from the scriptures? We have vainly sought from Genesis to Revelation for the slightest hint of the existence of such a thing as a "human species" or a "race of men."

The terms "species" and "races" are scientific terms; they belong to natural science, and are used to describe what is termed "natural relations." But the terms "human species" and "races of men" belong exclusively to the atheistic school of Natural Development, which teaches that man is a highly developed species of ape—the human species—and that this human species of ape is divisible into five or more "races of men." On the other hand, the terms "tribes," "nations" and "empires" are political terms, and are used to describe political relations. And it is a significant fact, and one which the professed Christian would do well to observe, that these political terms—tribes, nations and empires—are invariably employed by the inspired authors in describing the relations of men. The terms "human species" and "races of men" are conspicuous in scripture by their absence.

The first reference to the "races of men" which we find in ancient history is found in the fragment of Plato's history of the lost continent of Atlantis. Plato lived 300 years B. C. He was the descendant of Solon, the great lawgiver of Athens. Solon spent ten years of his life in Egypt. In his discussions with the Egyptian priests Solon first heard of Atlantis and of the records concerning it to be found in the sacred registers of Egypt. Permission having been granted to examine them, Solon obtained from the sacred registers the necessary data from which to write in Greek a history of Atlantis. But before completing his work, Solon died. It seems that in the course of time his data or his manuscript fell into the hands of Plato, who decided to write a history of Atlantis. But after writing a description of the continent, its population, products, religion, wealth, culture, power, etc., Plato died, leaving a mere fragment of what, if completed, would have been one of the most invaluable contributions to the literature of the world.

The sacred registers of Egypt from which the data of Plato's history of Atlantis were obtained were far more ancient than the Bible. They were so much more ancient than any historical records of the Greeks, that an Egyptian priest said to Solon, "You have no antiquity of history, and no history of antiquity." Throughout Plato's narrative frequent allusion is made to "the human race" and to the "race of men." These atheistic terms could only have originated in the atheistic school of evolution. And they are always employed by the advocates of the theory of man's descent from the ape. The presence of these terms in the sacred registers of ancient Egypt clearly indicates that "The Theory of Descent" was universally taught in perhaps as systematized and elaborated a form in that remote period as it is in our day. And that in the dark ages which followed the crucifixion of the Saviour, this theory, in its systematized, elaborated form, in common with all literature, art, and science, was lost amid the crash of falling empires. But unfortunately the pernicious influences of this infamous theory upon the minds of men, together with its atheistic terms, survived its literature, and was handed down in a traditional way from generation to generation.

Thus we find that the "Theory of Descent," so far from being a product of the Christian era, was an old, demoralizing, degrading theory at the advent of our Saviour. And that so far from its having been first outlined by Linnæus, or Lamark, or Blumenbach, or to whomsoever belongs the discredit, and more recently systematized and elaborated by Darwin and his disciples, it actually antedates the Christian era thousands of years. It was the pernicious influence of this atheistic theory which was advocated by the

33

idolatrous authors who lived and taught prior to the
advent of the Saviour which so demoralized and degraded man and removed him so far from his God as
to necessitate the sacrifice of the Son of God to redeem
him.

Upon the revival of learning in modern time, the
theory of evolution was again systematized, and is
now as universally disseminated among men as it was
in ancient time.

But who are they, and to what school do they
belong, who would teach us that man is merely an
animal and must take his position in "the zoological
system" with the rest of the animals; that man is
simply a highly developed species of ape—"the human
species"—and that this "human species" of ape is
divisible into five "races of men"—the Negro, the
Malay, the Indian, the Mongolian, and the Caucasian?
Darwin, Haeckel, Huxley, Tyndall, Spencer, Voltaire,
and their disciples; that class of philosophers who
would teach us the existence of a universe without a
God, a creation without a Creator, man without religion, and the world without a Sabbath or a Bible.

How do these philosophers treat God's word, which
the devotees of "enlightened Christianity" profess to
so much revere? Ordinarily, in attempting to explain
the existence of "the heaven and the earth," with all
the phenomena which characterize each, they make
no reference to scripture, but treat it with silent contempt. The Bible occupies no place in their theory.

[3]

But when compelled to allude to it from any cause, they denounce it as a Semitic myth, a Hebrew legend, or a Jewish tradition.

Further evidence of the antiquity of "The Theory of Descent," and of its prevalence in the days of the Apostles, is shown by the great opposing declaration of St. Paul that "all flesh is not the same flesh; but there is one kind of flesh of men, another flesh of beasts, another of fishes, and another of birds." A careful comparison of this teaching with that of "The Theory of Development" must convince us that this inspired declaration was a blow aimed directly at "The Theory of Development," which teaches that the most complex organism is merely a development from the most simple. Hence, "all flesh" is akin.

What is most directly opposed to the inspired declaration of the great apostle that "all flesh is not the same flesh?" Necessarily we must decide that it is the theory that all flesh is the same flesh. What theory is this? It is the theory which teaches that animal life originated in the monera by "spontaneous generation" out of simple compounds of carbon, oxygen, hydrogen, and nitrogen." And that from this little monera, the lowest form of animal life, on up to and including man, all flesh is the same. It-is the theory which teaches, in direct opposition to the Bible, that man is merely a highly developed species of ape—the "human species"—and that this "human species" of ape is divisible into "five races of men." It is the Theory of Development.

What is most directly opposed to the inspired declaration of the great apostle that "there is one kind of flesh of men, another flesh of beasts, another of fishes, and another of birds, making in all four different kinds of flesh, as separate and distinct from each other as if the one made its first appearance upon and inhabited the earth, the other the Moon, the other Jupiter, and the other Mars? Necessarily we must decide that it is the theory which teaches that, from the little monera on up to and including man, there is just one flesh in different stages of development. It is the Theory of Development.

How do you professed believers in God's word— you professed followers of the Saviour—you professed admirers of St. Paul—how do you treat this atheistic theory which God did all in his power, short of physical force, even to the sacrifice of his Son, to blot from the face of the earth; this infamous theory which Christ died to obliterate from the minds of men; this blasphemous theory which St. Paul, with his accustomed force and skill, dealt what will yet prove its death blow? How do you professed Christians treat this ante-scriptural theory that man is merely a highly developed species of ape—the "human species"—and that this "human species" is divisible into five "races of men"—the Negro, the Malay, the Indian, the Mongolian, and the Caucasian? You teach it at your fireside, you teach it in the social circle, you teach it on the highways and on the by-ways, you teach it in the kindergarten, you teach it in the Sabbath school, you teach it in your higher institutions of learning, you teach it through the press, you teach it from the lecture platform, and Oh! blasphem of blasphemies! you teach it at the altar!

And what is the result? To say nothing of the disastrous results which must inevitably accrue to you in eternity from your adherence to and your promulgation of this infamous theory in every relation in life from the cradle to the grave, what is the result to you in time? With those Divine promises ever held out imploringly to you—"Ask and ye shall receive," "and no good thing will he withhold from those who walk up rightly;" you pray for a rain, and you get a drouth; you pray for fair weather, and you get a flood; you pray for prosperity, and want stares you in the face; you pray for happiness, and wretchedness and misery and degradation and disappointment and grief are your constant companions from the cradle to the grave; you pray for peace, and you get a war. Is God unable or unwilling to redeem his promises, or do you fail to walk uprightly?

It cannot be disproven that the theory now universally taught that man is a "species" divisible into "races" is an inseparable part of the theory of man's descent from the ape. Neither can it be denied that it is directly opposed to the plain teaching of the Bible that man, unlike the fish and fowl and beast, was created a single pair; hence, is not divisible into

"species" and "races." The effort of modern Christianity to mix this atheistic theory that man is a
"species" divisible into "races" with the scriptural
teaching that man is a distinct creation, "in the
image of God," must prove disastrous both in time and
in eternity. Take any two different elements and
mix them, and the product is neither the one nor the
other of the originals; each of the originals in their
purity no longer exist; and the product resulting from
their mixture is merely a compound in which is
blended the characters peculiar to each. So it is in
this case. The teachings of the Bible that man is a
distinct creation, "in the image of God," and the theory that man is a "species of ape divisible into races
of men" are opposites. Hence, the effort of professed
Christians to mix the two has resulted in the destruction of Christianity from the earth; and also the destruction of the theory of Natural Development, to the
extent to which it has been mixed with scripture.
The theory of Natural Development in its purity is
only found among those who reject the Bible in its
entirety. And pure Christianity will never again
shed its radiance upon man's pathway to the grave
until the church as an organization, and each individual member of it utterly repudiates the atheistic theory of Natural Development, with all its demoralizing
teachings, its degrading influences, and its misleading
terms.

Man alone was created "in the image of God;" the fish and fowl and beast, like the plants, were made after their kinds. Man alone is responsible to God for his acts; the lower animals are responsible to man, under whose "dominion" they were placed in the creation, and into whose "hands" God delivered them after their preservation from the deluge. Man alone in his "first estate" was clothed with Divine authority to "have dominion" and he alone fell from this high "estate" by his wanton violation of Divine ,law. Hence, man alone is the subject of redemption.

Man was created "in the image of God"—male and female—a single pair—distinct from the fish and fowl and beast, which, like the plants, were made after their kind. This is the teaching of the scriptural narrative of Divine creation.

Man is a highly developed species of ape—the human species—and this human species is divisible into five races of men—the Negro, the Malay, the Indian, the Mongolian, and the Caucasian. This is the teaching of the atheistic theory of Natural Development, which thrusts God aside and declares that man, the most complex organism, is merely a development from the most simple. Hence, according to this theory, man traces his pedigree back through the beast and fowl and fish to the lowest form of animal.

The absolute conflict between the teachings of these opposing schools—Divine Creation and Natural Development—is apparent. Hence, if that most com-

plex organism, man, is merely a development from
the most simple; if he has descended from the ape,
and is simply a highly developed species of ape—the
human species—and this "human species" is divisible
into five "races of men," it follows that he was not
created "in the image of God"—a single pair—and his
flesh is not, as Paul tells us, a different kind of flesh
from that of the fish and fowl and beast, but is akin
to it.

If, on the other hand, that most complex organism, man, was created "in the image of God"—a single pair—and if, as Paul tells us, his flesh is a different kind of flesh from that of the fish and fowl and
beast, then he is not a development from the most simple organism, and there is no kinship between man
and the animals.

Let us now compare the teachings of the gospel
with reference to the origin and mission of the Saviour
and the ultimate basis of the gospel, with the teaching
of the modern Christian church upon this subject, and
the ultimate basis of the church.

We are taught by the gospel that Jesus Christ was
the Son of God, and that he came into the world and
suffered and died to redeem fallen man. What is the
ultimate basis of this teaching? The narrative of
Divine creation, which teaches that man was "created" "in the image of God"—a single pair—distinct
from the fish and fowl and beast, which, like the
plants, were made after their kind. (St. John i.)

In apparent harmony with the teaching of the gospel, the modern Christian church teaches that Jesus Christ was the son of God; and that he came into the world and suffered and died to redeem fallen man. But what is the ultimate basis of this teaching of the modern Christian church? The theory that man is a species (and of course if he is a species of anything, he is a species of ape)—the human species—and that this human species is divisible into five races of men— the Negro, the Malay, the Indian, the Mongolian, and the Caucasian. Thus it cannot be disproven that the teachings of the modern Christian church find their ultimate basis, not on the scriptural narrative of Divine creation, but upon the atheistic theory of Natural Development.

Evidently the church which Jesus Christ established on the narrative of Divine creation has been transferred to the theory of Natural Development. Surely nothing could be more absurd, nothing more blasphemous than the attempt on the part of professed Christians to confuse the teachings and terms of these opposing schools.

The product resulting from the mixture of the teachings of these opposing schools is what its devotees are pleased to term "Enlightened Christianity." But a glance at its atheistic teachings, its degrading influences, and its misleading terms, suffice to convince us that it is merely a counterfeit, in which is blended and distorted the teachings peculiar to scripture with those peculiar to atheism. Énlightened Christianity, indeed! How enlightened, and enlightening, is this modern Christianity which, under the influence of the atheistic theory of Natural Development, upon which it is based, ignores the broad distinction which God made in the creation between man and the ape, and places them in the same family as different races of one species of animal.

Christ.

CHRIST – THE SON OF GOD.
Man was created in the image of God.
Is the negro in the image of God's son – Christ?

Chapter II.

Biblical and Scientific Facts Demonstrating that the Negro is not an Offspring of the Adamic Family.

The White, the highest, and the Negro the lowest of the so-called "five races of men," present the strongest contrast to each other in their physical and mental characters; and in their modes of life, habits, customs, language, manners, gestures, etc.

White is not a color; neither is black a color; yet the white, colorless complexion of the white, finds its strongest contrast in the black, colorless complexion of the Negro.

The long, fine, silken hair of the White, finds its strongest contrast in the short, coarse, woolly hair of the Negro. Each individual hair of the white "is cylindrical." Hence, "its section is circular." In striking contrast to that of the white, each individual hair of the Negro "is flattened like a tape." Hence, its section is oval." (Haeckel, *Hist. of Creation*, Vol. 11, pp. 414, 415.)

The relatively short, broad skull of the White, finds its strongest contrast in the long, narrow skull of the Negro. This length and narrowness of the Negro's skull is a character of the ape. Winchell says, "A certain relative width of skull appears to be connected with energy, force, and executive ability." Hence the narrowness of the Negro's skull denotes his lack of energy, force, and executive ability. This is significant, when considered in connection with the design of God in creating man, and the great task to which he was assigned in the Creation. Winchell quoting from the measurements of Broca says, (1) "The face of the Negro occupies the greater portion of the total length of the head. (2) His anterior cranium is less developed than his posterior, relatively to that of the White. (3) His occipital foramen is situated more backward in relation to the total projection of the head, but more forward in relation to the cranium only. In other words, the Negro has the cerebral cranium less developed than the white; but its posterior is more developed than the anterior." (*Preademites*, pp. 169, 170.) "In the Negro skull the sphenoid does not, generally, reach the parietals, the coronal suture joining the margin of the temporals. The skull is very thick and solid, and is often used

for butting, as is the custom of rams. It is flattened
on the top, and well adapted for carrying burdens."
(*Ibid*, p. 171.) The cephalic index * * * among
Noachitis (whites), ranges from 75 to 83 degrees;
among negroes, from 71 to 76 degrees. (*Ibid*, p.
246.)

In discussing cranial capacity, Dr. Winchell says,
"Capacity of cranium is universally recognized as a
criterion of psychic power. No fact is better established than the general relation of intellect to weight
of brain. Welker has shown that the brains of
twenty-six men of high intellectual rank surpassed
the average weight by fourteen per cent. Of course
quality of brain is an equally important factor; and
hence not a few men with brains even below the
average have distinguished themselves for scholar-
ship and executive ability. The Noachites possess a
mean capacity of 1,500 cubic centimeters. * * *
Among Negroes, 1,360 cubic centimeters." (*Ibid*, p.
246.)

"The average weight of the European brain,
males and females, is 1340 grammes; that of the
Negro is 1178; of the Hottentot, 974, and of the Australian, 907. The significance of these comparisons
appears when we learn that Broca, the most eminent
of French anthropologists, states that when the
European brain falls below 978 grammes (mean of
males and females), the result is idiocy. In this
opinion Thurman coincides. The color of the Negro

brain is darker than that of the White, and its density
and texture are inferior. The convolutions are fewer
and more simple, and, Agassiz and others long ago
pointed out, approximate those of the quadrumama.
(*Ibid*, pp. 249, 251.)

The atheism, which, for ages has enveloped the
world in darkness, erroneously teaches that all bipeds,
with articulate speech, the erect posture, a well developed hand and foot, and the ability to make and
handle tools, are men. Hence, no table exists, in
which the average brain weight of the adult male, of
pure Adamic stock is given. But, we feel assured,
that this average may safely be placed at not less
than 1,500 grammes. Winchell, Topinard, Quatrefages, and other scientists give the following table of
"comparative weights of brains compiled from observations collected by Sanford B. Hunt, made during
the civil war in the United States."

"State of hybridization.	Wt. of Brain. Grammes.
24 Whites	1,424
25 three-parts white	1,390
47 half-white or mulattoes	1,334
51 one-quarter white	1,319
95 one-eighth white	1,308
22 one-sixteenth white	1,280
141 pure Negroes	1,331"

(Anthropology)

Had these estimates extended to every class of
people in the United States the average of whites
would doubtless have been raised to 1,500 grammes.

This average is far exceeded by many individual whites; for example:

Weight of brain.

grms.   oz.

Cuvier—63 years old—Naturalist......1829.96 (64.54)
Byron—36 years old—Poet...........1807.00 (63.73)
Lejisene Dirichlet—50 years—Mathe-
    matician.................... ....1520.00 (53.61)
(Quatrefages, *Human Species*, p. 411.)

In the table from which the above weights were taken, the brain weight of several distinguished individuals are given which fall below the average. This indicates that the weight and volume of the brain, is not the only factor to be considered in determining the relative intelligence of individuals. Quatrefages, while admitting "that there is a certain relation between the development of the intelligence and the volume and weight of the brain," says, "But, at the same time, we must allow that the material element, that which is appreciable to our senses, is not the only one which we must take into account, for behind it lies hidden an unknown quantity an x, at present undetermined and only recognizable by its effects." (*Ibid*, p. 413.) This is a truth which is easily demonstrated by comparing the achievements of the white, with those of the Negro, and the mixed-bloods.

The relatively short, narrow jaw of the White finds its strongest contrast in the long, broad jaw of the Negro. This is another character of the ape which the Negro presents. The jaws of the Negro, like those of the lower apes, "extend forward at the

expense of the symmetry of the face, and backward at
the expense of the brain cavity." Quartrefages, says:
"It is well known that in the Negro, the entire face,
and especially the lower portion, projects forward. In
the living subject it is exaggerated by the thickness
of the lips. But it is also apparent in the skull, and
constitutes one of its most striking characters." It is
this trait which is opposed to the orthognathism of
the White. (*Ibid*, p.p. 390, 391.)

Dr. Winchell says, "The amount of prognathism
is another marked criterion of organic rank. One
method of expressing this is by means of 'auricular
radii,' or distances from the opening of the ear to the
roots of the teeth, and to other parts of the head.
Among Europeans, the distance to the base of the
upper incisors is 99, but among negroes it averages
114. On the contrary, the average distance to the top
of the head is, among Europeans, 112; but among
negroes, 110. The distance to the upper edge of the
occipital bone is, among Europeans, 104; among negroes, 104. The measurements prove that the Negro
possesses more face, and particularly of jaws, and less
brain above. Other measurements furnish a similar
result; and show, also, that the development of the
posterior brain, in relation to the anterior, is greater
in the Negro. Prognathism is otherwise expressed
by means of the 'facial angle,' or general slope of the
face from the forehead to the jaws, when compared
with a horizontal plane. Among the Noachites, the

facial line is nearest perpendicular, giving an angle of 77 degrees to 81 degrees. Among negroes, it averages only 67 degrees." (*Preademites*, p. 247.)

The prominent chin of the White finds its strongest contrast in the retreating chin of the Negro. This is another character of the ape which the Negro presents. Winchell says, "The retreating contour of the chin as compared with the European, approximates the Negro to the chimpanzee and lower mammals." (*Ibid*, p. 251.)

The front teeth of the White, set perpendicularly in the jaw, find their strongest contrast in the front teeth of the Negro, which set slanting in the jaw. This is another character of the ape which the Negro presents. Haeckel describes as Prognathi those "whose jaws, like those of the animal snout, strongly project, and whose front teeth, therefore, slope in front; and men with straight teeth Orthognathi, whose jaws project but little and whose front teeth stand perpendicularly."

The relatively thin lips of the White find their strongest contrast in the thick, puffed lips of the Negro. This is another character of the ape which the Negro presents. In referring to the differences presented by the mouth, in the so-called races of men, Quatrefages says, "The thousand differences of form and dimensions which exhibit, from the Negro of Guina with his enormous and, as it were, turned-up lips, to certain Aryan or Semitic whites can neither be measured nor described. * * * 'It may, however, be remarked, that the thickness of the lips is very marked in all negroes, in consequence of their projection in front of the maxillary bones and the teeth. The mouth of the Negro presents . another character which seems to me to have been generally neglected, and which has always struck me. It is a kind of clamminess at the outer border of the commissures, and seems to prevent the small movements of the corner of the mouth which play such an important part in the physiognomy. The dissections of M. Hamy have explained these facts. They have shown that in the negroes the muscles of this region are both more developed and less distinct than in the whites." (*The Human Species*, p. 367.)

The prominent nose of the White finds its strongest contrast in the flat nose of the Negro, which has the appearance of having been crushed in. This is another character of the ape which the Negro presents.

In contrasting the Negro skull and face with those of the White, Topinard says, "The Norman verticalis is of an elliptical shape. The supra-iniac portion of the occipital is frequently projecting, its portions are flat and vertical, the curved temporal lines describe an arc corresponding with the mass of temporal muscles which are inserted beneath them; the temporal shell itself is longer than that of the White. The frontal is articulated frequently with the

temporal; the greater wings of the sphenoid are consequently not articulated with the parietal. The
cranial sutures are more simple than in the white
type, and are obliterated sooner (Gratiolet). The
squamo-temporal and the spheno-parietal frequently
form a horizontal straight line. The forehead is narrow at the base, sometimes receding and rather low,
sometimes straight and bulging (bombe) at the summit. The frontal bosses are often confluent, or replaced by a single and median protuberance. * * *
'The orbits, moreover, are microsemes, that is to say,
short from above downwards. * * * 'The eyeballs
are close to the head, and the palpebral apertures are
nevertheless small and are on the same horizontal
line. * * * 'The nose is developed in width at
the expense of its projection; its base is larger and
crushed in, owing to the softness of the cartilages, and
spreads out into two divergent alæ, with elliptical
nostrils more or less exposed. This extremity is sometimes tri-lobed. The skeleton of the nose is platyrr-
hinian (54-78); the two bones proper are occasionally
united, as in apes. * * * The prognathism of
the Negro extends within certain limits to the entire
face. All the parts of the superior maxilla contribute
to it, and even the pterygoid processes, which are
drawn forward by the development of the jaw; but it
is only characteristic and considerable in the subnasal
region and in the teeth. It frequently exists also in
the lower jaw; that is to say, the chin recedes, and

the teeth project obliquely forward. The teeth are wider apart than in the white races, beautifully white, very firm and sound. Lastly, the ears are small, round, their border not well curled, the lobule short and scarcely detached, and the auditory opening wide. The neck is short." (*Anthropology*, p.p. 488, 489, 490.)

The long, slender neck of the White finds its strongest contrast in the short, thick neck of the Negro. In this, the Negro presents another character of the ape. Burmeister, quoted by Hartman, says, "The Negro's thick neck is the more striking, since it is generally allied with a short throat. In measuring negroes from the crown of the head to the shoulder, I found the interval to be from nine and a quarter to nine and three-quarters inches. In Europeans of normal height this interval is seldom less than ten inches, and is more commonly eleven inches in women and twelve in men. The shortness of the neck, as well as the relatively small size of the brain-pan, and the large size of the face, may the more readily be taken as an approximation to the Simian type, since all apes are short-necked. * * * This shortness of the neck of the Negro explains his greater carrying power, and his preference for carrying burdens on his head, which is much more fatiguing to the European on account of his longer and weaker neck." (*Anthropoid Apes*, p.p. 100, 101.)

"The clavicle is longer in proportion to the humerus than in the White. His radius is perceptibly longer in proportion to the humerus—thus approximating to that of the ape. The scapular is shorter and broader. (*Preadimites*, p. 171.) "Among negroes the forearm is longer, in proportion to the arm, than is the case with whites. The same is true of anthropoid apes. The Negro's arm, when suspended by the side, reaches the knee-pan within a distance of only four and three-eighths per cent of the whole length of the body. The white man's arm reaches the knee-pan within a distance which is seven and one-half per cent of the whole length of the body. This length of the arm is a quadrumanous characteristic. (*Ibid,*, p.p. 248, 249.) Topinard says, "The arm * * * is shortest in whites, longest in negroes. * * * Frequently, in the latter, the extremity of the middle finger touched the patella; once it was twelve millimeters below its upper border, as in the gorilla." (*Anthropology*, p. 335.) Quatrefages says, "I have already observed that the upper limb is a little longer in the Negro than in the White. The essential cause of this difference is the relative elongation of the forearm." M. Broca, after comparing the radius and humerus of the two races, gives 79.43 for the Negro, and 73.82 for the Europeans. (*The Human Species*, p. 399.)

Mr. Hartman says, "In the case of an adult male gorilla the first glance at this member reminds us of the knotty fist of a black laborer or lighterman, like those who, at Rio de Janeiro, Bahia, or La Guayra, lift the heavy bags of coffee and place them on their heads or on their herculean shoulders." (*Anthropoid Apes*, p. 102.)

Winchell says, "Among the Negroes the capacity of the lungs is less than among the Whites; and the circumference of the chest is less." (*Preadimites*, p. 173.)

Quatrefages says, "The thoracic cage presents some interesting facts sufficiently well proved. In consequence of the form of the sternum, the greater or less curvation of the ribs, it is generally broad and flattened in the White, narrow and prominent in the Negro." (*The Human Species*, p. 397.)

Topinard says, "M. Pruner-Bey speaks of two important characters which remind one of the ape. The three curvatures of the spine are less pronounced in the Negro than in the White; his thorax is relatively flat from side to side, and slightly cylindrical. The shoulders, he adds, are less powerful than in the European. The umbilicus is nearer the pubis; the iliac bones in the male are thicker and more vertical. The neck of the femur is less oblique." (*Anthropology*, p. 490.)

Topinard says, "The pelvis, formed by the two iliac bones and the sacrum, is divided into two parts— the great pelvis, or wide upper portion, and the small pelvis, or pelvic cavity, through which the fœtus passes at birth. Camper and Soemmering observed that the pelvis of the Negro in its *ensemble* is narrower than that of the White.—'In 1826 Vrolik came to the conclusion that the pelvis of the male negro—from its strength and thickness—from the want of transparency in its iliac fossœ—from the higher projection of its superior extremity, and from the spinous processes of the iliac bones being less projecting and less separated from the cotyloid cavities, approximates to that of animals, while the pelvis of the negress maintains a certain slenderness. In 1864 Joulin asserted that the transverse diameter of the inlet is always greater antero-posteriorly in the female. * * * In the negress, he says, the iliac bones are more vertical, the transparency of the fossœ, the capacity and depth of the cavity less, the pubic arch, as well as its angle greater." (*Ibid*, pp. 305, 306.) "Weber found that in each of the races which he had studied, the pelvis presented a predominant form, which, on that account alone, became characteristic. He regarded the inlet as being generally oval and of large transverse diameter in the White. * * * Cuneiform and of large antero-posterior diameter in negroes. * * * M. Verneau confirms the assertions of the greater number of his predecessors, as to the reality of the characters of race to be found in the pelvis. Amongst these characters, there are some which have been pointed out in the negro as *indications of animalism.* * * * In fact the verticality of the ilia, and the increase of the antero-posterior diameter of the pelvis in the Negro, have been chiefly insisted upon as recalling characters which may be observed in mammalia generally, and particularly in apes." (*The Human Species*, pp. 397, 398.)

Winchell says, "The Negro pelvis averages but 26½ inches in circumference; that of the White race is 33 inches. In the Negro it is more inclined, which is another quadrumanous character. It is also more narrow and elongated." (*Preadamites*, p. 249.) In the greater length and slenderness of the pelvis, the Negro presents another character of the ape.

Topinard gives the relative length of the femur to the tibia as 67.22 in the Negro and 69.73 in the White. (*Anthropology.*)

The highly developed calves of the White, find their strongest contrast in the thin calves of the Negro. This slenderness of the Negroe's calves is another character of the ape. The calves of the White, situated low on the leg, find their strongest contrast in the calves of the Negro, set relatively high on the leg. The elevated position which the calves of the Negro occupy in the leg, is another character of the ape.

The short, narrow heel of the White, finds its strongest contrast in the long, broad heel of the Negro. The latter is another character of the ape.

The short, highly arched foot of the White, finds its strongest contrast in the long, flat foot of the Negro. The latter is another character of the ape.

Topinard in contrasting the following characters of the Negro with those of the White, says: "The femur is less oblique, the tibia more curved, the calf of the leg high and but little developed, the heel broad and projecting, the foot long, but slightly arched, flat, and the great toe rather shorter than in the White. Negresses age rapidly, their breasts elongate after the first pregnancy, and become flabby and pendulous." (*Anthropology*, p. 490.)

In discussing the differences presented by the muscles, viscera, vessels, and nerves of the so-called "races of men." Topinard says, "Their study, equally with that of the bones, forms part of the comparative anatomy of man. * * * 'The anatomy in ordinary use with physicians has been acquired in our dissecting rooms, on white subjects, of which there is always a plentiful supply. Some few Negroes and Mongolians have also been submitted to dissection, but without much attention being paid to the subject. It is only now that this branch of anthropology is beginning to spring into life. We begin to find that there are as many reasons why we should search into the differences which exist in internal organs as into the features of the countenance. Some splendid works on the anatomy of foreign races have already appeared; anatomical variations, supposed anomolies, are no longer passed by as matters of no interest. * * * 'One fact has been already ascertained—namely, that the muscular system is the seat of differences: some as to the nature of the characters which we have termed unimportant; others produced by arrangements which are found normally in various classes of the Mammalia. The variations exhibited by the cutaneous muscle, the muscles of the face or of the ears, the adductors of the arm, the rectus abdominus muscle, the muscles of the hand and foot, the glutæi, and the triceps of the calf of the leg are in this category. * * * 'All the internal parts of the body are subject to variety in different races: the peritoneum, the ilso-cœcal appendix, the liver, the larynx; and if the small number of cases observed did not lead us to fear pronouncing as an individual variation one of an ethnic character, we might mention many examples of them. No doubt special peculiarities in the internal generative organs will be discovered. The nervous system has been the subject of closer study. Soemmering, and after him Jacquart, demonstrated that the nerves of the Negro, particularly those of the base of the brain, are larger than those of the European. It has been ascertained that his cerebral substance is not so white. (*Anthropology*, pp. 307, 308, 309.)

Quatrefages says: "Relatively to the white, the Negro presents a marked predominance of peripheral nervous expansians. The truneks are thicker, and the fibres more numerous, or perhaps merely easier to isolate and to preserve on account of their volums alone. On the other hand, the cerebral centres, or at least the brain appear to be inferior in development. "(*The Human Species*, p. 401.)

"There are also some slight variations between the respiration, circulation, animal temperature secretions, etc., of the White man and the Negro; the muscular energy and the manner in which it is employed, sometimes vary considerably in different races; general sensibility, and consequently aptitude for feeling pain, are very unequally developed." (*Ibid* p, 409.

Dr. Mosely quoted by Winchell says, Negroes are void of sensibility to a surprising degree. They are not subject to nervous diseases. They sleep soundly in every disease, nor does any mental disturbance keep them awake. They bear chirurgical operations much better than white people; and what would be the cause of insupportable pain to a white man, a negro would almost disregard." (*Preadimites*, p, 178.)

Dr. J. Hendree, of Aniston, Alabama, writing to Dr. Winchell says; "Let me mention one fact especially, drawn from my own experience of forty years. The coarseness of their (the negroes) organization makes them require about double the dose of ordinary medicine used for the whites." Dr. M. L. Barrow, of Drayton, Georgia, writing to Dr. Winchell say: "I have practiced among the negroes over forty years * * *Your information in respect to the doses of medicine for the colored people corresponds with my experience—except as regards opiates; and perhaps they will bear large quantities of these, as I have known some to take very large doses with impunity." (*Ibid*, p. 177.)

The highly developed pilions system of the white, finds its strongest contrast in the deficient pilious system of the negro. Of the latter Topinard says, "The beard is scant and developed late. The body is destitute of hair, except on the pubis and armpits." *Anthropology*, p, 483.) Winchell says, "As to the pilions sys-

tem it is deficient in the Negro. The hairs of the head
are black and crispy, with a transverse section, and
are inserted vertically in the scalp. The skin is
black, velvety and comparatively cool. (*Ibid*, p, 174.)

"In the Negro, the development of the body is generally in advance of the white. His wisdon teeth are
cut sooner; and in estimating the age of his skull, we
must reckon it as at least five years in advance of the
white." (*Ibid*, p, 175) "The temperament of the Negro
is more sluggish than that of the White man." In
Africa, the Negroes are extremely indolent, and use
little exertion for their well-being. Every person who
has resided in the midst of a Negro population in our
Southern States has been compelled to remark their
incapability of intense effort, and their constitutional
sleepiness and slowness. This inability to make great
exertions secures them from fatigue, and diminishes the
demand for regular periods for total repose and invig-
orating sleep. "In a true sense, they are in a state of
partial sleep during the day, and hence are able to pass
night after night without a total suspension of their
usual activity." (*Ibid*, pp. 175, 176.)

The person of the White exhales an order which
is scarcely perceptable, and not especially offensive.
In striking contrast to this, the Negro is characterized
by a very strong offensive odor. Topinard says, "The
characteristic effluvium from the hold of a slave-ship
can never be got rid of."—(*Ibid.*)

Dr. Winchell says, "The exemption of the Negro from malarial diseases, and sundry other pathological affections of the White race is another significant diagnostic. "If the population of New England, Germany, France, England, or other northern climates, should come to Mobile, "or to New Orleans, a large proportion die of yellow fever, and if one hundred such individuals landed in the latter city, at the commencement of an epidemic of yellow fever, probably half would fall victims to it. On the contrary, Negroes, under all circumstances, enjoy an almost perfect exemption from this disease, even though brought in from our northern states."—*Preadimites*, p, 180.) Quatreages says, "Of all human races the White is the most sensitive to marsh fevers, and the Black the least so. On the other hand the Negro race suffers more than any other from phthisis."—(*The Human Species.* p. 426.)

Dr. Winchell says, "The mental indolence of Negroes is further shown in the comparative records of insanity and idiocy. While among Whites, mania occurs in the proportion of 0.76 per thousand, among Negroes it is only 0.10 per thousand. While idiocy, among the former, is 0.73 per thousand, among the latter it is 0.37 per thousand."—*Preadimites*, p. 182.

Dr. Winchell quotes Mr. William Morrow, Chesterville, Ohio, (The Transcript, published by the students of the Ohio Wesleyan University, Delaware, Ohio, Oct. 1878), who says:

"'In early life I had conceived a horror of slavery in all its forms, and had long held to the opinion that the Negro, once free, and having a fair opportunity, would surely make rapid progress toward becoming a good and honorable citizen. I expected a good deal more than I have found.'" "After narrating the extent and variety of his experiences in New Orleans, Huntsville [Alabama], and Nashville, he gives his conclusions lead as follows:" "'As a rule, the Negro does not learn as well as do children of this state [Ohio]. Some things they seem to master readily; but when they come to any reasoning they usually fail. They read well if they have a good teacher, and nearly all write well. In arithmetic, grammer, geography and the higher branches, they are mostly deficient. They learn definitions tolerable well, but fail in the application. In arithmetic, a class may learn a method of solving examples, and will work them with wonderful facility. You pass on a week or so with the class, come to a place requiring the use of the principle formerly learned, and it is gone. I had in my charge a class in arithmetic that had been half way through the book; upon examination, I found that not a single one of them could work an example in long division. * * *Some of those who are teaching, of course, are more intellgent, many being able to teach arithmetic as far as decimals and interest. I meet very few who know anything about grammar. * * *'Fear is usually the only thing that controls them. Very few of the finer feelings find any lodgment in their natures. Having been once taught to obey, they do moderately well. The coarse nature is easily aroused, and they have never heard tell of such a thing as self-control. Their anger knows no bounds, often attacking a teacher in open school * * * A Negro knows no bashfulness; no feeling of diffidence in the presence of superior ever troubles him. If accused of anything, they assume a look of injured innocence that would credit the veriest saint in the calendar. They never plead guilty, and have an excuse for any and all occurrences."—[*Ibid*, pp. 183, 184.]

The doctrine was once universally taught, and is still entertained by many that, the dark complexion of the Negro, and that of the other so-called "colored races of men" is due to climatic influence. Scientific research has long since demonstrated the fallacy of this absurd hypothesis. In discussing this subject, Dr. Winchell says:

"The yellow-tawny Hottentots live side by side with the black Kaffirs. The ancient Indians of California, in the latitude of 42 degrees, were as black as the Negroes of Guinea, while in Mexico were tribes of an olive or reddish complexion, relatively light. So in Africa, the darkest Negroes are 12 or 15 degree north latitude; while their color becomes lighter the nearer they approach the equator." "The Yoloffs," says Goldberry, "are a proof that the black color does not depend entirely on solar heat, nor on the fact that they are more exposed to a vertical sun, but arises from other

[5]

causes; for the further we go from the influence of its rays, the more the black color is increased in intensity.'' So we may contrast the dark-skinned Eskimo with the fair Kelts of temperate Europe. If it be thought that extreme cold exerts upon color an influence similar to that of extreme heat, we may compare the dark Eskimo with the fair Finns of similar latitudes. Among the black races of tropical regions we find generally some light colored tribes interspersed. These sometimes have light hair and blue eyes. This is the case with the Tuareg of the Sahara, the Affghans of India, and the aborigines of the banks of the Orinoco and the Amazon. The Abyssinians of the plains are lighter colored than those of the heights; and upon the low plains of Peru, the Antisians are of fairer complexion than the Aymaras and Quichuas of the high table-lands. Humboldt says: ''The Indians of the Torrid Zone, who inhabit the most elevated plains of the Cordillera of the Andes, and those who are engaged in fishing at the 45th degree of south latitude, in the islands of the Chonos Archipelago, have the same copper color as those who, under a scorching climate, cultivate the banana in the deepest and narrow- est valleys of the Equinoctial region.'' (*Ibid*, pp. 185, 186. See also Topinard's *Anthropology*, pp. 386, 387.)

In explaining the real cause of the differences in *Complexion*, which we observe among the so-called ''races of men,'' Topinard says:

''The color of the skin, hair and eyes is the result of a general phenomenon in the organism, namely, the production and distribution of the coloring matter. The skin of the Scandinavian is white, almost without color, or rather rosy and florid, owing to the transparency of the epidermis allowing the red coloring matter of the blood to be sun circulating through the capillaries. * * * "The skin of the Negro of Guinea, and especially of Yoloff, the darkest of all, is, on the contrary, jet black, which is caused by the presence in the minute cellules on the deep surface of the epidermis of black granulus, known by the name of pigment. The black layer thus formed by these cellules, which used to be called *rete mucosum* of Malpighi, remains adherent sometimes to the dermis and sometimes to the epidermis on removing the latter, after previously submitting the skin to maceration. This pigment is found in all races, whether black, yellow or white, but in very different quantity; hence their various tones of color, from the lightest to the darkest whites, who readily become brown on exposure to light, are undoubtedly provided with it. It is always more abundant in the scrotum and round the nipple. It is very visible on the mucous membrane of negroes, which are frequently surrounded by masses of it, notably on the vault of the palate, the gums, and the conjunctiva, which we have also met with in young orangs. (*Anthropology*, pp. 342, 343.)

In discussing this subject Quatrefages says: "With all anthropologists I recognize the high value of the color of the skin as a character. * * * We know that it does not result from the existence or disappearance of special layers. Black or White, the skin always comprises a white *dermis*, penetrated by many capillaries, and *epidermis*, more or less transparent and colorless. Between the two is placed the *mucous layer*, of which the *pigment* alone in reality varies in quantity and color according to the race. All the colors presented by the human skin have two common elements, the white of the dermis and the red of the blood. Moreover, each has its own proper element, resulting from the colorings of the pigment. The rays reflected from these different tissues combine into a resultant which produces the different tints and traverses the epidermis. The latter plays the part of roughened glass. The more delicate and the finer it is, the more perceptible is the color of the subjacent parts.   *   *   *   From the preceding, we can also understand why the White alone can be said to turn pale or to blush. The reason is, that in him the pigment allows the slightest differences in the afflux of blood to the dermis to be perceived. With the Negro as with us, the blood has its share in the coloring, the tint of which it deepens or modifies. When the blood is wanting, the Negro turns gray from the blending of the white of the dermis with the black of the pigment." (*The Human Species*, pp. 356, 357.)

Thus, it is shown by the highest scientific authorities, that the black, colorless complexion of the Negro, is not the result of climatic influence; but it is due solely to the black pigment, which intervenes between the dermis and the epidermis. This pigment, like every other part of the organism, is subject to disease. One of the diseases to which the pigment is liable is known as albinism. The victims of this disease are termed albinos. In discussing albinism, and albinos, Dr. Topinard says:

"Albinos are individuals in whom the pigmentary matter is so far deficient that the skin and hair are colorless, the iris is transparent, and the choriod coat destitute of the dark pigment for the absorption of redundant rays of light. In consequence of this, they are unable to bear sunlight, and see better at night than during the day. Their eyeballs are affected with a perpetual oscillating movement, their skin and hair are colorless, or of a dull white, the eyes reddish, the transparency of the tissues showing the blood circulating through the capillaries. They are often indolent, and without muscular vigor. There are partial aibinos, in whom the above symptoms are observed, but in a less degree. They easily pass unnoticed among the white races, but are very observable among the black; their hair is flaxen red, their skin coffee-colored or speckled, their eyes are light blue or reddish. Both are met with among all races and under all climates. In some of the native courts on the west coast of Africa, especially in Congo, they are an object of veneration, and go by the name of 'dondos.' Dr. Schweinfurth has seen a great number of them with the King of the Menbouttous on the banks of the Bahr-el-Ghazel. From their presence among the blackest populations, Prichard framed an important argument in favor of the influence of external circumstances, and of the derivation of the human race from one primitive pair. He delighted to reiterate it, and, moreover, he was the first to establish the fact that their hair was as wooly, and their features were as negro as their fellow countrymen of the same tribe. We say again, albinism is only a monstrosity, a pathological condition which has been cured, and we must take care how we place implicit reliance on the confused accounts given of it by travellers." (*Anthropology*, p. 161.)

Scientific research has also demonstrated that the differences which we observe in the form and texture of the hair, among the so-called "races of men," is not the result of climatic influence. Dr. Winchell says:

"The condition of the hair is found to sustain relations to climate no more exact than the complexion. The Tasmanians, in latitude forty-five degrees, had hair as wooly as that of the Negroes under the equator. On the contrary, smooth hair is found extensively in tropical latitudes, as among the Australians, the Blacks of the Deccan (India), and the Himejarites of the Yemen, in Arabia. * * * Similar absence of correlation between stature and the environment has been ascertained." [*Preadimites*, pp. 186, 187.]

Dr. Topinard says, "No explanation can be given as to the varieties of the hair in its fundamental types. For example, the straight and the round, the wooly and flat hair, as seen under the microscope. In this lies the most serious objection to the theory of the derivation of characters from one another. In the present state of science we have no explanation to give on the subject,'' —(*Anthropology*, pp. 391, 392.)

The utterance of this eminent anthropologist should receive our most serious consideration. With his occustomed candor, he frankly admits that science can give no explanation as to why the hair of the white is long, smooth, fine and round, and is inserted obliquely in the scalp; while in striking contrast to these charac- ters, the hair of the Negro, is short, coarse, woolly, and flat; and is inserted vertically in the scalp. [2] He calls attention to the fact that, in these opposite characters, ''lies the most serious objection to the theory of the derivation of characters from one another,'' or, in other words in these opposing characters, lies the most serious objection to the theory that either the Negro or the White, is the result of development, the one from the other; and also presents the most serious objection to the theory that the White and the Negro, are the descendants of one primitive pair.

Thus it is shown by comparative anatomy that the Negro, from the crown of his woolly head, to the sole of his flat foot, differs in his physical and mental organisms from the White; and that ''just in proportion as he differs from the White, he approx- imates the lower animals,''

DOES LIKE BEGET LIKE?

Could that negro child be the child of pure Adamic parents? If the negro is an offspring of Adam and Eve, then it is possible.

Chapter III.

The Theory of Evolution Exploded; Man was Created a Man, and did not Develop from an Ape.

When we approach the modern Christian with the inquiry, "If the results of comparative anatomy, which indicates that the negro is an ape, are of no value; and if he is a man—a descendant of Adam—from what branch of the Adamic family did he descend; and how do you account for his structural inferiority to the white, and his approximation to the ape?" he naively replies: "The negro is the son of Ham, and his inferiority to his white brother is the result of a curse which Noah put upon Ham for his disrespectful conduct toward him."

This monstrous theory was conceived in, and has been handed down to us from, the dark ages of ignor-

ance, superstition and crime; and because the Church
gave it to us, the devotees of Enlightened Christianity
accepted it as "both sound and sacred." But fortu-
nately, this blind acceptance of church theories is
rapidly giving place to intelligent, systematic investigation, which must inevitably lead to the happiest·
results.

Since the Hamitic origin of the negro, as explained by the church, is at once opposed to the results of all scientific research, and to all observation
and experience, it is proper, even at this late day, to
inquire, Does it harmonize with scripture?

We are taught by the Bible that, after the Deluge,
"Noah began to be an husbandman, and he planted
a vineyard: And he drank of the wine and was
drunken; and he was uncovered in his tent. And
Ham, the father of Canaan, saw the nakedness of his
father, and told his brethren without. And Shem
and Japheth took a garment and laid it upon their
shoulders, and went backward, and covered the nakedness of their father; and their faces were backward,
and they saw not their father's nakedness. And Noah
awoke from his wine, and knew what his younger
son had done unto him. And he said, cursed be
Canaan; a servant of servants shall be unto his
brethren. And he said, blessed be the Lord God of
Shem; and Canaan shall be his servant. God shall
enlarge Japheth, and he shall dwell in the tents of
Shem; and Canaan shall be his servant." (Gen. ix.:
20, etc.)

Thus, the Bible clearly teaches that though Ham offended Noah, there was no curse put upon Ham in consequence of it. Forced by the plain teaching of the Bible to abandon his original position, the modern Christian hastily seeks shelter for his "brother in black" in the theory that it was Canaan whom Noah cursed and changed into a negro. Now, let us investigate and see what we are called upon to believe. in order to accept this absurd proposition.

1. We must believe in direct opposition to the plain teaching of the Bible, that Noah had any authority, or any power, to visit such a calamity upon Canaan or anyone else.

2. We must believe that a just, merciful, loving God would approve the drunken desire of Noah to visit so dire a calamity upon Canaan, an unoffending individual; and would consent that it should be perpetuated in his descendants throughout all time.

3. We must believe that Noah's curse deprived Canaan of the exalted physical and mental characters which distinguish the white from the negro, and gave him the degraded physical and mental characters which approximates the negro to the organisms below; that it changed his complexion from the colorless white to the colorless black; that it changed his long, smooth, silken hair, to the short, coarse, woolly hair of the negro; that it changed each individual hair of h_s head from the cylindrical to the flat; that it changed the manner in which his hair was inserted

into the scalp from the oblique to the vertidal; that it
lengthened and narrowed his cranium; that it thickened his skull and discolored his brain; that it reduced
the number and increased the size of the convolutions
of his brain, thus simplifying and approximating it
to that of the lower animals; that it lengthened and
broadened his jaw; that it extended his jaws forward
at the expense of the symmetry of the face, and backward at the expense of the brain cavity; that it
thickened his lips, sloped his front teeth, and flattened
his nose; that it shortened and thickened his neck;
that it rendered his "clavicle longer in proportion to
the humerus;" that it rendered his "radius perceptibly
longer in proportion to the humerus;" that it reduced
his muscular system; reduced his chest measurement;
that it reduced his lung capacity; that it wrought
other radical changes in the viscera, vessels, etc.; that
it lengthened and narrowed his pelvis, and set it
more obliquely to the spinal column; that it rendered
his "tibia longer as compared with the femur;" that
it reduced the size of his calves, and placed them at
a higher elevation on the legs; that it lengthened and
broadened his heel, and flattened his foot.

Having consented to believe all this absurdity, in
order to accept the best explanation which the modern
clergy has offered us as to the origin of the negro, we
should be excused for indulging the hope that our
credulity had been sufficiently taxed, and that no
further draft would be made upon it; but this fond

hope, however comforting, was but born to be blighted; a glance at the scriptural narrative reveals the fact that Noah manifested no disposition to visit this dire calamity upon any other individual than Canaan; there was no female cursed and changed into a negress to mate with Canaan, and thus enable him to produce a progeny of negroes. Hence, he had no alternative than to take a wife from among the whites, for he was the father of the Canaanites; the offspring resulting from this union would not have been negroes, but half castes—mulattoes. These, upon reaching maturity, would not have taken husbands and wives from among their brothers and sisters, but would have intermarried with the whites; the offspring resulting from these unions would not have been negroes, but three-quarter white. Thus, through their intermarriage with the whites, each succeeding generation of the descendants of Canaan would have grown whiter, and their hair straighter, until, in the course of time, it would have been difficult, if not impossible, for the ordinary observer to distinguish them from pure whites; and when Canaan had lived out his days and died, he would have been the last, as the clergy would have us believe he was the first negro, and the presence of the negro in subsequent ages would remain unexplained. Hence, whether we view this most important subject from a scriptural, or from a scientific standpoint, it at once becomes plain that the negro is not the son of Ham.

When Noah awoke from his wine, and knew what his younger son had done unto him, "he was offended;" and evidently supposing that it would be more hurtful to Ham's feelings to say something offensive to Canaan, than it would be to say the same thing of Ham himself, Noah said: "Cursed be Canaan, a servant of servants shall he be unto his brethren." By way of further manifesting his displeasure toward Ham, and his appreciation of the service his other sons had rendered him, Noah said: "God shall enlarge Japheth, and he shall dwell in the tents of Shem; and Canaan shall be his servant."

That this curse was merely the spiteful babble of an old man just "coming out of his cups," and was not sanctioned by God, and had no effect upon Canaan and his descendants is shown by the fact that it was never fulfilled. It is a matter of scriptural record that while the Israelites, who were a branch of the family of Shem, were in bondage to the Egyptians, who were a branch of the family of Ham, the descendants of Canaan, whom Noah cursed, were the masters of one of the finest countries in the world; a country which God described as "a goodly land;" "a land flowing with milk and honey."

Further evidence that Noah's drunken spite toward Ham had no effect upon the relations of Canaan and his descendants to Shem and Japheth and their descendants, is shown by the language of Moses in explaining to Israel why God dispossessed the Canaanites of their country, and gave it to Israel. It was not in fulfillment of Noah's curse upon Canaan; neither was it because of the "righteousness" of Israel, "but for the wickedness of those nations." (Deut. ix.:4.) And when the land of Canaan was given to the Israelites, they were not commanded to enslave the Canaanites, but to "utterly destroy them," and "save alive nothing that breatheth." [Deut. xx.:16-17.]

This absurd church theory of the Hamitic origin of the Negro is at once irrational, unscientific and anti-scriptural, and should be repudiated. With the rejection of this ridiculous theory, we have absolutely no explanation of the origin of the Negro which makes any claim to a scriptural basis. On the contrary, our present social, political and religious systems, so far as our relations to the Negro are concerned, are based solely on the atheistic theory of evolution.

When we approach the atheist with the inquiry, From whence came the Negro, and what are his relations to the Whites? he proceeds to inform us "that the most ancient ancestors of man, as of all other organisms, were living creatures of the simplest kind imaginable, organisms without organs, like the still living monera. They consisted of simple, homogeneous, structureless and formless little lumps of mucous or albuminous matter [plasson], like the still living *protamoeba primitiva.* The form value of these most ancient ancestors of man was not even equal to that

of a cell, but merely that of a cytod; for, as in the
case of all monera, the little lump of protoplasm did
not as yet possess a cell-kernel. The first of these
monera originated in the beginning of the Laurentian
period, by spontaneous generation, or archiogeny,
out of so-called 'inorganic combinations,' namely, out
of simple combinations of carbon, oxygen, hydrogen
and nitrogen." [*Haeckel.*]

According to Haeckel, from this "first ancestral
stage" the progenitors of man evolved through the
fish and fowl and beast, to reach the "twenty-third
ancestral stage" in the anthropoids, or man-like apes,
the gibbon, ourang, chimpanzee and gorilla. Describing what he terms the "twenty-fourth ancestral
stage," Mr. Haeckel says:

"Although the preceding ancestral stage is
already so nearly akin to genuine men that we scarcely
require to assume an intermediate connecting stage,
still we can look upon the speechless primæval men
[alali] as this intermediate link. These ape-like men,
or Pithecanthropi, very probably existed toward the
end of the tertiary period. They originated out of
the man-like apes, or anthropoids, by becoming completely habituated to an upright walk and by the corresponding stronger differentiation of both pairs of
legs. The fore hand of the anthropoids became the
human hand; their hinder hand became a foot for
walking. We may, therefore, distinguish a special
[24th] stage in the series of our human ancestors,

namely, speechless man [Alalus], or ape-man [Pithe-canthropus], whose body was indeed formed exactly like that of man in all essential characteristics, but who did not, as yet, possess articulate speech. The origin of articulate language, and the higher differentiation and perfecting of the larnyx connected with it, must be looked upon as a later and the most important stage in the process in the development of man. It was doubtless this process which, above all others, helped to create the deep chasm between man and animals, and which also first caused the most important progress in the mental activity and the perfecting of the brain connected with it."

While admitting that geological research, which has discovered some remains of about everything that ever existed on the earth, has failed to discover the slightest vestige of such a creature, Mr. Haeckel proceeds, with his accustomed audacity, to describe it. He says:

"We as yet know of no fossil remains of the hypothetical primæval man [Protanthropos atavus — Homo primigenius]. But considering the extraordinary resemblance between the lowest woolly-haired men and the highest man-like apes, which still exist at the present day, it requires but a slight stretch of the imagination to conceive an intermediate form connecting the two, and to see in it an approximate likeness to the supposed primeval men, or ape-like men. The form of their skull was probably very long, with slanting teeth; their hair woolly; the color of their skin dark, of a brownish tint; the hair covering the whole of the body was probably thicker than in any of the still living human species; their arms comparatively longer and stronger; their legs, on the other hand, knock-kneed, shorter and thinner, with entirely undeveloped calves; their walk but half erect.'"

According to the opinion most generally entertained by the leading advocates of this theory, this purely hypothetical creature, speechless, ape-like man, differentiated into the Negro with articulate speech. The great bulk of the Negros developed no higher; and thus present a case of "arrested development;" but at some period in the remote past, a branch of the Negros differentiated into Malays. The great bulk of the Malays developed no higher; and thus present another case of "arrested development;" but in the course of time a branch of the Malays differentiated into Indians. The great bulk of Indians developed no higher; and thus present another case of "arrested development." But in the course of time a branch of the Indians differentiated into Mongolians. The great bulk of the Mongolians developed no higher: and thus present another case of "arrested development." But in the course of time a branch of the Mongolians differentiated into Caucasians (Whites.)

Thus, according to this theory, the colorless black, in violation of that well established principle that like produces like, emerged through the various shades of

colors, brown, red, and yellow, to emerge—again colorless—but white. The advocates of this theory would
have us believe that these "differentiations" were accomplished with the aids of "natural selection," "the survival of the fittest," etc.

Mr. Haeckel says: "A great many reasons might be
advanced in favor of the opinion that the primaeval men
of the Lissotrichous species (the primary forms of
straight-haired men) were derived from South Asiatic
anthropoids, whereas the primaeval men of the Ulotrich-
ous species (as the primary forms of the four wooly-
haired tribes) were derived from Central African man-
like apes."

Thus, according to this atheistic theory, man is not
a distinct creation in the image of God, but is merely a
highly developed species of ape—the "human species"—
and this human species of ape is divisable into five or
more "races of men," dependent upon the whim of the
naturalist who makes the classification. That of Blumenbach, who divides the "human species" of ape into
five "races of men," is universally accepted and
taught by enlightened Christians, perhaps in deference
to the scriptural injunction: "Train up a child in the
way he should go; and when he is old he will not de-
part from it." The classification of other naturalists
vary from that of Blumenbach on up to that of Haeckel,
who divides the "human species" into thirty-six "races
of men."

The atheistic theory of man's descent from the ape, which seeks to establish a blood relationship between man and the lowest orders of animal life, though no more anti-scriptural, is really as irrational, and as unscientific as that of the church, that the Negro is the son of Ham. However, a comparison of its teachings with those of the Bible enables us to realize that it was not through the scriptural teaching that man is a distinct creation in the image of God, that the Negro obtained his present unnatural position in the family of man: but through the pernicious influence of this atheistic theory, that man is merely a highly developed "species" of ape—the "human species"—of which the Negro is the lowest race Hence, our social, political, and religious relations with the Negro are not based upon scripture, but upon atheism. But modern Christians should pause to consider that in their vain, criminal attempt to establish a blood relationship between the flesh of man and that of the ape, they have, to all intents and purposes, repudiated the declaration of Paul, that the flesh of man is a different kind of flesh from that of the beast, and have accepted this atheist theory, that all flesh is akin; that they have repudiated the scriptural teaching that man is a distinct creation, in the image of God, to accept this atheistic theory that man is a highly developed species of ape—the "human species"—of which the White is the highest, and the Negro the lowest race, with the browns, reds and yellows as intermediate races, in d10-ereut stages of development. They should bear in mind that in yielding to the degrading influence of this atheistic theory, they practically renounced their kinship with God to claim kin with the ape.

All scientific investigation of the subject proves the Negro to be an ape; and that he simply stands at the head of the ape family, as the lion stands at the head of the cat family. When God's plan of creation, and the drift of Bible history are properly understood, it will be found that the teachings of scripture upon this, as upon every other subject, harmonize with those of science. This being true, it follows that the Negro is the only anthropoid, or man-like ape; and that the gibbon, ourang, chimpanzee and gorilla are merely negro-like apes. Hence, to recognize the Negro as a ''man and a brother,'' they were compelled to declare man an ape. Thus the modern Christian, like the atheist, takes man, whom God created ''in his own image,'' and takes the Negro, whom God made ''after his kind''—the ape kind —and places them in the same family, as different ''races'' of one ''species'' of animal. The only difference between them is, that the atheist perpetuates this enormity in supreme contempt of God's plan of creation, and in open defiance of his law, while the modern Christian commits this infamous crime in the name of the Father, Son and Holy Ghost.

While there are a few who claim to be ''Christian evolutionists,'' whatever that may mean, we are happy to state, in simple justice to them, that the great majority of the modern Christian priesthood who teach this infamous theory, which degrades man to the level of the brute, do so in ignorance of its infidelity, and of its destructive results, both in time and eternity.

Thus, the history of the ancient Jewish church and its priesthood repeats itself in that of the modern Christian church and its priesthood, as shown by the following: God looked down from heaven upon the children of men, to see if there were any that did understand, that did seek God. Everyone of them is gone back; they are altogether become filthy; there is none that doeth good, no, not one." [Ps. liii.:2-3.] "My people hath been lost sheep; their shepherds have caused them to astray; they have turned them away on the mountains; they have gone from mountain to hill; they have forgotten their resting place." [Jer. 1.:6] "Many pastors have destroyed my vineyard; they have trodden my portion under foot; they have made my pleasant·portion a desolate wilderness. The whole land is made desolate because no. man layeth it to heart." [Jer. xii.:10-11.] "Woe be unto the pastors that destroy the sheep of my pasture! saith the Lord." [Jer. xxiii.:1.)

The scriptures abound with assurances that there will come a time when all men shall "worship God in the beauty of holiness." But fully appreciating the strength of man's blind attachment to the Negro, in disregard of the most positive evidence of his inferiority, we refrain from speculating upon the course which will be pursued by the modern Christian priesthood when brought face to face with the fact that they must either absolutely renounce God, and the Bible, and all pretentions to religious worship, or utterly repudiate this atheistic theory, that man is a species, divisible into races, together with their present social, political and religious relations with the Negro and his offspring by man.

Let us bear in mind that men may legitimately divide themselves into as many tribes, nations, or empires, as suits their pleasure, their convenience, or their interest; but that God alone can make a species or a race. And that in creating man God made first the male; and it is significant, that with the whole earth out of which to make the female, without drawing upon the male, he made woman out of man. Thus, Adam truthfully said of her, "This is now bone of my bones, and flesh of my flesh." This single pair were of one flesh, or, as Paul terms it, were one kind of flesh; a kind of flesh distinct from that of the fish, or fowl, or beast.

To twist the narrative of Creation into any semblance of harmony with The Theory of Descent, we must suppose that, when Adam was the sole representative of man on the earth, he, a single individual, was divisible into "species and races." The whole proposition is absurd. No amount of reasoning can ever harmonize the scriptural teaching of Divine Creation with this atheistic theory of Natural Development. They are opposites. Hence, when the scriptural teaching of Divine Creation is accepted in its entirety, and the atheistic Theory of Development, which first introduced the

Negro into the family of man, and which keeps him there, as one of the lower "races of men," is repudiated, the Negro will make his exit from the Adamic family with it, and will resume his proper position with the apes.

The Bible plainly teaches that man was created a single pair, "in the image of God." And we feel assured that a careful consideration of this subject must lead any rational mind to decide that the White, with his exalted physical and mental characters, and the Negro with his ape-like physical and mental characters, are not the progeny of one primitive pair. This is admitted by the great thinkers of the earth. Mr. Haeckel says: ."The excellent paleontologist Quenstedt is right in maintaining that, "if Negroes and Caucasians were snails, zoologists would universally agree that they represented two very distinct species, which could never have originated from one pair by gradual divergence.—*History of Creation.*

This being true, it follows that, if the White was created "in the image of God," then the Negro was made after some other model. And a glance at the Negro indicates the model; his very appearance suggests the ape. Mr. Darwin says, "The resemblance to a Negro in miniature of Pithecia satanus with his jet-black skin, his white rolling eyeballs and his hair parted on the top of the head, is almost ludicrous."

Prof. Wyman says: "It cannot be denied, however wide the separation, that the Negro and ourang do afford the points where man and brute, when the totality of their organizations is considered, most nearly approach each other."

Mr. Haeckel quotes "a great English traveler, who lived a considerable time on the west coast of Africa," as saying: "I consider the Negro as a lower species of man, and cannot make up my mind to look upon him as a man and a brother, for the gorilla would then also have to be admitted into the family."

Prof. Winchell says: "The inferiority of the Negro is fundamentally structural. I have enumerated the points in his anatomy in which he diverges from the White race, and have indicated that, in all these partienlars, he approximates the organisms below. It follows that what the Negro is structurally, at the present time, is the best he has ever been. It follows that he has not descended from Adam." (*Preademites.*) When we turn upon the statement of this distinguished American scientist the light of Paul's declaration, that "there is one kind of flesh of men, another flesh of beasts, another of fishes, and another of birds, we find that the Negro, who "has not descended from Adam," and is consequently not of the "flesh of men," belongs to one of the other three "kinds of flesh," and that being a land animal—an ape—he belongs to the "flesh of beasts."

Such is the striking contrast between the Negro and the White, that even the poet has made it his theme. A distinguished American poet has very forcibly said:

"When I am told the human race,
    Are all from Adam seed,
That kinky—headed coons and I,
    Are from one common breed;
I think that apes and darned baboons,
    Must be my brothers too;
But then I don't believe the tale,
    I cant! O, can you?"*

DOZIER.

The Bible teaches us that when the fish, and fowl, and beast, were all made after his kind, "The Lord God said, Let us make man in our own image, after our likeness; and let them have dominion over the fish of the sea, and over the fowl of the air, and over the cattle, and over all the earth, and over creeping things that creepeth upon the earth. Thus the Bible teaches that the work for which man was designed was a mental work. We are also taught that in the execution of Divine proposition to 'make man,' God created man in His own image, in the image of God created He them, and God blessed them, and God said unto them, Be fruitful, and multiply, and replenish the earth, and subdue it; and have dominion over the fish of the sea, and over the fowl of the air, and over every living thing that moveth upon the earth." (Gen. 1.)

To "subdue" the earth means to develop its resources; for, just in .proportion as man subdues the earth from its wild, uncultivated state he necessarily develops it into a cultivated state. Hence the biblical

---

*Note— Dr. Dozier will kindly excuse the changes made in the punctuation of our, quotation from his "Cant-O."

term "subdue," in this command, and our term develop
are synonymous, To have "dominion" means to have
control. Hence the language of God in assigning man
to the duties upon the earth for which he was desig-
nated, was equivalent to commanding him to develop
the resources of the earth, and exercise control over
fish, and fowl and beast.

In our age, God's Plan of Creation is utterly ignored.
Hence, we should not be surprised to find that his Plan
of Redemption is wholly misunderstood. For nothing
could be more absurd than to suppose that man can understand the Plan of Redemption, in ignorance of the
Plan of Creation. The former may be termed an out-
growth of the latter, or a superstructure based upon it;
in any event, they are now inseparable parts of a general system.

Man, by disregarding the design of God in his creation, and by violating those original statutes assigning
him to the duties upon the earth for which he was designed, removed himself so far from God as to necessitate
the sacrifice of the Son of God to redeem him. Hence,
the Plan of Redemption was a final effort upon the part
of God to induce man to respect the design of God in
creating him, and to discharge the duties upon the earth
to which he was assigned in the Creation.

These original statutes, which define and fix man's
relation to the earth and to the rest of created things, are
distinct in every essential feature, from those divine
statutes, which define and fix man's form of religious

worship, and the manner of his approach to God. This is shown by the fact that man may obey one class of these statutes to the very letter, and violate the other class. For example: An Israelite, in the days of David, might have obeyed to the very letter the law prescribing the ritual of the Jewish Church, and yet never make the least effort to develop the resources of the earth and exercise control over fish and fowl, and beast. On the other hand, he might, in deference to his own material interests, do all in his power to develop the resources of the earth, and exercise control over fish and fowl, and beast, and yet utterly ignore the divinely prescribed ritual of the Jewish Church. In either case he must answer at the judgment bar of God, for his violation of divine law. And we should bear in mind that it is the violation of divine law that constitutes sin, and that it is sin that damns. He should have obeyed all the law. He should have observed the Jewish ritual. His efforts to develop the resources of the earth so far as lay in his power, should not have been made merely in deference to his material interests, neither should he have exercised control over fish, and fowl, and beast, so far as he was brought in contact with them, simply because of his intellectual superiority over them; but out of respect for the design of God in creating him, and in obedience to divine law.

This argument applies with equal force to man under gospel dispensation, which, with its fewer ceremonies, the simplicity of its form of worship, and its approach to God through the Saviour, replaced that of the Jews, with its complicated forms and ceremonies, its animal sacrifices, and its approach to God through the priesthood.

That these original statutes defining and fixing man's relation to the earth, and to the animals, were not in the least impaired by any subsequent divine legislation changing man's form of religious worship, and the mode of his approach to God, is shown by the declaration of the Saviour: "Think not that I came to destroy the law or the prophets: I am not come to destroy, but to fulfill. For, verily I say unto you, Till heaven and earth pass, one jot, nor one title shall in no wise pass from the law till all be fulfilled." (Matt, v.:17-18.) This being true, it follows that man will yet subdue the earth, and have dominion over fish and fowl and beast.

Any subsequent legislation which would relieve man of the obligations imposed upon him by those original statutes, would thwart the design of God in creating man. Hence, it would change, in many respects, man's relation to God. It would change man's relations to the earth and the animals; it would nullify God's Plan of Creation. A moment's reflection should convince us that no such result was contemplated. Hence, the obligation to subdue the earth, and have dominion over fish, and fowl and beast, is as binding upon man to-day as it was upon Adam. This being true, it follows that, to be in favor with God, man must make those original statutes the basis of his social, political and religious systems; and any social, political, or religious system

which fails to make those original statutes its ultimate
basis, is simply a delusion and a snare. Hence, in order
to discharge intelligently the duties upon the earth for
which man was designed, and to which God assigned
him in the Creation, it is essential that we should be
able to distinguish man from the ape; and it is also
essential that we recognize and maintain the relation
between man and the ape which God established in
the Creation.

The great task to which man was assigned in the
Creation, was one of such magnitude as only the
mind of Deity could have conceived, and its accomplishment would require ages; and demanded that
man be endowed with mind almost God-like in its
power; mind at once legislative, executive and judicial.
And all history, and all tradition, and all scientific
research combine to teach us that man is thus endowed. The perfect harmony of God's Plan of Creation, demanded that man, the crowning work of God's
creative mind, should present in his physical structure
the very perfection of mechanism; and that the almost
limitless power of his mind to combine and utilize the
various resources of the earth should verge closely
upon the creative. This power is peculiar to man.
It is this wonderful intellectual power which enables
man to tower above the mere animal, like the snow
crowned mountain height towers above the brooklet
at its base.

When we reflect upon man's history, and of his wonderful achievements, and pause to consider that the great intellectual qualities which he has displayed were inherited from Adam, upon whom they were a divine bestowal, we feel free to assert that Adam, fresh from the hands of his Creator, presented in his physical, mental and spiritual organisms, the grandest specimen of manhood that ever graced the earth; and that Eve, fresh from the hands of her Creator, presented in her physical, mental and spiritual organisms, the most sublime specimen of that lovely sex, upon whose fair brow is stamped the image of her God.

We presume it will not be denied, that the obligation to "subdue" the "earth," as far as lay in his power, was binding upon Adam from the moment of his assignment to this task; yet it is a significant fact that it was not until after he had violated divine law, that "the Lord God sent him forth" from the garden of Eden to personally "till the ground," and thus "eat bread," "in the sweat" of his "face." (Gen. iii.)

But suppose that Adam had never sinned, would God have driven him forth from the garden of Eden to personally till the ground? Would he have sentenced him to "eat bread" "in the sweat" of his "face," even if he had not violated divine law? To entertain this idea, we must decide in disregard of the plain teaching of the Bible. that man, so far from having been created the subject of divine love, was simply designed as the victim of divine whim. But how was man to subdue the earth, and not personally till the ground? How was he to develop all the resources of this globe and not eat bread in the sweat of his face? Upon the impulse of the moment, we would naturally decide that no amount of reasoning could possibly reconcile these apparently irreconcilable propositions. But when we pause to reflect that each of these are divine propositions; that they had a common origin in the fountain of all truth, then our reverence for God — if we have any reverence for God—forbids the thought that there can by possibility be the slightest contradiction between them; for we know that just as harmony pervades all of God's works, so does consistency characterize his every utterance. Thus, when we turn upon the Narrative of the Fall, the inspired light of the Narrative of Creation, the fact becomes plain that it was not the original design of the Creator that man, the son of God, should be the subject of physical toil, beyond such as is inseparable from mental toil. Hence, we have no alternative than to decide that there must be among the animals some creature upon which God bestowed mental ability and physical form in such near approach to man, as would enable him, in the capacity of servant, to perform the manual labor necessary to subdue the earth under man's control.

When we appeal to science to identify this creature, she promptly invades the so-called "human species" and points us to the negro, as the highest grade of ape and the only creature among the lower "kinds of flesh," which possesses the essential characteristics of a servant. The negro possesses the erect posture, a well-developed hand and foot, articulate speech, and is, withal, a tool-making, tool-handling animal. These characteristics pre-eminently fit him for the position of servant, while the low order of his mentality disqualifies him for a higher sphere. Prof. Huxley says: "The difference in weight of brain between the highest and the lowest men is far greater, both relatively and absolutely, than that between the lowest man and the highest ape." (Man's Place in Nature.) "The average weight of the European brain, males and females, is 1,340 grammes; that of the negro is 1,178." [Winchell.]

The gulf is far too wide and deep, which separates between the mental indolence and incapacity of the negro, which accomplishes nothing, and the flashing intellect, the restless energy, and the indomitable courage of the white, which enables him to discover, conquer, and develop continents.

Theodore Parker says: "The Caucasian differs from all other races; he is humane; he is civilized, and progresses. He conquers with his head as well as with his hand. It is intellect, after all, that conquers not the strength of man's arm. The Caucasian has been often master of the other races—never their slave. He has carried his religion to other races, but never

taken theirs. All the great limited forms of mon-
archies are Caucasian. Republics are Caucasian. All
the great sciences are of Caucasian origin; all inven-
tions are Caucasian; literature and romance come
from the same stock; all the great poets are of Caucasian origin. No other race can bring up to memory
such celebrated names as the Caucasian race."

De Gobineau says: "The white race has great
vigor, capacity and endurance. It has an intensity
of will and desire which is controlled by intellectuality. Great things are undertaken readily, but not
blindly. It manifests a strong utilitarianism, united
with a powerful imagination, which elevates, en-
nobles and idealizes its practical ideas. The Negro
can only imitate, the Chinese only utilize, the work
of the white; but the latter is abundantly capable of
producing new works. He has as keen a sense of order as the yellow man, not from a love of repose, however, but from the desire to protect and preserve his
acquisitions. He has a love of liberty far more intense than exists in the black and yellow races, and
clings to life more earnestly. His high sense of
honor is a faculty unknown to the other races, and
springs from an exalted sentiment of which they
show no indications. His sensations are less intense
than in either the black or yellow, but his mentality
is far more developed and energetic."—*Moral and Intellectual Diversity of Races.*

This is shown by the highest authorities of the age
that the pure-blooded white alone possesses the great

mental qualities which are essential in the creature whom God designed should develop the resources of the earth, and have dominion over fish and fowl and beast; and it is significant that these exalted characteristics find their opposites in the Negro. Mr. Morris says: "It may be remarked that all the savage tribes of the earth belong to the Negro or the Mongolian races. No negro civilization has ever appeared. No Mongolian one has ever greatly developed. On the other hand, the Caucasian is pre-eminently the man of civilization. No traveler or historian records a savage tribe of Caucasian stock." (The Aryan race.)

Thus, scientific research demonstrates that man [the pure-blooded white], whom God designed, equipped, and clothed with authority to subdue the earth, never descends to savagery. On the other hand, the Negro, when uncontrolled by the White, becomes "a mere wanderer in the woods," and like any other animal, subsists upon the spontaneous products of the earth, and the proceeds of the chase. This indicates that the natural relation between the White and the Negro is that of master and servant.

Mr. Morris says: "The Negro is normally peaceful and submissive. His lack of enterprise must keep him so. Education with him soon reaches its limit. It is capable of increasing the perceptive, but not of strongly awakening the reflective faculties. The Negro will remain the worker. Of the * * *

workers and the thinkers, the Negro belongs by nature to the former class." [*Ibid.*]

The Duke of Argyle, quoted by Lubbock, while
admitting that monkeys use stones to crack nuts, says:
"Between these rudiments of intellectual perception
and the next step [that of fashioning an instrument
for a particular purpose] there is a gulf in which lies
the whole immeasurable distance between man and
brutes." [Origin of civilization.] This modern idea
that the ability to fashion an "instrument for a particular purpose" is peculiar to man, is one of the results of placing man and the ape in the same family.

This mass of scriptural and scientific evidence
clearly indicates that the pure-blooded White is the
creature whom God designed should perform the mental labor necessary to subdue the earth; and that the
Negro is the creature whom God designed to perform
the manual labor. The Negro, in common with the
rest of the animals, made his appearance upon the
earth prior to the creation of man. With the Negro
and the animals of draught, burthen and food, it was
possible for man to develop all the resources of the
earth and not personally till the ground. With the
Negro as a servant, it would have been easy for man
to have accomplished this great task with only such
physical labor as is inseparable from mental labor.

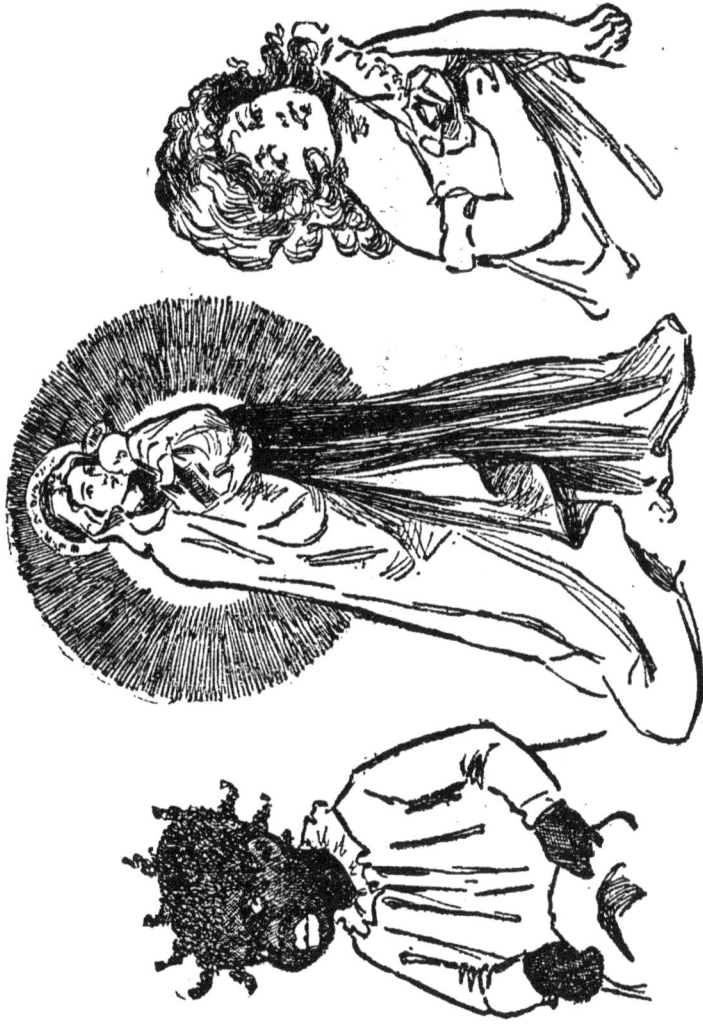

The VIRGIN MARY and the CHILD CHRIST.
Could the Child Christ possibly be of the same flesh as the Negro?

Chapter IV.

Convincing Biblical and Scientific Evidence that the Negro is not of the Human Family.

The following measurements of brain weights collected by Sanford B. Hunt, in the Federal army during the late war in the United States, demonstrates that the White blood is the lever which elevates; and that the Negro blood is the lever which lowers the mental grade of individuals, tribes, nations, continents, and the world at large.

	Weight of brain Grammes.
" 24 Whites	1424
25 Three parts white	1390
47 Half-white, or mulattoes	1334
51 One-quarter white	1319
95 One-eighth white	1308
22 A sixteenth white	1280
141 Pure negroes	1331"

[*Topinard's Anthropology*, p. 312.]

These estimates are accepted by the scientific world, are quoted by Topinard, Quatrefages, Winchell, and others. Though these measurements are fair to the Negro, and to the classes of mixed bloods to which they refer, they are obviously unfair to the pure Whites, for the following reasons: (1) They were evidently taken from the common soldiers of the Federal army; the higher grades of army officers and the more intelligent classes in the various peaceful vocations in the United States were not represented. Had they been, the average brain weight of the Whites would have been raised to the average of the Noachites—1500 grammes. (2) More or less of the soldiers whom Dr. Hunt recognized as pure whites may have had some admixture of negro blood; and this, as shown by his table, would have reduced the brain weight of such individuals; and would, of course, have reduced the average to this extent. Hence, in the present amalgamated condition of the world, it is evident that it would be unjust to take the average of brain weights in almost any assemblage of individuals, or in any nation, or continent, as representing that of the pure whites.

Topinard, in discussing Hunt's measurements, says, "This would lead us to believe that the mixed breeds assimilate the bad more readily than the good." (*Ibid*, p. 312.)

These measurements are invaluable in that they prove that man is a distinct creation. They also demonstrate that the whites and the negroes are not different races of the same species. One of the great difficulties which breeders experience in their attempt to produce new varieties by crossing is the strong disposition of the offspring to resort to one or the other of its parent stocks. But not so with the offspring of whites and negroes. As has been shown, the offspring of man and the negro, if bred continuously to pure whites for ages, could never become pure white; you could never breed the ape out, nor breed the spiritual creation in. Hence, they would remain simply mixed bloods, without reference to what their physical and mental characters might be. These measurements demonstrate that if the offspring of whites and negroes were bred continuously to negroes for ages they would never become negroes, but would remain mixed bloods.

If whites and negroes were different races of the same species, their immediate offspring should take a position, in point of brain weight, midway between the two; thus presenting a brain weight of at least 1377½ grammes. But, instead of this, the half-whites present an average of 1334 grammes, only three grammes in excess of the Negro, and 90 grammes less than that of the common white soldier of the Federal army. Then mate the half-white with pure negroes and you would reduce the white blood from one-half to one-quarter, and increase the negro blood from one-half to three-quarters; and the offspring presents a brain weight of 1319 grammes, which is 12 grammes less than that of the pure negro. Then mate the one-quarter white with pure negroes and you reduce the white blood in their offspring from one-quarter to one-eighth, and increase the negro blood from three-quarters to seven-eighths; and the offspring presents a brain weight of 1308 grammes, which is 23 grammes less than that of the pure negro. Then mate the one-eighth white with pure negroes, and you reduce the white blood in the offspring from one-eighth to one-sixteenth, and increase the negro blood from seven-eighths to fifteen-sixteenths, and the offspring presents a brain weight of only 1280 grammes, which is 51 grammes less than that of the pure negro.

This is as far as Dr. Hunt's measurements extended. But, it is evident that, with this rapid fall of brain weight in each succeeding generation, if the process were continued, their offspring would finally descend in point of brain weight to the level of the gorilla, whose brain weight is placed by Huxley at 600 grammes.

When we compare the brain weight of whites with that of "the Hottentot, 974," and with that of "the Australian, 907 grammes," we find that, as Winchell says, "The significance of these comparisons appears when we learn that Broca, the most eminent of French anthropologists, states that when the European brain falls below 978 grammes [mean of males and females], the result is idiocy. In this opinion Thurman coincides."

[*Preademites*, pp. 249. 259] Dr. Schaaffhausen, quoted by Huxley, says the brain weight of ''the diminutive Hindoos falls to as little as 27 ounces.'' [*Man's Place in Nature*, p. 160.]

These diminutive brain weights, carrying with them a corresponding dimunition of intelligence, would, in a civilized community, place the individuals in the lowest grades of society; at the same time they might never suffer for the want of food. Hence, their physical development might not be impaired. But, if driven into the forest and compelled to battle with adverse conditions, of climate, etc., they would suffer long periods of want, and this repeated at frequent intervals for many centuries would necessarily impair their physical development; and finally their physical organisms would become as degraded as their mental. Thus, it becomes evident that the mixed bloods in whom the blood of the Negro largely predominates over that of the White, are more degraded and ape-like in their physical and mental organisms; and consequently are more depraved in their modes of life, customs, habits, language, manners, gestures, etc., than the pure Negro. This alone can explain the following facts cited by Winchell, who says:

''The measurements already given show the Australians to possess an organism quite inferior to that of the Negro. In intelligence he is said to be so low as to be unable to count over four or five. Of the Aetas of the Phillippines, De la Geronniere says that they gave him the impression of being a great tribe of monkeys;

their voices recalled the short cry of these animals, and their movements strengthened the analogy. Buchner says that the toes of these savages, who live partly in grottoes, partly on trees, are 'very mobile,' and more separated than ours, especially the great toe. They use them in maintaining themselves on branches and cords, as with fingers. According to Buchner, 'the language of the savages of Borneo is rather a kind of warbling, or croaking, than a truly human mode of expression.' 'The Veddahs of Ceylon,' says Sir Emerson Tennant, 'communicate among themselves almost entirely by means of signs, grimaces, gutteral sounds, resembling very little true words, or true language.' 'The Dokes of Abyssinia,' according to Krapt, 'are human pigmies; they are not more than four feet high; their skin is of an olive brown. Wanderers in the woods, they live like animals, without habitations, without sacred trees, etc. They go naked, nourishing themselves by roots, fruit, mice, serpents, ants, honey; they climb trees like monkeys. Without chief, without law, without arms, without marriage, they have no family, and mate by chance like animals; they also multiply rapidly. The mother after a short lactation, abandons her child to itself. They neither hunt nor cultivate, nor sow, and have never known the use of fire. They have thick lips, a flattened nose, little eyes, long hair, hands and feet with great nails, with which they dig the soil.' Some of the American tribes remain at the lowest point of degrada-tion. This is the case with the Fuegians, and the Bote-

cudos of Brazil have often been cited. Of the latter
Lallimand says, 'I am sadly convinced that they are
monkeys with two hands.' " [*Preademites*, pp. 267,
268.]

The following is Cuvier's description of the "Hottentot Venus," a female Bojesman, "who died in Paris
on the 29th of December, 1815:" "She had a way of
pouting her lips exactly like that we have observed in
the Orang-Outang. Her movements had something
abrupt and fantastical about them, reminding one of those
of the ape. Her lips were monstrously large; her ear
was like that of many apes, being small, the tragus
weak and the external border almost obliterated behind.
These are animal characters. Again, I have never seen
a human head more like an ape than that of this woman."
Referring to the "fatty proturberances" of the haunches,
he says: "They offer a striking resemblance to those
which exists in the females of the mandritts, the papions,
etc., and which assume, at certain epochs of their life,
an enlargement truly monstrous."

"In the dissection of a Bojesman by M. L. Testut
[Acad., des Sci., Paris, 7 July, 1884; Science, xxx.,
284] a muscular system in a more or less rudimentary
state was revealed—such as exists in a normal condition,
in various anthropoid and other apes, and in some instances even in the mammals of other orders." [*Preademites*.]

These facts taken in connection with Hunt's
measurement of brain weights, showing the effects

of amalgamation on cerebral development, fully con-
firm the following conclusions. (1) When whites
and negroes are mated the brain weight of their
offspring is neither that of the white nor that of the
negro; the same is true of his physical characters, he
is neither white nor black, but colored. You would
thus produce a new, so-called race of men, with an
average brain weight of 1,334 grammes. Let us
suppose that there are 1,500 of these half-breeds, and
that 500 of them find mates among themselves; their
offspring would be half-breeds with a brain weight of
1,334 grammes. Then suppose that we mate another
500 of the half-breeds with pure whites, this offspring would be three-quarter white; and would
present a brain weight of 1,390 grammes. You would
thus produce another so-called, "race of men." Then
suppose we mate the remaining 500 half-breeds with
pure negroes, their offspring would be one-quarter
white; and would present a brain weight of 1,319
grammes. You would thus produce another "race of
men," making in all three new and distinct classes of
creatures, as widely different in their physical, as in
their mental characters. If each class of these creatures now isolated from the rest of the world and their
marriage relations confined to their own class, they
would finally settle down to some fixed type. It is
easy to say that the number of these so-called "races
of men," could be increased almost indefinitely, by
mating the mixed bloods with pure whites, with pure

negroes, and with mixed bloods of different grades; the progeny of each cross would present a new type of man, when viewed from the standpoint of Natural Development. We observe that, between the white Federal soldier and the negro there is a difference in point of brain weight, of 93 grammes; while between the three-quarter white, and the one-sixteenth white, there is a difference in point of brain weight, of 110 grammes. Thus we have a greater difference in point of brain weight, between the extremes of mixed bloods, as shown by Hunt's measurements, that exists between the whites and negroes. Hence, we might lay the whites and negroes aside, and still have a wider range for the production of new "races of men," by crossings among the different grades of mixed bloods; and this range could be largely increased by mating the progeny of the three-quarter whites, with whites; and by mating the progeny of the one-sixteenth white with negroes. In the former the increase of brain weight would correspond with the increased predominance of white blood; while in the latter the decrease in brain weight would correspond with the increased predominance of negro blood; and these differences in their mental characters, would be accompanied with corresponding differences in their physical characters. The rapid decrease in brain weight resulting from each infusion of negro blood, as shown by Hunt's measurements, demonstrates that, if the progeny of the one-sixteenth white was

[7]

mated continuously with negroes for generations, they would finally descend as low, or perhaps lower in point of brain weight, than "the diminutive Hindoos" —"27 ounces." There are doubtless other tribes of mixed bloods whose brain weight is even nearer that of the gorilla. The brain weight of many of the lower grades of mixed-blooded tribes have never been ascertained.

(2) They prove that the White and the Negro are not the same kind of flesh, from the fact that the offspring resulting from their unions cannot revert to either of its parent stocks.

(3) They prove the truth of Paul's declaration that "All flesh is not the same flesh; but there is one kind of flesh of men, another flesh of beasts," etc.

(4) They prove that the Negro belongs to the flesh of beasts, from the fact that his offspring by man, though mated continuously with negroes will not revert to the Negro, but approximates a lower grade of animal. Further evidence of this is found in the fact that the mixed bloods frequently develop characters which are never found in either the pure white or the pure negro, but which are peculiar to lower grades of animals. From the many which the want of space forbids us to enumerate, we shall select the following:

"A character of the humerus, or arm bone, was remarked ·by Cuvier, which approximates the Bush-men to monkeys, dogs and other carnivores, as well as to the wild boar, chevrotian and the daman. It was the non-ossification of the wall separating the anterior cubital fossa from the posterior fossa of the humerus—something which will be intelligible to persons versed in anatomy." (*Preadimites.*) Such also is "tablier" and "steatopygia." Of these Topinard says, "Hitherto we have met with many opposite characters in the human groups, but few so remarkable as these. We have seen the marked difference between woolly and straight hair, between the prognathous and the orthognathous, the jet black of the Yoloff and the pale complexion of the Scandinavian, between the ultra-dolichocephalic Esquimau or New Caledonian and the ultra-brachycepalic Mongolian. But the line of separation between the European and the Bosjesman as regards these two characters is, in a morphological point of view, still wider, as much so as between each of the anthropoid apes, or between the dog and the wolf, the goat and the sheep." (*Anthropology*, p. 363.) The Bushman, or Bosjesman, and the Hottentots are classed by Winchell as one race. Topinard describes the Hottentots as "an agglomeration of ancient races."

These, and other animal characters in the mixed breeds, have been seized upon by the advocates of the Theory of Development as proof that man developed from a lower form; and that these animal characters were transmitted from his "animal ancestors." The very reverse is true. The creatures possessing these characters are the result of amalgamation between two different kinds of flesh; the flesh of men and the flesh of beasts. The mere fact that these creatures frequently develop characters which are common to the "flesh of beasts," should occasion no surprise when viewed in the light of Paul's declaration as to the different kinds of flesh. The wonder is that they don't develop a tail; and if one or more individuals of these so-called "lower races of men" is found either alive or in a fossil state, with such an appendage, an intelligent examination of his anatomy will reveal the evidences of crossing. Let us bear in mind that the Negro, the lower apes and the quadrupeds, all belong to "one kind of flesh," the "flesh of beasts." Hence it should rather be surprising, than otherwise, if the Negro did not transmit to the offspring resulting from his unnatural union with man, characters which are not only common to the lower apes, but even those which are common to quadrupeds. The mixed-bloods are "an unnatural production," and being altogether "out of the common order of nature," they are simply monstrosities, no odds what their social, political, or religious standing may be. Even the atheist, who denies the existence of a God and the inspiration of the scriptures, will insist that amalgamation between Whites and Negroes is "a violation of the natural law." For thousands of years these base-born creatures have been found in every position in life, from the jungle to the throne. In thousands of cases they live sumptuously, and are arrayed in "purple and fine linen," and be-

decked with jewels and all the paraphenalia of their inherited wealth and rank. In other cases, like that of
many of our newly acquired "brothers and sisters of the
Phillipines," they obtain a bare subsistence from the
spontaneous products of the earth, and the proceeds of
the chase, and are simply attired "in atmosphere and
smiles."

For further evidence of the frequent appearance
of "animal characters" in the so-called "lower races of
men," see the works of Cuvier, Winchell, Darwin,
Huxley, Haeckel, etc.

The existence of a tool-making animal should occasion us no surprise, when we consider the fact that
lower grades of ape than the Negro handle tools for a
particular purpose. Mr. Darwin says,

"It has often been said that no animal uses any
tool, but the chimpanzee in a state of nature cracks a
native fruit, somewhat like a walnut, with a stone.
Renger easily taught an American monkey thus to
break open hard palmnuts, and afterward of its own
accord it used stones to open other kinds of nuts, as
well as boxes. It thus also removed the soft rind of
fruit that had a disagreeable flavor. Another monkey
was taught to open the lid of a large box with a stick,
and afterward it used the stick as a lever to move
heavy bodies; and I have myself seen a young ourang
put a stick into a crevice, slip his hand to the other
end, and use it in the proper manner as a lever.
*   *   *   In these several cases, stones and sticks were

employed as implements; but they are likewise used as weapons. Brehm states, on the authority of the well-known traveler, Schimper, that in Abyssinia when the baboons belonging to one species (C. gelada) descend in troops from the mountains to plunder the fields they sometimes encounter troops of another species (C. hamadoyas), and then a fight ensues. The Geledas roll down great stones, which the Hamadoyas try to avoid, and then both species, making a great uproar, rush furiously against each other. Brehm, when accompanying the Duke of Coburg-Gotha, aided in an attack with firearms on a troop of baboons in the pass of Mensa in Abyssinia. The baboons in return rolled so many stones down the mountains, some as large as a man's head, that the attackers had to beat a hasty retreat, and the pass was actually closed for a time against the caravan. It deserves notice that these baboons thus acted in concert." (*Descent of Man,* pp. 91, 92.)

Mr. Hartman says, "Buffon's Chimpanze offered people his arm, walked with them in orderly manner, sat down to table like a man, opened his napkin and wiped his lips with it, made use of his spoon and fork, poured out wine and clinked glasses, fetched a cup and saucer and put in sugar, poured out tea, let it get cold before drinking it. * * * He ate all the ordinary food of men, but preferred fruit. * * * He was friendly with every one, coming close to them, and taking pleasure in their caresses. He took such a fancy to one lady, that when other people approached her he seized a stick and began flourishing it about, until Buffon intimated his displeasure at such conduct." (*Anthropoid Apes*, p. 267.)

According to the account of Captain Grandpre, a female chimpanzee on board his vessel would heat the oven, taking care that no coals fell out, and carefully watching until it was of the right heat, of which she would inform the baker. She fulfilled all the duties of a sailor, such as drawing up the anchor, furling and making fast the sails. She patiently endured maltreatment by a brutal mate, stretching out her hands imploringly to ward off the blows. But after this she refused all food, and died in five days of grief and hunger." (*Ibid*, p. 268.)

Mr. Darwin says, "Monkeys seize thin branches or ropes, with the thumb on one side and the fingers and palm on the other, in the same manner as we do. * * * They seize nuts, insects, or other small objects with the thumb in opposition to the fingers. * * * Monkeys open mussel shells with two thumbs. * * * With their fingers they pull out thorns and burrs, and hunt for each other's parasites. They roll down stones, or throw them at their enemies; nevertheless, they are clumsy in these various actions, and, as I have myself seen, are quite unable to throw a stone with precision." (*Ibid*, pp. 56, 57.)

"A male chimpanzee, which was kept in the Berlin Aquarium in 1876 * * * was on particularly friendly terms with Dr. Hermes' two-year-old-boy. When the child entered the room, the chimpanzee ran to meet him, embraced and kissed him, seized his hands and drew him to the sofa, that they might play together. The child was often rough with his play-fellow, pulling him by the mouth, pinching his ears, or lying on him, yet the chimpanzee was never known to lose his temper. He behaved very differently to boys from six to twelve years old. When a number of school·boys visited the office, he ran towards them, went from one to the other, shook one of them, bit the leg of another, seized the jacket of a third with the right hand, jumped up, and with the left gave him a sound box on the ear; in short he played the wildest pranks. * * * One day when Hermes gave his nine-year-old son a slight rap on the head, on account of some miscalculation in his arithmetic, the chimpanzee, who was also sitting at the table, gave the boy a smart box on the ear. * * * When he saw that Hermes was writing, he often seized a pen, dipped it in the inkstand, and scrawled upon the paper. He displayed a special talent for cleaning the window-panes of the aquarium. It was amusing to see him squeezing up the cloth, moistening the pane with his lips, and then rubbing it hard, passing quickly from one place to another." (*Anthropoid Apes,* pp. 270, 271.) "An ourang brought by Montgomery to Calcutta in 1827 * * * tried to scour his tin vessel with a cloth, throwing one end over his shoulder, as he had seen the servants of the house do." (*Ibid*, p. 279.)

Mr. Hartman says, "Mafuca was a remarkable creature, not only in her external habits, but in her disposition. At one moment she would sit still with a brooding air, only occasionally darting a mischievous, flashing glance at the spectators, at another she took pleasure in feats of strength, or she seemed to roam to and fro in her spacious enclosure like an angry beast of prey. She would insert the index finger of her right hand in the opening of a vessel that weighed thirty pounds, climb up the pole with it, and let it fall with a crash and clatter from a height of six feet. * * * She hardly obeyed any one except Mr. Schopf, the director of the Dresden Zoological Gardens, and when in a good humor she would sit on his knee and put her muscular arms around his neck with a caressing gesture. In spite of this, Schopf was never secure from Mafuca's roguish tricks, since her good humor was of short duration. She was rather fond of the keeper, but not always obedient to him. * * * Mafuca was able to use a spoon, although somewhat awkwardly, and she could pour from larger vessels into smaller ones without spilling the liquor. She took tea and cocoa in the morning and evening, and a mixed diet between whiles, such as fruit, sweet-meats, red wine and water, and sugar. * * * If she was left alone for any time, she tried to open the lock of her cage without having the key, and she

once succeeded in doing so. On that occasion she
stole the key, which was hanging on the wall, hid it
in her axilla, and crept quietly back to the cage.
With the key she easily opened the lock, and she also
knew how to use a gimlet. She would draw off her
keeper's boots, scramble up to some place out of reach
with them and throw them at his head when he asked
for them. She could wring out a wet cloth and blow
her nose with a handerkerchief. * * * Just before
her death from consumption, she put her arms around
Schopf's neck when he came to visit her, looked at
him placidly, kissed him three times, stretched out her
hand to him and died. The last moments of anthropoids have their tragic side!" (*Ibid*, pp. 271, 72,
73.)

Mr. Darwin says, "Sir Andrew Smith, a zoologist
whose scrupulous accuracy was known to many persons, told me the following story, of which he himself
was an eye-witness: At the Cape of Good Hope an officer had often plagued a certain baboon, and the animal, seeing him approach on Sunday for parade,
poured water into a hole and hastily made some thick
mud which he skillfully dashed over the officer as he
passed by, to the amusement of many bystanders.
For a long time afterward the baboon rejoiced and
triumphed whenever he saw his victim." (*Ibid*, p.
78.)

Mr. Darwin says, "Mr. Wallace on three occa-
sions saw female ourangs, accompanied by their

young, breaking off branches and the great, spicey fruit of the Durian tree with every appearance of rage, causing such a shower of missiles as effectually kept us from approaching too near the tree." As I have repeatedly seen, a chimpanzee will throw any object at hand at a person who offends him; and the before-mentioned baboon at the Cape of Good Hope prepared mud for the purpose. In the zoological gardens a monkey, which had weak teeth, used to break open nuts with a stone; and I was assured by the keepers that after using the stone he hid it in the straw and would not let any other monkey touch it." (*Ibid*, p. 92.)

Mr. Topinard says: ''Many species of monkeys, like Man, select a chief, who directs their operations and to whom they submit. The howlers, or mycites, belonging to the Cebin family, hold meetings in which one of them speaks for hours at a time in the midst of a general silence, succeeded by great excitement, which ceases as soon as the speaker gives the word of command. Other monkeys combine together to plan an excursion; divided into detachments, some plunder and tear up roots, others make a chain for the purpose of carrying them from hand to hand; others are placed as sentinels to keep watch. In unexpected danger, the sentinel gives the alarm and all decamp. It has been remarked that if the troop is surprised, owing to the fault of the sentinel, there is a grand hub-bub in the neighboring forest during the night, and on the morrow the body of one of the plunderers is found, to all appearance having been put to death by his companions." (*Anthropology*, p. 151.)

These, and many other proofs which might be adduced, enable us to see how closely the lower apes approach the Negro, in their ability to handle tools. Yet we must admit that, the lower apes, and even the so-called anthropoids, are unfit for general domestic purposes. They could never handle domestic animals, work metals, level forests, break the soil, plant, cultivate, and harvest crops, and erect mechanical structures; in short perform the multitudinous duties of servants. Besides, no one of the so-called anthropoids, can be said to be "most absolutely like man. The Gorilla approaches nearest to Man in the structure of the hand and foot, the Chimpanzee in important structural details in the skull, the Ourang in the development of the brain, and the Gibbon in that of the thorax." (Haeckel, *The Evolution of Man*, p. 181.)

Darwin says, "One can hardly doubt that a manlike animal who possessed a hand and arm sufficiently perfect to throw a stone with precision or to form a flint into a rude tool could, with sufficient practice, as far as mechanical skill alone is concerned, make almost anything which a civilized man can make." (*Ibid*, p. 56.)

The force of Mr. Darwin's reasoning upon this subject is plain. It is easy to see that an animal who could realize his need of a weapon and was possessed of mechanical skill sufficient to enable him to fashion for himself a rudely-chipped weapon of stone, which he could handle with precision, could, if properly trained, make and handle any implement that a man could make and handle. Add to this the fact that the Negro is the highest grade of ape and that the disposition of this family of animals to imitate the actions of man are more highly developed in the Negro than in any other ape, and his ability to discharge all the duties of servant, for which God designed him is fully explained. Desor, quoted by Darwin, "has remarked that no animal voluntarily imitates an action performed by man, until, in the ascending scale, we come to monkeys, which are known to be ridiculous mockers." (*Ibid*, p. 82.)

The great intellectual qualities which the men of this and preceeding ages have displayed, are the result of inheritance from Adam, upon whom they were a Divine bestowal. Hence, they are transmittible. The low order of the Negro's mentality—his lack of inventive skill—is demonstrated by his meager accomplishments in his undomesticated state, which, as has been shown, are confined to the fashioning of a few rude weapons of stone; while the greater achievements of the domesticated Negro are due solely to the influence of man. Hence, if from any cause he is relieved of this influence and is thrown upon his own resources in the forest, he soon relapses into savagery and descends to the use of stones for weapons.

Among the older naturalists the opinion prevailed that the apes were quadrumana, or four-handed animals. But this delusion has long since been dispelled. There is no four-handed animal.

But for the existence of the lower apes we, at this late day, would have no alternative than to decide that the Negro is the sole representative of his species or that he is a man. But with this family, shading up from the Lemur to the Negro, we are enabled, with the aids of Scripture and the sciences, to determine that the Negro is a member of it. Thus this interesting family of animals, though unfit for general domestic purposes, are invaluable to man in that they enable him to determine the Negro's proper position in the universe—that he is simply an ape.

But, says the Enlightened Christian, the Negro possesses the moral faculty. Is not this the most positive evidence that he is a man—that he has a soul? Not the least evidence! In discussing this question it is essential that we bear in mind that there were just three Creations—Matter, Mind and Soul, and that these made their appearance in the Universe in the order stated. When we accept the teachings of the Bible, we must admit that everything belongs to, and is a part of one or the other of these three creations and necessarily made its appearance in the material universe simultaneously with the Creation of which it is a part. Hence, the question is, which of these three creations is the moral faculty a part of?

Evidently it is not a part of matter, since it does not exist in the plant. Hence, it belongs either to the mind creation, or to the spiritual creation. If it is a part of the latter creation it is peculiar to man. If it is a part of the former creation it is common to man and the animals. It is this faculty—the moral faculty—which enables man to distinguish between right and wrong; and that it is right to obey, and wrong to disobey God. But for the existence of this faculty in man, he could not in justice, be held responsible to God for his acts   This leads us to realize that it is the moral faculty in the animals which makes it possible for man to teach them that it is right to obey, and wrong to disobey their master. But for their possession of this faculty the animals would be un-fit for domestic purposes. Hence, inasmuch as the moral faculty does not exist in the plant, in which the matter creation is alone represented, and inasmuch as it is not peculiar to man, in whom the soul creation is alone represented, we have no alternative than to decide that it is a part of the mind creation. Further evidence of this is found in the fact that this faculty, like any phy-sical or mental character, is subject to accident or disease. If from accident or from disease, the mind creation of man, or woman is impaired, the moral faculty is correspondingly impaired. If, as in the case of an insane person, the mind is so impaired as to temporarily, or permanently, destroy the reasoning faculty, the moral faculty is temporarily or permanently destroyed as the case may be. The soul creation of the individual cannot be

impaired, and the matter creation as presented in the
physical structure may not be impaired by its combination with mind that has been injured or become diseased.
The individual may live long after his reasoning faculties
have been destroyed. But the very moment he ceases
to be a rational being, he ceases to be a moral being.
Then, if his mind is restored his moral faculty is restored. The same argument holds good with the animals. The moral, like any faculty of the mind, may be
cultivated and developed, or it may be neglected and
dwarfed. This can be demonstrated by comparing the
cultivated with the uncultivated man; the domesticated
with the undomesticated Negro; or our domesticated
quadrupeds with the same class of animals in their undomesticated state. When the world of mankind is
freed from the thralldom of atheism, and its great intellects are turned upon the Mosaic Record, and the characters peculiar to each of the three Creations are already
ascertained (as they will be), our present opinions as to
the characters peculiar to man will be very materially
modified. Under the influence of The Theory of Natural Development, the Negro has been taken into the
family of man: the result is, that we have been led to
believe that mind, with its intellectual and moral faculties, articulate speech, the erect posture, a well developed hand and foot, the ability to fashion and handle
implements, are characters peculiar to man. This is a
sad mistake. It will yet be ascertained that man has
just two characters peculiar to him. (1.) His flesh is

a different kind of flesh from that of the lower animals (2.) Man possesses immortality, while the animals are mere creatures of time.

"But," says the enlightened Christian, "If a man is married to a negress, will not their offspring have a soul?" No; it is simply the product resulting from God's violated law, and inherits none of the Divine nature of the man, but, like its parent, the ape, it is merely a combination of matter and mind. "Then, if the half-breed marries a man, will not their offspring have a soul?" No! "Then if the three-quarter white marries a man will not their offspring have a soul?" No. "If the offspring of man and the Negro was mated with pure whites for generations, would not their ultimate offspring have a soul?" No! In discussing this question we must bear in mind that there were just three Creations—matter, mind and soul. That these three creations made their appearance in the order stated. That matter is the basis of all formations in the material universe; whether it exists alone as in the plant, or in combination with mind as in the animal, and with soul as in man. Let us also bear in mind that, the reproduction of these Creations as they exist in the plants, in the animals, and in man, was not left to chance, but is governed by laws which God established in the Creation, and which are unerring and positive in their operations and results.

[9]

In order to acquaint ourselves with the operations
and results of these laws, let us first discuss the reproduction of plants, in which the matter creation is
alone represented; and, since the manner of their
reproduction is more generally understood, let us take
as an illustration, the flowering plants, in which the
sexes are represented in the male, and in the female
flower. As is well known reproduction results from
the union of the pollen, or fecundating dust, of the
stamen of the male flower with the pollen of the pistil
of the female flower. This indicates that one side or
part of the matter creation, exists in the male flower;
and that its corresponding side or part exists in the
female flower. These opposite sides or parts, each
act as a magnet which attracts its corresponding side
or part in the opposite sex; and, when united, the
matter creation is perfected and reproduced in the
young plant. But if, from any cause, the matter
creation, as it exists in its imperfect state in the
respective germs of the male and the female flowers,
are not united and perfected in the female flower,
these vital elements are wasted, and the reproduction
of the matter creation in the young plant is not
accomplished. The same law holds good with the
animal, in which the two Creations- Matter and
Mind, exist in the respective germs of the male, and
the female. One side or part of the Matter Creation,
and one side or part of the Mind Creation, exists in
an imperfect state in the male germ; the correspond-

ing sides or parts of these imperfect Creations exists
in the female germ. By uniting these imperfect
creations in the female, they are perfected and reproduced in the young animal. This indicates that each
of these creations maintains its individuality in their
respective male and female germs; and that each side
or part of these creations, act as a magnet, which
attracts its corresponding side or part in the opposite
sex. When sexual union takes place, each side or
part of these two creations—Matter and Mind—are
united and perfected in the female, conception and
birth ensues, and the combination of matter and
mind is reproduced in the offspring.

But, if from any cause these imperfect matter and
mind creations, as they exist in the respective germs
of the male and the female animal, are not united and
perfected in the female, these vital elements are
wasted, conception does not ensue, and the reproduction of these two creations in a young animal is not
accomplished. The strength of our position on this
subject is demonstrated by the actions of our domestic
fowls; it frequently occurs that the female fowl, when
not associated with the male fowl, will lay eggs.
But only one part of the two creations—matter and
mind—as they existed in an imperfect state in the
germ of the female were represented in the egg; their
corresponding side or part in the male, which was
necessary to perfect the creations, was absent. The
result of the effort of the female to reproduce these

two creations without their corresponding side or part
in the male, was abortion—the egg would not
"hatch."

The same law holds good with man, in whom the
three creations—matter, mind and soul—exist. As in
the plant and in the animal, so it must be in man; one
side or part of the matter creation, and one side or
part of the mind creation, and one side or part of the
soul creation exists in the male germ; the corresponding side or part of each of these creations exists in
the female germ. Each side or part of these three
creations maintains its individuality in their respective male and female germs; and each side or part of
these three creations acts as a magnet which attracts
its corresponding side or part in the opposite sex.
When sexual union takes place, each side or part of
these three creations unite and are perfected in the
female germ; conception ensues and the three creations—matter, mind and soul—are reproduced in the
offspring. But when no corresponding side or part of
one of these creations exists in the opposite sex, this
creation finds no attraction and is passive. Hence, if
the sexual act results in conception, this passive creation is not perfected and forms no part of the offspring. For example: In the Negro, as in any other
animal, but two creations—matter and mind—are
combined. On side or part of each of these creations
exists in the male germ; their corresponding side or
part exists in the female germ, as mutually dependent

sides or parts of the life system of the animal. In the sexual act each of these creations acts as a magnet, which attracts its corresponding side or part in the opposite sex, and, if united, these two creations are perfected; conception ensues and the combination of matter and mind is transmitted to the offspring.

Thus, while but two creations—matter and mind— combine to perfect the Negro, three creations—matter, mind and soul—combine to perfect man. While these two creations—matter and mind—exist in an imperfect state in the germs of the male and female Negro, as mutually dependent sides or parts of the life system of the animal, three creations—matter, mind and spiritual life—exist in an imperfect state in the germs of the male and female man, as mutually dependent sides or parts of the life system of man; and such is the attraction between matter and mind as they exist in their imperfect state in the germs of man and the Negro that sexual intercourse between the two will unite and perfect these two creations. But the soul creation in its imperfect and dependent state in the germ of the man, finds no corresponding side or part in the negress. Hence, this creation having no attraction remains passive, and if conception ensues from the union of the germs and the consequent perfecting of the matter and mind creations of man and the Negro, this passive creation forms no part of the offspring of this unnatural union. Thus, it is impossible for either side or part of the life system of man—the male or the female—to transmit these three creations—matter, mind and soul to their offspring by the Negro, in whom matter and mind alone exists. In other words, the male and the female can only transmit to their offspring such creations as are common to both.

Let us bear in mind that prior to the creation of man there was no connecting link—no tie of kinship between the Creator and His creatures. All things in the material universe were material, there was nothing spiritual; all was mortal, there was no immortality; but when the Lord God formed man out of "the dust of the ground," this "dust of the ground" being a part of the original creation—matter—"and breathed into his nostrils the breath of life," spiritual, immortal life, "man became a living soul." This spiritual, immortal life, "this living soul," was a part of the substance of God. Hence, its combination with matter and with mind, as presented in man's physical, mental and spiritual organisms, formed the connecting link—the link of kinship—between the Creator and creature. Thus, man became "the Son of God." His failure to form this link of kinship between Himself and the fish, or fowl, or beast, clearly demonstrates the design of God that no kinship should exist between them. Hence, when man becomes so degenerated as to associate himself carnally with the Negro, the very act brings into operation the law which governs the reproduction of the creations, which makes it impossible for man to transmit to his offspring by the beast the slightest vestige of kinship with God.

This law becomes active and operates with the same result when man associates himself carnally with the mixed breeds; without reference to what their proportions of white and black blood may be. The immediate offspring of man and the Negro—the half breed—like the Negro, is merely a combination of two creations—matter and mind. Hence, but two—matter and mind—of the three creatures—matter, mind and soul—as they exist in their imperfect state in the germ of the man find their corresponding sides or portion in the opposite sex of the half breed. The result is, that the one side or part of the soul creation, as it exists in its imperfect state in the germ of the man, finding no corresponding side or part in the opposite sex of the half breed, with which it may be united and perfected, is not attracted and remains passive. Hence, if the matter creation and the mind creation as they exist in their imperfect state in the respective germs of man and the half breed, are united and perfected, and conception ensues, this passive creation forms no part of the offspring. This unvarying law would hold good through millions of generations. Man, in associating himself carnally with the mixed-breeds, would continually oppose three creations—matter, mind and soul—as they exist in their imperfect state in his germ, to only two creations—matter and mind—as they exist in their imperfect state in the germ of the mixed bloods. As a result it could only be possible to unite and perfect the matter and mind creations as they exist in their imperfect state in the respective germs of man and the mixed bloods, and thus reproduce and transmit them to the offspring. But the soul creation as it exists in its imperfect state in the germ of man, finding no corresponding side or part in the opposite sex of the mixed bloods with which it might be united and perfected, is not affected in the sexual act and remains passive, hence it is not represented in the offspring.

ADAM and EVE in the GARDEN of EDEN.
Is the negro an offspring of Adam and Eve?
Can the rose produce a thistle?

Chapter V.

Cain's Offspring Souless, as they were of Amalgamated Flesh.

The atheist takes the negro which God made an ape and thrusts him violently into the family of man as "a lower race of the human species," and enlightened Christianity receives him with open arms; the atheist then points to the remnant of the animals and tells us with much the appeaeance of truth that there is no beast with which man may associate himself carnally and produce offspring; and enlightened Christianity responds with a hearty Amen! This theory may be good modern philosophy, but it is not scripure, as shown by the following:

"And Adam knew Eve his wife, and she conceived and bare Cain, and said, I have gotten a man from the Lord. And she again bare his brother Abel. And Abel was a keeper of sheep, but Cain was a tiller of the ground. And in process of time it came to pass that Cain brought of the fruit of the ground an offering unto the Lord. And Abel, he also brought of the firstlings of his flock and of the fat thereof. And the Lord had respect unto Abel and to his offerring. But unto Cain and to his offering he had not respect. And Cain was very wroth, and his countenance fell." (Gen. iv, 3-4-5.)

It will be observed that these brothers were not rivals in business; they were engaged in different pursuits; each offered the products of his labor and skill; and had each of them walked uprightly before God, there could have been no reason why their offerings would not have been alike acceptable to God. But such was not the case. Abel was a good man; he had faith in God (Heb. ii, 4) and respected and obeyed his laws. Hence, "the Lord had respect unto Abel" as a man, and consequently, to his offering. But Cain was a bad man; the little faith which he had in God, was not expressed in obedience to his laws; he had no respect for the laws of God. Hence, God had no respect for his offering. Cain was a violater of the laws of God, as shown by the following:

"And the Lord said unto Cain, Why art thou wroth, and why is thy countenance fallen? If thou doest well, shalt thou not be accepted? And if thou doest not well, sin lieth at thy door; and unto thee shall be his desire, and thou shalt rule over him." (Gen. iv, 6-7.)

This indicates that Cain had not only violated the law of God, but that he had an associate in the crime. To have desire requires life, and also requires intelligence; no inanimate object can have desire. In view of the fact that individuals of the same sex have no desire for each other, it would seem natural to decide that this creature which had desire for this fine young man, Cain, was a female; and the mere fact that the inspired writer refers to it in the masculine gender is no evidence that it was not a female. In describing the animals, it is common in the scriptures to find both sexes referred to in the masculine gender. For example: God made "every winged fowl after his kind." "Let the earth bring forth the living creature after his kind," etc. (Gen. i.: 22–24.) David refers to the Sun, which is without sex, in the masculine, as follows: "His going forth is from the end of the heaven, and his circuit from the ends of it. (Ps. xix, 6.)

We should observe (1) that God charged Cain with sin; (2) that "Unto thee shall be his desire and thou shalt rule over him," was a sentence which God imposed upon Cain and his partner in crime. We should also note the striking similarity of God's language in imposing this sentence to that which he employed in imposing his sentence upon Eve. To the woman who had committed sin, God said, "Thy desire shall be to thy husband, and he shall rule over thee." (Gen. iii, 16.) To the man Cain, who had committed sin, God said, "Unto thee shall be his desire, and thou shalt rule over him." Thus it is shown that the sentence which God imposed upon Eve was identical with that which he imposed upon Cain's partner in sin. In this identity of sentence we find the most positive evidence that Cain's accomplice in the crime which cost him the respect of God was a female. In each case God decreed that the desire of the female should be to a particular male, and that the male should "rule over" the female which had desire for him.

In the epistle of Jude we find not only the most positive proof that Cain's partner in sin was a female, but that she was not of Adamic flesh. It will be observed that Jude at once arraigns the men of his day on the charge of amalgamation—"giving themselves over to fornication, and going after strange flesh." And appeals to the followers of the Saviour to "keep" themselves "in the love of God."

Jude says: "Beloved, when I gave all diligence to write unto you of the common salvation, it was needful for me to write unto you and exhort you that ye should earnestly contend for the faith which was once delivered to the saints. For there are certain men crept in unawares, who were before of old ordained to this condemnation; ungodly men, turning the grace of our God into lasciviousness, and denying the only Lord God, and our Lord Jesus Christ. I will therefore put you in remembrance, though ye once knew this, how that the Lord, having saved the people out of the land of Egypt, afterward destroyed them that believed not. And the angels which kept not their first estate, but left their own habitation, he hath reserved in everlasting chains under darkness unto the judgment of the great day. Even as Sodom and Gomorrah, and the cities about them, in like manner, giving themselves over to fornication, and going after strange flesh, are set forth for an example, suffering the vengeance of eternal fire. Likewise these filthy dreamers defile the flesh, despise dominion, and speak evil of dignitaries. Yet Michael, when contending with the devil, he disputed about the body of Moses, durst not bring against him a railing accusation, but said, The Lord rebuke thee. But these speak evil of those things which they know not; but what they knew naturally as brute beasts, in those things they corrupt themselves. Woe unto them, for they have gone in the way of Cain, and ran greedily after the error of Balaam for reward, and perished in the gainsaying of Core."

Thus Jude, after stating various events, which occurred in the past, distinctly charges the people of Sodom and Gomorrah with giving themselves over to fornication, and going after strange flesh. And says that they are set for an example, suffering the vengenance of eternal fire. Continuing, Jude says: "These filthy dreamers defile the flesh (this is precisely the offense with which God charged the ante-

diluvians and the Canaanites), despise dominion (preferring social equality with the negro to that dominion
which God designed them to have and commanded
them to exercise), and speak evil of dignitaries."

In closing his charges against "these filthy dreamers, who defile the flesh by giving themselves over to
fornication and going after strange flesh," Jude
says: "Woe unto them! for they have gone in the way
of Cain."

Thus the inspired apostle Jude, a New Testament writer, specifically charges that Cain was one of
these filthy dreamers, who despise dominion, defile
the flesh, by giving themselves over to fornication,
and going after strange flesh.

By comparing the sentence which God imposed
upon Eve, and in which Adam was made a participant, with the sentence which he imposed upon Cain's
paramour, and to which Cain was made a participant,
we find that in each case the result to the parties in-
terested was identical. The relation of husband and
wife, which existed between Adam and Eve, was established in the days of their innocence, and was sanctioned by the law given man in the creation, "Be
fruitful and multiply." But in their fallen state God
saw fit, by special edict, to bind and confine them in
their sexual relations to each other, changing their
former relations only so far as to place the offending
woman in subjection to her husband, whom she had
misled.

Lest we should be misunderstood upon this most important subject, we desire to state most emphatically that there is not a single passage of Scripture which warrants the slighest suspicion that either Adam or Eve ever descended to amalgamation. On the contrary, we are plainly taught that Cain led off in this wicked course. Hence, Jude describes it as "the way of Cain."

When Cain committed fornication with this female of strange flesh, he at once outraged the design of God in creating man and violated that Divine law given man in the Creation—"Have dominion * * * over every living thing that moveth upon the earth." "Dominion" means control, and control is the very opposite of social equality; and social equality, to a greater or less extent, is inseparable from sexual intercourse. And God in his wrath and disgust determined that he would visit upon Cain for his wanton, shameless, loathsome crime, the most degrading penalty. Thus, as in the case of Adam and Eve, God bound Cain and his paramour of strange flesh in the relation of husband and wife and confined them, in their sexual relations, to each other; and at the same time placed Cain's wife of strange flesh in subjection to him.

In the ordinary course of events, the first female born to the Adamic family, upon reaching maturity, would have been given in marriage to Cain, the first born son. But Cain's shameless crime in cultivating

sexual relations with a beast had rendered him unfit
for the companionship of a pure woman. Besides, God's
decree bound Cain in the relation of husband all his life
long to this beast, and forever debarred him from holding sexual relations with women. Hence, the beautiful
Adamic woman, who, in all her virgin loveliness, would
have been the wife of Cain, would now become the wife
of his brother, Abel. In his jealous rage upon realizing
this, we might find an explanation of why "Cain rose
up against Abel his brother and slew him."

The correctness of our interpretation of God's sentence upon Cain and his accomplice in sin—that it
bound them together in the relation of husband and wife
—is fully sustained by the scriptural record, which
shows that subsequent to this event Cain is accredited
with a wife, while prior to this event he is merely accredited with a paramour of strange flesh, with whom he
committed fornication. The record is as follows:

"And Cain went out from the presence of the Lord,
and dwelt in the land of Nod, on the east of Eden. And
Cain knew his wife, and she conceived and bare Enoch."
(Gen. iv, 16-17.)

This scriptural record forms a part of a genealogical
table, which shows the line of descent for five generations, and gives the name, occupation, etc., of the most
prominent character in each generation of his descendants during that period of time.

We desire to call special attention to the fact that
there is absolutely nothing in this record which indicates

that Cain obtained his wife in the land of Nod. On the other hand, his previous history, as above shown, proves that she was formerly his paramour, and sustained that relation to him at the time when he and his brother Abel brought their offerings unto the Lord. And that, immediately after that event, God, by special decree, and as a punishment upon Cain for his criminal relations with her, bound them to each other in the relation of husband and wife. After their arrival in the land of Nod, "Cain knew his wife," in the sense that she conceived and bare Enoch; just as, after their expulsion from the garden of Eden, "Adam knew Eve his wife," in the sense that she conceived and bare Cain. (See also Luke i, 36.) Cain and his wife disappear from the records, and all trace of them is lost after the birth of Enoch and the building of the city which Cain named after his son Enoch.

If, as many suppose, Cain had taken his sister to wife, sin would not have lain at his door as the result of his act. He would simply have obeyed the law given man in the creation: "Be fruitful and multiply." The only way the sons of Adam could have preserved and increased the pure Adamic flesh was by taking their sisters to wife. This course was evidently pursued by Seth and his younger brothers, and they were never censured for it. On the contrary, Seth, the third son of Adam, was very highly honored in that his taking his sister to wife placed his name in the line of descent from Adam to Jesus Christ. Hence, he stands in the genealogical tables of the Bible as one of the ancestors of the Messiah.

Thus, the testimony of the inspired writers, Moses, Jude and St. Paul, sweeps away the veil of mystery which for so many centuries, has enveloped the marital relations of Cain, and lays bare the most important and instructive events in his history, as follows:

1. That it was the sin which lay at Cain's door, which cost him the respect of God, and led to the rejection of his offering. The nature of his offering had no bearing on the result; any offering which he might have made would have shared the same fate. God had no respect for Cain as a man; hence, for his offering he had not respect.

2. That Cain had an associate in his crime.

3. That his associate in crime was a female.

4. That this female was not of the flesh of man; she was not a woman, but was a creature of strange flesh with which he was committing fornication. Just here, as in many other portions of the Bible, Paul's declaration that "There is one kind of flesh of men; another flesh of beast, another of fishes, and another of birds," proves invaluable, in that it enables us to fathom many of the so-called mysteries of the Bible. When we turn it upon the statement of Jude that Cain was of those filthy dreamers who were guilty of giving themselves to fornication, and going after strange flesh, we can see at a glance that this creature with which Cain committed fornication was not of the flesh of man; that she was not a woman, but that she belonged to one of the three other kinds of flesh; and being a land animal, she nec-

essarily belonged to the flesh of beasts.   Hence, Cain's paramour was a beast.

5.   That God in His wrath and disgust at the depravity thus displayed by Cain, in descending to sexual relations with a beast, bound Cain and his paramour of strange flesh in the relation of husband and wife, and confined their sexual relations to each other, thus forever debarring Cain from holding sexual relations with woman.

6.   That Cain's wife of strange flesh conceived by him and bore him Enoch.

7.   That Cain's son Enoch, begotten of his wife of strange flesh, was indefinitely fertile; and that he had numerous descendants, children, grandchildren, great-grandchildren, etc.

8.   That the descendants of Cain by his wife of strange flesh raised domestic animals, mined and worked metals and fashioned them into implements, and were skillful musicians, and for generations retained a knowledge of God and his dealings with Cain; and all circumstances indicate that they cultivated domestic plants, especially the food plants.

When called upon to identify this creature of strange flesh which bore Cain offspring as above described, science promptly invades the so-called human species, and points to the negro, the lowest of the so-called races of men, as the only creature among the lower kind of flesh with which man may associate himself carnally and produce offspring which will at once be indefinitely fertile and capable of being taught a knowledge of God and the arts of civilization.

Man's strong disposition to abandon himself to this loathsome, destructive crime, as shown by his whole past history, is made even more conspicuous by the fact that Cain, the first child born to the Adamic creation, fell the victim of amalgamation.

The history of Cain and his descendants presents little to interest, and is practically of no value when viewed from the atheistic standpoint that man is a species divisible into races. But when viewed in the lights of revelation and the sciences, it is at once transformed into a subject of the most absorbing interest and importance. In the disasters which resulted to Cain from his association with his paramour of strange flesh, we find the most positive evidence of God's utter abhorrence of amalgamation; while in his formation and preservation of the genealogical table of Cain's descendants we find additional evidence of his unerring wisdom, his infinite mercy, and of his wondrous love for man in thus making it a matter of scriptural record that there is a beast with which man may associate himself carnally and produce offspring, which will at once be indefinitely fertile and capable of acquiring a knowledge of God and of the arts of civilization.

Cain's wife being a negress, it follows that her offspring by Cain were mixed-bloods. This explains why Cain and his descendants were thrust out of the line of descent from Adam to the Saviour. Cain was the sole representative of the Adamic creation in his famiiy.. Hence, the only living soul, the last vestige of immortality in his family, disappeared when the spirit of Cain, whose crimes of murder and amalgamation made him a fugitive and a vagabond in time, took its flight from earth to receive the doom of the outcast in eternity.

The value of Paul's teaching that there are four different kinds of flesh is thus shown, in enabling us to see what Adam meant when he said: "Therefore shall a man leave his father and his mother and shall cleave unto his wife, and they shall be one flesh." In their ignorance of the true value of Paul's teaching, modern theologians have been led to believe that what Adam meant was, that when a couple were joined in marriage, their respective individualities were merged to a certain extent and they became one in aspiration, interest, etc., or, as the Bible terms it, one flesh. But when viewed in the light of Paul's teaching as to flesh, and in the general teaching of the Bible that there is a beast with which man may associate himself carnally and produce offspring, we find that what Adam meant was, that the husband should not be of one "kind of flesh," and the wife of another "kind of flesh;" they shall be one flesh; or, as Paul terms it, one "kind of flesh." And Cain and his wife were not of one flesh; they were of different kinds of flesh.

Further evidence that Cain's wife was not of the flesh of man—that she was not a woman—is found in the fact that Seth was the third child born to Adam, and took the place of Abel, whom Cain slew (Gen. iv, 25), and there were no daughters born to Adam until after the birth of Seth (Gen. iv, 4). Yet Cain had a wife before Seth was born. Thus, it is shown that Cain had a wife before there was a female child born to the Adamic family.

The degrading punishment which God visited upon Cain for his loathsome crime failed to deter other men from "going after strange flesh," as shown by the statement of Jude, as follows: "The angels which kept not their first estate, but left their own habitation * * * giving themselves over to fornication, and going after strange flesh * * * These filthy dreamers defile the flesh, despise dominion, and speak evil of dignitaries * * * Woe unto them, for they have gone in the way of Cain.'"

These "angels" were not celestial beings, but were creatures of flesh. They were the early descendants of Adam who went in the way of Cain. They "left their own habitation"—the Adamic flesh—"going after strange flesh;" that is, flesh that was of a different "kind of flesh" from their flesh. They "despised dominion," preferring social equality with the Negro to that "dominion" which God designed them to have, and commanded them to exercise, Such was the prevalence of amalgamation in the days of Enoch, the seventh from Adam, that he warned the people that God would "execute judgment" upon them for their shameless violation of his law. (Jude.) Further evidence of the prevalence of

this crime in antediluvian time is found in God's charge
that "The sons of God saw the daughters of men that
they were fair; and they took of them wives of all which
they chose." (Gen. vi, 2.) The punishment—a universal deluge—which God visited upon the "sons of
God" and "the daughters of men" and their progeny,
proves that their relations were criminal. Hence, this
text has been the subject of endless speculation. Men
have even gone so far as to suppose that the "sons of
God" were celestial beings—angels—who became enam-
ored of the charms of the women of the earth—"the
daughters of men"—and had intercourse with them,
which resulted in producing offspring (see Lenormant's
"Beginnings of History," chap. vii.) But when we lay
aside our atheism, and accept the teachings of scripture
that man (the white) is a distinct creation, "in the
image or God," and that the Negro is an ape, the mystery with which atheism has enveloped this text disappears, and, it becomes plain that "the sons of God"
were the white males who traced their pedigree through
a line of pure-blooded ancestors to Adam; and that "the
daughters of men" were mixed-blooded females who
traced their pedigree to men, on the paternal side, and to
negresses, on the maternal side. Their fathers were
men, but their mothers were negresses—apes—beasts.
Hence, the unions between the male descendants of
Adam and these mixed-blooded females resulted in further corrupting the flesh of the earth, and finally led God
in His wrath and disgust to destroy them with the deluge
as shown by the following:

"And God saw that the wickedness of man was great in the earth, and every imagination of the thoughts of his heart was only evil continually. And it repented the Lord that he had made man on the earth, and it grieved him at his heart. And the Lord said, I will destroy man whom I have created from the face of the earth; both man and beast, and the creeping things, and the fowls of the air; for it repenteth me that I have made them." (Gen. vi, 5-6-7.)

But just at this critical juncture, the most critical that man has ever known, when the hand of Almighty God was raised in his just wrath to destroy from the earth which their shameless crime had corrupted the last vestige of the seed of man, "Noah found grace in the eyes of the Lord." (Gen. vi, 8.) Why? "Noah was a just man and perfect in his generations, and Noah walked with God." (Gen. vi, 9.)

It will be observed that there are three characteristics here recorded of Noah, which are assigned as so many reasons why "Noah found grace in the eyes of the Lord:" (1) "Noah was a just man;" (2) he was "perfect in his generations;" (3) "Noah walked with God." The first and third characteristics are happily not uncommon, for in sacred history various individuals are accredited with similar characteristics. The second characteristic is common to every pure-blooded descendant of Adam. But the record of it, unlike the choracistic itself, is peculiar to Noah. It is not significant that in all sacred history there is just this one individual of whom it is recorded in just so many words that he was "perfect in his generations?" No such record is found of Abraham, the father of all Isarel; nor of Moses, the great law-giver of Isarel; nor of David, the sweet singer of Israel; nor even of the Messiah. This characteristic in Noah, that he was "perfect in his generations," was not the result of any act upon his part; and all credit for his possession of it is due solely to his ancestors, who transmitted to him from Adam in uncorrupted line of descent the pure Adamic stock. This characteristic as-signed as one of the reasons why "Noah found grace in the eyes of the Lord," with its attendant circumstances, necessarily carries with it the implication that there were others in Noah's day who were not perfect in their gen-erations. Now, if Noah was "perfect in his genera-tions" because his ancestors transmitted to him from Adam in uncorrupted line of descent the pure Adamic stock, and there were others in Noah's day who were not perfect in their generations, by association with whom did their ancestors transmit to them a corrupted line of descent from Adam? The morals of man may be cor-rupted by illicit intercourse between the sexes, but the offspring will be of pure Adamic stock, whether the rela-tions of its parents are legitimate or otherwise. Hence, as long as man's sexual relations are confined to the Adamic family—to the "flesh of men"—their genealogy will be "perfect," and the line of descent uncorrupted. This being true, it follows that the genealogy or the ante-diluvians—their line of descent from Adam—could only have been corrupted by their sexual relations with some other "kind of flesh." which resulted in the production of offspring that was indefinitely fertile.

While the most depraved conditions of their morals is implied in his arraignment of them, the sole charge of the Almighty against the descendants of Adam in Noah's day, is, that under their administration the flesh of the earth was corrupted." "The earth also was corrupt before God, and the earth was filled with violence, And God looked upon the earth, and behold it was corrupt; for all flesh had corrupted his way on the earth." (Gen. vi, 11–12.)

This term "all flesh" suggests to our mind the inquiry as to how many kinds of flesh there are on the earth, and what in God's eye would constitute the difference between them. An intelligent reply demands that we turn upon this record the inspired light of Paul's declaration that "there is one kind of flesh of men, another flesh of beasts, another of fishes, and another of birds," making in all four distinct kinds of flesh; and then turn upon it the inspired light of the Mosaic Record, which teaches that the fish were made to inhabit the waters; that the fowl were made to fly above the earth in the open expanse of heaven, and that man and the beasts were made to inhabit the dry land. We are thus taught that there are just two kinds of flesh on the earth, which belong strictly to the earth—the flesh of man and the flesh of beasts. As has been shown, no form of lust which man can indulge within the pale of the Adamic

family can corrupt the flesh of man.   However illicit the
unions, the offspring is of pure Adamic flesh, unadulterated by any foreign element.   The same rule holds good
with the beasts.   No hybridization which may occur between the different species or races of beasts can corrupt
the flesh of beasts.   The offspring resulting from these
unions is the pure flesh of beasts, unadulterated by any
foreign element.   To corrupt the flesh there must be
sexual contact between two different kinds of flesh; and
the ''corrupted'" flesh must express itself in the offspring.
Hence, in discussing this question we should bear in
mind that however loathsome the lust, no corruption of
the flesh can result to the participants in it.   To illustrate: The flesh of man is a kind of flesh distinct from
that of beasts, while the Negro, being merely a race of
the ape species, belongs to the flesh of beasts.   Now,
let a man associate himself carnally with a negress;
the flesh of that man is not corrupted by his contact with that beast, neither is the flesh of the
beast corrupted by her contact with the man;
the flesh of each is as pure after the contact
as it was before.   But when the contact results in conception and birth, the corrupted flesh which is the sole
charge of the Almighty against the antediluvians, expresses itself in the offspring—in the mulatto- which is
not born the pure flesh of man, as was its Adamic parent,
neither is it the pure flesh of beast, as was its parent the
negress; it is what God so fitly describes it as being
corrupted flesh, resulting from amalgamation between

the flesh of man and the flesh of beast. Further evidence that there is a beast with which man may associate him-self carnally, and produce offspring, is found in God's law to Israel, in which is assigned his reasons for the destruction of the Canaanites. After enumerating and forbidding every form of illicit sexual intercourse which it is possible for man to indulge within the pale of the Adamic family, God closes his law on the subject as fol-lows: "Neither shalt thou lie with any beast to defile thyself therewith; neither shall any woman stand before a beast to lie down thereto; it is confusion. (Lev. xviii.:23.) Confusion, mixing, mingling, are synony-mous terms. Hence, there should be no mixing, no mingling, no confusion of man's blood with that of a beast.

Continuing, God said: "Defile not ye yourselves in any of these things; for in all these the nations are de-filed which I cast out before you; and the land is defiled; therefore I do visit the iniquity thereof upon it; and the land itself vomiteth out its inhabitants. Ye shall there-fore keep my statutes and my judgments, and not com-mit any of these abomination. * * * That the land spue not you out also when ye defile it, as it spued out the nations that were before you." (Lev. xviii, 24, 25, 26, 28.)

A careful investigation of the laws of God will demonstrate that the violation of this statute forbidding man to lie with a beast is the only crime that man can commit that will have the three results described in the narrative of the deluge and that of the Canaanites: (1) The corruption of flesh; (2) the corruption of the earth itself in the eyes of God; (3) the penalty of death under the law of God. Prior to the deluge, God looked upon the earth and said it was corrupt; for all flesh had corrupted his way upon the earth. God thus describes a condition of the flesh of the earth, which could only have resulted from amalgamation. Prior to the arrival of the Israelites in Canaan, God said of the land of Canaan, "The land is defiled." Defile and corrupt are synonymous terms. He specifically charges the Canaanites with lying with beasts, which, as shown in the case of the antediluvians, would result in corrupting the flesh of Canaan. In each case the penalty of death was visited upon this corrupted flesh and those who were instrumental in corrupting it. In the case of the antediluvians by a universal deluge; in that of the Canaanites by a war of extermination.

Thus, to accept the teachings of the Bible, we must admit that there is a beast with which man may associate himself carnally and produce a fertile offspring. As we have shown, the teachings of science prove the Negro an ape; and all history and all scientific research and all observation combine to teach us that the Negro is the only one of the lower animals with which man may associate himself carnally and produce a fertile offspring. Hence, we have no alternative than to decide that it was their criminal relations with the Negro which brought the curses of God upon the antediluvians and the Canaanites and led to their destruction by Divine edict.

Nothing could place God in a more ridiculous light than to suppose that He enacted a statute forbidding man to commit an act which it was impossible for him to commit, and then, as if to emphasize the absurdity, to affix the death penalty to the violation of the law. Hence, if we accept the Bible as the expression of God's will to man, we have no alternative than to decide that the very presence of this Divine law forbidding man to "lie with a beast," or a woman "to lie down thereto," proves the existence of a beast which a man may lie with just as he would with a woman; or to which a woman, if she desired carnal association with, might lie down to just as she would to a man. Had this great law of God's been obeyed, no mulatto would ever have "defiled" this beau- tiful earth with his presence; a presence at once degrad- ing to man and loathsome to God; or had the just pen- alty which God attached to the violation of his law been enforced, no mulatto would have lived to see the light of day: "And if a man lie with a beast, he shall surely be put to death, and ye shall slay the beast. And if a woman approach unto any beast and lie down thereto, thou shalt kill the woman and the beast; they shall surely be put to death; their blood shall be upon them." (Lev. xx, 15-16.) Which is equivalent to God's saying to man, "Have no superstitious fears that their blood will be upon your hands, no conscientious scruples that their blood will be upon your head; kill them for their shame- less violation of Divine law; slay them in obedience to Divine command—their blood shall be upon them."

Thus, the immediate offspring of man and the Negro
—the mulatto—was doomed by Divine edict to instant
death in the very moment of conception. Hence,
neither the mulatto nor his ultimate offspring can ac-
quire the right to live. This being true, it follows that
these monstrosities have no rights social, financial, political or religious that man need respect; they have no
rights that man dare respect—not even the right to live.
We find an illustration of this in God's command to
Israel to "utterly destroy" the Canaanites of all ages and
sexes, and "leave nothing alive that breatheth," and
take their country with its accumulated wealth of ages.
The offspring of Man and the Negro is not upon the
earth in deference to Divine will, but in violation of Divine law. Hence, it is not a part of God's creation.
And there can never be any peace between God and man
so long as this corrupted flesh is permitted to "defile"
the earth with its presence. Inasmuch as the immediate
offspring of Man and the Negro is corrupted flesh, it fol--
lows that its ultimate offspring could never become
pure. If mated continuously with pure whites for
millions of generations, you could never breed the ape
out, nor breed the spiritual creation in, the offspring of
Man and the Negro. It was not a part of God's creation
to begin with, and could never become so. Surely the
great Architect of the universe has not become so im-
becile, His creative power so far waned, that he must
needs accept and appropriate to himself this loathsome
product of His creatures' crime.

[11]

THE BEAST AND THE VIRGIN.

Can you find a white preacher who would unite in holy wedlock, a burly negro to a white lady? Ah! parents, you would rather see your daughter burned and her ashes scattered to the winds of heaven.

Chapter VI.

Red, Yellow and Brown Skin Denotes Amalgamation of the Human Family with the Beast, the Negro.

The mere fact that, under the influence of the law of heredity, the ultimate offspring of whites and negroes, when mated continuously with whites, present to a greater or less extent the elevated physical and mental characters of the white, does not make them men and women. They lack the spiritual creation, which forms the link of kinship between God and man, and is only transmitable to his offspring through pure Adamic channels. Nothing could be more absurd, nothing more blasphemous, than to suppose that God, who declined to establish any kinship between himself and the animals, would make it possible for man to do so, by an act, which of itself, is a

(165)

violation of that divine law, "Thou shalt not lie with any beast." Hence, the mixed-bloods, the corrupted flesh, inherit none of the immortality of their Adamic parent—they have no soul. But, like the negro, and the rest of the animals, they are merely combinations of matter and mind. They were not in existence at the time of Adam's transgression; and are not included in the Plan of Salvation. Man alone fell, and he alone is the subject of redemption. Hence, "Go ye into all the world, and preach the gospel to every creature." (Mark xvi.:15.) Remembering that God "hath made of one blood all nations of men." (Acts xvii.:26.) But, "Give not that which is holy unto the dogs, neither cast ye your pearls before swine, lest they trample them under their feet, and turn again and rend you." (Matt. vii.:6.)

The existence of this prohibitory statute demonstrates the existence of an animal which man, in his criminal ignorance of God's plan of creation, might mistake for a man, and thus be misled into giving him the Bible with the view of conferring upon him the blessings of Christianity, which were intended alone for man. When we view this statute in the light of the sciences, and in that of Paul's declaration that "there is one kind of flesh of men, another flesh of beasts," etc., it becomes plain that the dog, the swine and the negro all belong to one kind of flesh—the flesh of beasts. The scriptures are described as "holy" (Rom. i, 2, etc.) The kingdom of heaven is

compared to "goodly pearls" (Matt. xiii, 45-46).
Hence, we are led to decide that "that which is holy,"
and which man is forbidden to "give unto dogs," is
the Bible. And that the pearls which man is forbidden to cast before swine is the kingdom of heaven.
This statute was evidently designed to confine the
use of the Bible and religious worship to man, and
exclude the lower kinds of flesh, which embrace the
negro. Hence, if it is criminal to give the Bible to
dogs, it is criminal to give it to the negro; if it is
criminal to undertake to Christianize swine, it is
criminal to undertake to Christianize the negro. In
these respects man can make no distinction between
one animal and another. This prohibitory law
applies with equal force to the mixed-bloods; they
possess none of the spiritual creation, but are wholly
animal. The "heathen" to whom the Saviour commanded that the gospel should be preached were the
pure-blooded descendants of Adam, who had lost
their knowledge of the true God, and of all religious
worship, or had descended to idolatry.

The Saviour's decree, "Go ye into the world, and
preach the gospel to every creature;" that is, to every
creature for whom it was designed, was fully exe-
cuted. Paul says that in his day the gospel "was
preached to every creature which is under heaven."
[Col. i, 23]. This sweeping statement of the learned
apostle was either true or false. We accept it as un-
questionably true. The gospel reached all for whom

it was intended. Yet it was not preached to the wild tribes of negroes and mixed-bloods of Africa; nor to the Laplanders, Finns, and Basques of Europe; nor to the Hindoos, Coreans, Chinese, Japanese, etc., of Asia; nor to the Australians, Malays, etc., of Oceanica; nor to the wild, hunting tribes of North and South America; nor to the Mexicans, Peruvians, etc. And no well-informed man or woman will assert that it was. This being true, it follows that Paul either misrepresented the facts when he said that in his day the gospel "was preached to every creature which is under heaven," or the Negroes, Hindoos, Chinese, Malays, Indians, Basques, etc., are not included in the Plan of Salvation.

If the gospel, as "published" by the primitive church, was confined to the pure white, and was not preached to the negro and the so-called "brown, red and yellow races" of the earth, where does the modern church obtain its authority to extend it to them? The explanation is simple. The primitive church which our Saviour established found its ultimate basis on the scriptural narrative of Divine creation, which teaches that man [the white] is a distinct creation "in the image of God." The modern church finds its ultimate basis on the atheistic theory of Natural Development, which teaches that man is a highly developed species of ape—the human species—of which the white is the highest, and the Negro, Malay, Indian and Mongolian are lower races of men.

Thus, it is clear that the modern Christian church derives its authority for recognizing the negro, the Indian, Malay, Chinese, etc., as lower races of men and for extending the gospel to them, not from scripture, but from atheism. The idea that the church can "present" these base-born mixed-bloods, "perfect in Christ Jesus," when their very existence is alone traceable to the most shameless violation of Divine law! This modern church theory that the negro and the mixed-bloods are included in the Plan of Salvation is another result of putting man and the ape in the same family.

When, in antediluvian times, amalgamation had corrupted the flesh of earth, God decided to destroy "all flesh," save Noah, "and they that were with him in the ark." Thus, the flesh of the earth was restored to its original purity. This illustrious family brought with them from their antediluvian home, and transmitted to their descendants a knowledge of the arts and sciences which had been accumulating in the Adamic family for ages. This explains why the most ancient artisans were the most skillful and accomplished, as shown by the fact that their architectural remains are invariably the most superb. Mr. Taylor says: "Among the ancient cultured nations of Egypt and Assyria, handicrafts had already come to a stage which could only have been reached by thousands of years of progress. In museums still may be examined the work of their joiners, stonecutters, goldsmiths, wonderful in skill and finish, and often putting to shame the modern artificer. * * * To see gold jewelry of the highest order, the student should examine that of the ancients, such as the Egyptian, Greek and Etruscan.'' (Anthropology.)

At the close of the deluge, Noah and his family set-tled upon one of the continents, and, with their negroes, proceeded to build for themselves homes, and in the course of time developed a great civilization. Having grown rich and populous, their descendants threw off colonies onto other continents. These colonists carried with them their negroes and other domestic animals, domestic plants, metallic implements, and all the appli-ances of civilized life, and in the course of time devel-oped the splendid civilizations, the remains of which are found upon every continent of the earth, and which even in their ruins command the admiration of the modern world. When we turn upon these ancient civilizations the light of modern science, we find that they were the work of the white—that ''no negro civilization has ever appeared; no Mongolian one has been highly devel-oped.'' The white ''is pre-eminently the man of civili-zation.'' The extent and splendor of their architectural remains indicate that those ancient whites who, with their negroes, developed those great civilizations, must have numbered their populations by the hundreds of millions. What became of them? What became of all those hundreds of millions of white-skinned, silken-haired whites? They have long since disappeared from three of the five continents, leaving no progeny of white-skinned, silken-haired whites. The remnant of their white descendants are practically confined to portions of Europe and America. What became of all those hundreds of millions of black-skinned, wooly-haired negroes? They have long since disappeared from four of the five continents, leaving no progeny of black-skinned, wooly-haired negroes. The remnant of their pure-blooded descendants have dwindled down to a few tribes in Africa. And where did all those so-called "brown, red and yellow races of men" come from, which we find in possession of these ancient civilizations, and which, in the sum of their physical and mental characters, are identical with the known offspring of whites and negroes in our midst? These degraded, worthless creatures never developed the civilizations which they possess, and as a rule they have no knowledge of who their builders were. Many of the ruins of the most magnificent civilizations are found in districts which are now occupied by wild, hunting tribes of savages.

The so-called "brown, red and yellow races" have no characters peculiar to them. No anthropologist will assert that the classification of the so-called "human species" into "five races of men" was based upon what the atheist would term "racial purity," but that it was based solely on geographical divisions. In Europe, the complexions range from pure white to brown; in Africa, we find the complexions to be nearly white, brown, red, yellow and pure black; in Asia, they range from light yellow to black; the same is true of Oceanica, the home

of the so-called "Malay race;" in America, previous to
its discovery by Columbus, the complexions were nearly
pure white, brown, red, yellow and black. Fontaine
says: "If a congregation of twelve representatives from
Malacca, China, Japan. Mongolia, Sandwich Islands,
Chili, Peru, Brazil, Chickasaws, Comanches, etc., were
dressed alike, or undressed and unshaven, the most skillful anatomist could not, from their appearance, separate
them." [How the World Was Peopled.]

Prof. Winchell says: "The ancient Indians of California, in the latitude of 42 degrees, were as black as the
negroes of Guinea, while in Mexico were tribes of an
olive or reddish complexion, relatively light. Among
the black races of tropical regions we find, generally,
some light-colored tribes interspersed. These sometimes
have light hair and blue eyes. This is the case with the
Tuareg of the Sahara, the Afghans of India, and the
aborigines of the banks of the Orinoco and the Amazon." [Preademites.] It will be observed that these
characters are identical with those presented by the offspring resulting from amalgamation between whites and
blacks in our midst. We have demonstrated here in the
United States that the way to produce these so-called
"brown, red or yellow races" is to mingle the blood of
the white with that of the negro.

Let us take a hasty glance at the conditions presented by the continent of America upon its discovery by
Columbus! There existed here the remains of an ancient civilization which extended from New York to Chili

and from ocean to ocean. While some of its cities and villages were preserved and occupied, its greatest and most ancient cities were abandoned and in ruins.

Mr. Donnelly says of Gran-Chimu: "Its remains exist today, the wonder of the southern continent, covering not less than twenty square miles, Tombs, temples and palaces arise on every hand, ruined but still traceable. Immense pyramidal structures, some of them half a mile in circuit; vast areas shut in by massive walls, each containing its water-tank, its shops, municipal edifices, and the dwellings of its inhabitants, and each a branch of a larger organization; prisons, furnaces for smelting metals, and almost every concomitant of civilization existed in the ancient Chimu capital. One of the pyramids, called the 'Temple of the Sun,' is 812 feet long by 470 wide and 150 high. These vast structures have been in ruins for centuries." [*Atlantis.*]

Such competent judges as Stevens, Dupaix, and Charnay pronounce the architectural remains of Central America to be equal, in point of solidity, beauty and finish, to those of Egypt, Rome or Greece in their best days. "The Peruvians made large use of aqueducts, which they built with notable skill, using hewn stone and cement, and making them very substantial. One extended four hundred and fifty miles across sierras and over rivers. * * * The public roads of the Peruvians were most remarkable; they were built of masonry. One of these roads ran along the mountains through the whole length of the empire, from Quito to Chili; another, starting from this at Cuzco, went down to the coast, and extended northward to the equator. These roads were from twenty to twenty-five feet wide, were macadamized with pulverized stone mixed with lime and bituminous cement, and were walled in by strong walls more than a fathom in thickness. In many places these roads were cut for leagues through the rock; great ravines were filled up with solid masonry; rivers were crossed by suspension bridges, used here ages before their introduction in Europe." [*Ibid.*]

The ancient Americans, like their brethren of other continents, built great mounds and truncated pyramids of earth, upon which to erect their magnificent palaces and temples; these were frequently from 50 to 100 feet high, and sometimes covered several acres. "The pyramid of Cholula is one of the greatest constructions ever erected by human hands. It is, even now, in its ruined condition, 160 feet high, 1,400 feet square at the base, and covers forty-five acres; we have only to remember that the greatest pyramid of Egypt—Cheops—covers but twelve or thirteen acres, to form some conception of the magnitude of this American structure." (*Ibid.*)

Our limited space forbids the mention of many other evidences of the enlightenment of the ancient Americans. But we have the most positive evidence that it was the work of whites, who, with their negroes, occupied this continent in the remote past.

(1) "Of the predecessors of the Toltecs in Mexico, the Olmecs and Xicalancans were the most im-

portant. They were the forerunners of the great races that followed. According to Ixtilxochitl, 'they came from the east in ships and barks.'" (*Ibid.*)

(2) "On the monuments of Central America there are representations of bearded men. How could the beardless American Indians have imagined a bearded race?" (*Ibid.*)

(3) Quelyatcoatl, the leader of the Nahuas, and who was deified, is described as having been a white man, with strong formation of body, broad forehead, large eyes and flowing beard. (*Ibid.*)

[4] "Very ancient ruins, showing remains of large and remarkable edifices, were found near Huamanga, and described by Cieca de Leon. The native traditions said this city was built by bearded white men, who came there long before the time of the Incas and established a settlement." [*Ibid.*]

"Prof. Wilson describes the hair of the ancient Peruvians, as found upon their mummies, as 'a lightish brown and of a fineness of texture which equals that of the Anglo-Saxon race.'" [*Ibid.*]

Short says: "The ancient Peruvians appear, from numerous examples of hair found in their tombs, to have been an auburn-haired race." [*North Americans of Antiquity.*]

Haywood says that in the early part of the century three mummies were found in a cave on the south side of the Cumberland river (Tennessee) who were buried in baskets as the Peruvians generally buried;

their skin was white and their hair auburn and of a fine texture. (*Natural and Aboriginal History of Tennessee.*)

[5]   Desare Charnay has published in the North American Review for December, 1880, photographs of a number of idols exhumed at San Juan de Trotihaucan, "which show striking negroid faces." [*Atlantis.*]

The Popol Vuh, the ancient book of the Quiches, refers to a period of great peace in the remote past, when the whites and blacks "lived together" and "all seem to have spoken one language." [*Bancroft's Native Races.*]

This harmonizes with the teaching of Scripture that there was a period in the remote past when "the whole earth was of one language and one speech." During this period the black servant spoke the language of his white master. This statement of the Popol Vuh. indicates that during this period of great peace, the whites and the blacks were the only inhabitants of the earth; no browns, reds or yellows are mentioned, which they certainly would have been had they then existed. It also indicates that the Popol Vuh was written by some ancient white. How could the so-called "red men" know anything of whites and blacks? The history of every nationality of ancient time, sustained by our experience with the Negro in the United States, demonstrates that the White must be the master of the Negro, else they can never live together in peace. This is the law of God. And it has cost every nationality of ancient times its existence to violate it. That, during this period of "great peace," the ancient whites, who, with their negroes, developed the splendid civilization of America, respected the law of God and maintained the relation of master and servant which God established between Man and the Negro in the Creation, is shown by the following:

Dr. Le Plongeon says: "Besides the sculptures of long-bearded men seen by the explorer at Chichen Itza, there were tall figures of people with small heads, thick lips and curly, short hair or wool, regarded as negroes. * * * We always see them as standard or parasol bearers, but never engaged in actual warfare." [*Maya Archæology.*]

Thus, it is shown that, in that remote age, the Negro was simply a menial. When America was discovered by Europeans in modern times, these ancient whites and their negroes had disappeared from the earth; their civilization was in ruins; their once fertile fields were transformed into a wilderness—a "desolalation"—the abode of colored barbarians and savages. Upon the discovery of these creatures, the atheist pronounced them a new and "lower race of men," which had descended from the ape, and attributed their degraded condition to arrested development. The Christians of the world promptly proceeded to hasten the development of this new-found "race of men" by civilizing, educating and Christianizing them. In this violation of Divine law they lost many a scalp, but never saved a soul.

Dr. Morton, an early writer upon the subject, misled the world into believing that the so-called "Indian race" possessed certain peculiar characteristics; that they were red or copper-colored men, with high cheek-bones, prominent noses, small black eyes, thin lips, with hair straight, coarse and black. The "Mortonian The-ory" has long since been exploded, yet it is persistently taught to the youth of the country. The Indian has no character peculiar to him; even the red or copper color is found in Africa. [Anthropology.] And it is signifi-cant that it is occasionally found among our mulattoes.

Catlin says: "A stranger in the Mandan village is first struck with the different shades of complexion and various colors of hair which he sees in a crowd about him, and is at once disposed to exclaim, 'These are not Indians.' There are a great many of these people whose complexions appear as light as half-breeds; and among the women particularly there are many whose skins are almost white, with the most pleasing symmetry and pro-portion of feature; with hazel, with gray, and with blue eyes. * * * Among the females may be seen every shade and color of hair that can be seen in our country, except red or auburn. * * * There are very many of both sexes, and of every age, from infancy to man-hood and old age, with hair of a bright, silvery gray, and in some instances perfectly white. * * * And by passing this hair through my hands I have found it uniformly to be as coarse and harsh as a horse's mane, differing materially from the hair of other colors, which, among the Mendans, is generally as fine and soft as silk." [Indians of North America.]

Prichard says: "It will be easy to show that the American races show nearly as great a variety in this respect as the nations of the old continent; there are among them white races with florid complexions, and tribes black or of a very dark hue; that their stature, figure and countenance are almost equally diversified." [Researches into the Physical History of Mankind.]

Short says: "The Menominees, sometimes called the 'White Indians,' formerly occupied the region bordering on Lake Michigan, Green Bay. The whiteness of these Indians, which is compared to that of white mulattoes, early attracted the attention of the Jesuit missionaries, and has often been commented on by travelers. Almost every shade, from the ash-color of the Menominees, through the cinnamon red, copper, and bronze tints, may be found among the tribes formerly occupying the territory east of the Mississippi, until we reach the dark-skinned Kaws of Kansas, who are nearly as black as the negro. The variety of complexion is as great in South America as among the tribes of the northern part of the continent." [*North Americans of Antiquity*.]

Thus, we find that in the remote past, this continent was settled by whites, who, with their negroes, developed a great civilization; then both whites and

negrces disappeared; their civilization crumbled into
ruins, and their country became a wilderness—the
abode of barbarians and savages, which, in their
physical and mental characters, are identical with the
offspring of whites and negroes in our midst.

Let us bear in mind that there are just two schools
of learning which propose to explain the phenomena
of the universe, of which these so-called "Malay,
Indian, and Mongolian races," are a part; and that
these are the schools of Divine Creation, and Natural
Development, respectively. Hence, we have no alternative than to decide that these so-called "Brown,
Red, and Yellow races," have developed from the ape,
and present so many cases of "arrested development;"
or we must decide that, they are the result of amalgamation between the whites and the negroes of ancient
time, just as the browns, reds, and yellows in our midst,
are the result of amalgamation between the whites
and negroes of modern times. How many ways are
there of producing these creatures? Are we to understand that, in the remote past, the same class of
creatures were produced by development from the ape,
that we now produce by amalgamation between whites
and negroes?

Many of these mixed-blooded nations, such as
these Chinese, Hindoos, Egyptians, etc., have preserved more or less of the literature of their white
ancestors. A careful investigation of their literature
reveals the fact that their remote ancestors were

monotheists (see the works of Renouf, Wilkerson, Rawlinson, Legge, Clark, Max Muler.) This should occasion us no surprise. Monotheism was the religion of Noah; and was handed down to his descendants. Yet, in every instance, their mixed-blooded descendants, when found far removed from the influence of the whites, have either lost all knowledge of a God, and of religious worship, or they have descended to idolatry.

Previous to the creation of man, the negro had no more idea of a God, or of religious worship, than any other animal. But God established between himself and man, the tie of kinship, which forms a bond of love and sympathy between them, and enables man to respect, confide in, and worship an all-wise, all-powerful, but invisible God. But no kinship exists between God and the mixed-bloods. Hence, though these creatures may inherit from their Adamic ancestors a knowledge of God, when relieved of the influence of the white, they soon lose all confidence in, and all respect for, an invisible God. They must have a god which they can see; and in the absence of such an one, they fashion for themselves gods of wood, stone, or metal; or deify some animate, or inanimate object, as their whim suggests. Thus, amalgamation becomes the parent of idolatry Hayti furnishes an illustration of this. In 1793, the negroes were emancipated. In 1825, England formally acknowledged the republic of Hayti. Thus, this fine country was turned over to the negroes and mixed bloods. They were given an organized system of political government, and an organized system of religion; with churches, schools, and all the appliances of civilization; yet despite the most persistent efforts of Catholics and Protestants, to hold them up to a civilized life, they have descended to fetish worship and cannibalism, in the shadow of scores of churches. They sacrifice their own offspring to snakes, and then eat the sacrifice; the ceremonies ending in a drunken debauch, which is characterized by the most indiscriminate intercourse between the sexes. (Sir Spencer St. John, *Hayti; or the Black Republic.*)

This reveals the startling truth that, underlying all of God's arraignments, and punishments of Israel, and her surrounding nations, for their idolatry, was this loathsome crime, amalgamation. It is not the idol, nor his confidence in it, but the obscene rites, and the indiscriminate intercourse between the sexes, which usually characterizes the worship of idols that induces man to renounce God, abandon his worship, and embrace idolatry. Their children are reared in a cess-pool of amalgamation, and trained to worship idols. Hence, in the course of time, they lose all knowledge of the true God, and of his worship, and become "heathen."

Man's social, political, and religious equality with the negro, inevitably leads to amalgamation; and this, in its turn, gives birth to idolatry; then, in order to get the negro and his amalgamated progeny into the family of man, the truth of Divine Creation is repudiated; and the Theory of Evolution is substituted in its stead. It was his desire to counteract the results of these destructive crimes, which led God to "raise up" for himself "a chosen people," in the Israelites, who would be "peculiar," in that they they would not descend to amalgamation and idolatry; and in order to disabuse their minds of, and counteract the degrading influences of the Theory of Evolution, which was universally taught in that day, God gave to Israel the Narrative of Creation, together with a history of the events which led up to the Israelitish occupancy of Canaan. It was God's desire that Israel would lead all men to renounce atheism, and abandon amalgamation and idolatry. But instead of respecting and executing the will of God, the Israelites abandoned themselves to the crimes they were designed to eradicate. Then God sent prophets to warn them of the results of their wicked course, and visited upon them war, pestilence, famine, etc., to induce them to return to their allegiance to him. Then, as a last resort, he sent the Savior, who established the Christian church on the Narrative of Creation. But evidently the primitive Christian church, which eliminated the negro and the mixed-bloods, did not long survive the Savior. For many centuries the modern church has found its ultimate basis on the Theory of Development; the negro and the mixed-bloods are recognized as "lower races of men," and the gospel extended to them; and ¦both the clergy and laity of to-day, are doing all in their power, socially, politcally, and religiously, to perpetuate on this earth a condition of affairs, which our Savior died to put an end to.

All the facts indicate that, for a long period, the descendants of Noah respected the design of God, in creating man; lived in obedience to his laws, and maintained the relation of master and servant, which God established between man and the negro, in the Creation. During this period, described in the "Popol Vuh" as one of "great peace," they prospered and were happy in the approving smile of heaven; and developed upon the various continents, the most superb civilizations. But, in an evil hour, they violated the law of God, by descending to amalgamation with their negroes; and the smiles of heaven were exchanged for its frowns; the blessings of God were withdrawn, and his curses were showered upon them in the forms of war, famine, pestilence, etc., to induce them to abandon their wicked course, and return to their duties. But, like the antediluvians, they persisted in their evil way; nation after nation was destroyed from the face of the earth, their civilizations laid in ruins, and their country turned over to the barbarians and savages their crime had produced.

These ancient people left in their great cities, sumptuous palaces, magnificent temples, gigantic pyramids, etc., the most enduring evidences of their enlightenment. But, when amalgamation has absorbed, and destroyed us, as it absorbed and destroyed them, what evidence will we leave to the explorers of thirty or forty centuries hence, that we were a great agricultural, commercial, and maritime people; that in eager quest of other avenues of trade, our ships had rode the billows of every ocean, and touched the shores of every continent of the earth? Absolutely none. Our frail civilization, of which we so highly boast, will disappear under the destructive influences of a few centuries, aided by the vandal hand of the savages we are producing, like mist before the morning sun; scarcely a vestige will remain. Hence, when we make monotheism, a knowledge of the arts and sciences, the number and magnitude of mechanical structures, the skill displayed in their construction, and their durability, the test of enlightened civilizations, we must admit that the great architects of these ancient civilizations were at least our peers.

In discussing the subject, we should carefully consider the stealthfulness with which amalgamation accomplishes its destructive results. This crime always begins between the white males and the black females. Quatrefages says: "In the crossings between unequal human races, the father almost always belongs to the superior race. In every case, and especially in transient amours, woman refuses to lower herself; man is less delicate." (*The Human Species.*) Thus, it is evident that the mixed-bloods must rapidly increase at the expense of both the pure whites, and the pure negroes. Upon reaching maturity, a very considerable percentage of the mixed-bloods, males and females, will take mates from among the negroes; again, many Adamic males will take concubines from among both negroes and mixed-bloods. Thus, the negro becomes the prey, not only of the white males, but also of the mixed-bloods of both male and female. Hence, it is easy to see that it is simply a question of time, when the negro will be absorbed and destroyed, and their descendants will all be mixed-bloods. This has been demonstrated in the United States. The first negroes from Africa, were imported here in A. D., 1619. Amalgamation at once began, to-day there is not a pure-blooded negro on this continent. Not one. Now it only remains for the mixed-bloods to complete the absorption and destruction of the pure whites, and we will leave this continent as we found i , populated with mixed-bloods. Hence, when we disabuse our minds of the atheism, which teaches that the white and the negro are but different races of the same species of animal, and accept the scriptural teaching, that they are different kinds of flesh, the progeny resulting from their unions appears in a very different light.

Woman, the female side, or part of man, is the great stronghold, the vital point, of the Adamic Creation. Hence, as long as the marriage relations of the pure Adamic females of a nation, or continent, is con-

fined to pure Adamic males, the pure Adamic stock of
that nation, or continent, cannot be absorbed and destroyed by amalgamation. In addition to their
Adamic wives, the Adamic males will, here and there,
have negro concubines. From their wives they will
produce pure Adamic offspring; from their negro concubines, they will produce mixed-bloods. The progeny
of the latter, are always mixed-bloods, without reference to whether their mates are whites, mixed-bloods,
or negroes.

While the absorbtion and destruction of the Negro, and the consequent increase of the mixed-bloods,
is progressing, the Adamic females declining to lower
themselves by association with their inferiors, the
Negro and mixed-bloods, are confining their married
relations to pure Adamic males; and are producing
pure Ádamic stock to very nearly the same extent as
if there was no amalgamation going on between the
Adamic males and the negroes and mixed-bloods.
The mixed-blooded females, for obvious reasons, pre-
fer the Adamic males, either in transient amours or
as permanent mates. Under the influence of the law
of heredity, the offspring resulting from these unhallowed unions, present more and more the physical and
mental characters of the White, with each succeeding
generation, until, in the course of time, it would never
occur to the ordinary observer that they were not of
pure Adamic stock. When this occurs, the mixed-
blooded males, by a change of residence to a distant part

of the country, find it easy to impose themselves on the whites as pure-bloods, and are thus enabled to form marriage alliances with Adamic females. When this lamentable result ensues, the Adamic Creation is successfully assaulted at its vital point—the female. The base-born products of God's violated law, resulting from these unions, will marry indiscriminately with pure whites. Then the doom of that nation is sealed. Nothing short of a direct intervention of Divine providence can save it.

When amalgamation begins in a nation, the relation of master and servant always exists between the whites and negroes. As this crime increases, no record is kept of the pure white, nor of the pure negroes, nor of the mixed-bloods. As in our own country, every individual whose skin is white, or relatively so, is recognized as pure white, unless he is known to be of negro extraction, or his antecedents are unknown. On the other hand, without reference to their complexion, all are recognized as negroes who are known to be tainted with negro blood. The result is, that at no time is it possible to discover that the mixed-bloods are rapidly increasing at the expense of both the pure whites and the pure negroes. Hence, each succeeding generation supposes that the conditions by which it is surrounded are such as always existed. In the meantime, God may visit his curses upon them in the form of war, famine, pestilence, etc., to compel them to abandon their crime and return to their allegiance to Him.

Failing in this, God, in his wrath and disgust, may destroy them from the face of the earth and lay their civilization in ruins. On the other hand, He may abandon them to the natural result of their shameless crime. In this case, as has been shown, the negroes will first be absorbed by their associations with the white males and the mixed-bloods. Then in their turn the whites will be absorbed through their associations with the mixed-bloods. This accomplished, the relation of that nation to God and its relation to the earth and the rest of created things, has undergone the most radical change. Its original population of whites and negroes, were parts of God's creation; while their amalgamated progeny is merely the product of His violated law. This change was so gradual, requiring many centuries for its completion, that it attracted no attention at the time. Hence, the cause which led to it is never investigated and understood. When the whites are finally destroyed, their country, with its civilization, wealth and national name, together with their religion, their knowledge of the arts, sciences, etc., is inherited by their mixed-blooded descendants. In many cases they are dispossessed of their civilization and driven into the forest where, with no capacity to develop a civilization for themselves, they descend to savagery. We find an illustration of this in the case of the Navajoes. At the time of the Spanish conquest, they were an agricultural community. Compelled by the Spaniards to

abandon their inherited possessions, they sought
shelter in the mountains. They never made the least
effort to develop a civilization, but became a wander-
ing band of as wild, blood-thirsty savages as ever in-
fested the border, and are such today. (Baldwin's
Ancient America.)

On the other hand, these mixed-bloods, in which
the white blood largely predominates, may, under
favorable conditions, retain more or less of their inherited possessions for an indefinite period. From
among the numerous examples of this kind which are
furnished by the various continents, we shall select
Greece as an illustration, since her history, both
ancient and modern, is more generally understood.

There was a period in the history of Greece when
her people were famed throughout the world for their
white skins, their fair hair and their possession of all
the exalted physical and mental characters which are
peculiar to that sublime creature whom God honored
in the Creation by the bestowal of His "likeness" and
His "image." In that remote age of her history,
Greece gave to posterity a galaxy of intellects, whose
names and whose achievements adorn the brightest
pages in the world's history. But alas! alas! Their
towering intellectuality, their boundless enterprise,
their restless energy, their dauntless courage, combined with their forgetfulness of God, paved the way
to their ruin. During their various wars, thousands
of negroes were captured and imported into Greece as

slaves, together with thousands of captives taken from the mixed-blooded tribes and nations against which Greece waged war. These were never exported, yet they have long since disappeared, leaving no progeny of negroes in their stead. And it is a significant fact, and one which no anthropologist, no historian and no traveler will deny, that the white-skinned, fair-haired Greek of ancient times has also disappeared, leaving no progeny of white-skinned, fair-haired Greeks. What became of them? A glance at our surroundings should convince us that, in an evil hour, amalgamation laid its blighting touch upon the vitals of Greece; and, in the course of centuries, under its destructive influences, the white-skinned, fair-haired Greek and the black-skinned, woolly-haired Negro disappeared, and were replaced by the dark-skinned, black-haired Greek of modern times. This radical change in the physical characters of her population was accompanied by a corresponding change in their mentality, and, consequently, in the status of Greece among the nations of the earth; and that fair land, once the home of the highest culture, became the abode of ignorance and superstition. Many a long century has dragged its weary length into eternity since Greece produced a Homer, an Aristides, a Herodotus, a Pericles, a Solon, a Plato or a Demosthenes.

Pausing amid the busy scenes of daily life to view the routes which man has trodden from the Creation to the Crucifixion, or even down to the fall of the

Roman empire, or down to our day, if you will, we observe that, however divergent these routes may be in
the ultimate, they all converge upon the Noachian
Deluge. Scattered thickly along these various routes,
we note the wrecks of principalities, kingdoms and
empires, with here and there one which, in the zenith
of its wealth and power, ruled the world. But alas!
Their glory has departed; their once intellectual, cultured and powerful populations no longer grace the
earth—their name is history; in many instances even
their national boundaries are stricken from the maps
of the world; their once fertile fields, that bloomed and
fruited in the smiles of heaven, and yielded an abundant harvest as the reward of intelligent, industrious
culture, are now barren wastes, which bear the numis-
takable impress of the curse of God and are properly
described in Scripture as desolations; their former
cities, once the flourishing marts of the world's commerce, are now buried beneath the earth; or, if any
vestige of them remains upon its surface still, a mass
of ruins alone mark their sites; their once splendid
capitals, within the palaces of which the royalty, the
nobility, the intellect, the culture, the beauty, the
chivalry, the wealth and fashion of those ancient
realms held high revel, are now swept from the earth;
or, if any vestige of them remains, they are in
ruins and, like Petra, Idumea's once proud capital,
they are degraded to a fold for herds and flocks; or,
like Nineveh, that city "that dwelt carelessly," they

have "become a desolation; a place for beasts to lie down in;" or, like Palenque, the ruins of their former beauties and grandeurs are now buried in the gloom and solitude of the jungle. Their histories or their traditions, if any, have descended to us; or their monuments, or their inscriptions, if any remain, all teach us that, in their prosperous days, tne White and the Black—Man and the Negro—were represented in their populations. But, strange as it may seem, it is nevertheless true, that any remnant of their descendants which can be identified, are colored—some shade of brown, red or yellow. If neither history, nor tradition, nor monument, nor inscription, nor any remnant of their descendants can be found, an investigation of the ruins of their civilization reveals the idol —the most infallible evidence that amalgamation destroyed them.

DID NATURE BLUNDER?

Would you believe that the above negro was the daughter of pure whites? Never, though it was written in letters of fire upon the face of the heavens.

Chapter VII.

That the Beast is a Biped Animal, and not a Quadruped, is Proven by the Bible.

We observe that God treats the land animals, with which man was to be more closely associated in his efforts to "subdue" the earth, very differently from the manner in which he treats the "fowl of the air," or the "fish of the sea," in that he divides them into three classes, as shown by the following: "And God said, Let the earth bring forth the living creature after his kind, cattle, and creeping thing, and beast of the earth after his kind; and it was so." (Gen. i:24.) This division of the land animals into the three classes named, "cattle," "creeping things," and "beast" is observed throughout the scriptures.

(197)

Theologians who have noted this classification, and have attempted to interpret it, base the distinction which God makes between "cattle" and "beast" upon the nature of the food upon which they subsist; that is, they consider the "cattle" to be herbiverous animals; and the "beasts" to be carniverous animals. (See Guyot's *Creation*, Kinn's *Moses and Geology*, etc.) This interpretation not only brings the Narrative of Creation in conflict with Bible history, as we shall hereafter show, but also brings it in conflict with the teachings of modern science. The first land animal to make its appearance on earth was a carniverous creature—an insect-eating marsupial. (Dana's *Manual of Geology*.) The distinction which God makes between "cattle" and "beast" is based upon the differences in their physical structure. The "cattle" are quadrupeds; the "beasts" are bipeds —apes. Blumenbach, Cuvier and the older naturalists, regarded the apes as quadrumana, or four-handed animals. But more recent and careful investigation shows there is no four-handed animal. Prof. Huxley has shown, by comparative anatomy, that the fore, or upper extremity of every ape, from the Lemur up, is an arm, which terminates in a hand; and that the hinder or lower extremity of every ape, from the Lemur up, is a leg, which terminates in a foot. (*Man's Place in Nature.*) Hence, the apes, like man, are bipeds. Our interpretation of God's division of the land animals, into the three classes named, harmonizes with the teachings of modern science. Geological researches show that these three classes of creatures made their appearance on the earth, in the order stated in the Narrative of Creation: (1) Marsupials—quadrupeds (cattle). (2) A variety of animal forms, consisting of insects, worms, snakes, etc. (creeping things). (3) Apes—bipeds (beasts). [See Dana's *Manual of Geology*.]

Inasmuch as the physical and mental organisms of the ape are in nearer approach to those of man, than are those of the quadrupeds, it follows that he is a higher grade of animal. Hence, while the "cattle" and the whole of the land animals are sometimes referred to in scripture as "beasts," this higher grade of animal, the "beast," is never referred to as "cattle." The quadrupeds are frequently referred to in the Bible as "cattle," "herds," or "flocks," and individual species of quadrupeds, or "cattle," are frequently referred to as the horse, ox, swine, dog, lion, etc. On the other hand, the ape is specially named, or referred to as "beasts;" but never as "cattle," or "herds," or "flocks." The careful observance of this unvarying rule will prove invaluable in our search of the scriptures. We must carefully observe the distinction which God makes between the "cattle," or quadrupeds, and the "beast," or ape.

We observe that, in addition to commanding the earth to "bring forth cattle and creeping things," God commanded it to bring forth the beast of the earth after his kind; that is, after the beast or ape kind. Theologians pay no attention to this command, supposing it to be a general term, which is applied to the carniverous animals. This is a mistake; it is the name which God applied to a particular ape, as shown by the following:

"And the fear of you and the dread of you shall be upon every beast of the earth and upon every fowl of the air, upon all that moveth upon the earth, and upon all the fishes of the sea; into your hand are they delivered." [Gen. ix.:2.] God thus names (1) the beast of the earth, (2) the fowl of the air, (3) "all that moveth upon the earth," [4] the fish of the sea. Thus we see that in this statement, the "beast of the earth" is separated from the rest of the land animals by the "fowl of the air." Thus it is shown that the term "beast of the earth," is not a general term applied to the carnivora, but is the name of a particular race of the "beast," or ape species. The importance and value of the "beast of the earth," in the execution of God's plan for the development of the resources of the earth, is indicated by the fact that he is the only animal specifically named in the Creation. No special mention is made of the horse, ox, etc. They are merely included with the rest of the quadrupeds under the general term cattle. In this respect he is on a par with man.

Bearing in mind the distinction which God makes between the "cattle," or quadrupeds, and the "beast," or ape, the following, in common with other punishments which God said he would inflict upon the Israelites if they violated His law, is significant: "And thy carcass shall be meat unto all fowls of the air and unto the beasts of the earth, and no man shall fray them away." [Deut. xxviii.:26.]

"Then," said David to the Philistine, "This day will the Lord deliver thee into my hand. * * * And I will give the carcasses of the host of the Philistines this day unto the fowls of the air, and to the wild beasts of the earth." [I. Sam. xvii. :45-46.]

This indicates that there were "wild beasts of the earth" in that region in that day. They had doubtless been emancipated. And it is significant that every one of the great nations of that region, with the exception of a scattered remnant of the Israelites, are destroyed from off the earth and their civilizations are in ruins. Later on, we shall have occasion to refer to the Philistine's challenge to David, with its accompanying threat. Thus, the Bible plainly teaches that there is a "beast," or ape, that is a man eater. Yet, not one of the recognized apes of to-day, are man eaters. What became of this great man-eating ape? When we appeal to science to solve this problem, she promptly invades the so-called "human species," and points us to the Negro, as the highest grade of ape, and the only ape that is a man eater. The Negro is not only a man eater, but he feeds upon the flesh of his own kindred, and even upon his own off-spring, as well as upon that of other apes. Though the Negro made his appearance upon the earth as the "beast of the earth," and is sometimes referred to by that name, it is not the only name. nor the one most frequently applied to him in scripture. This was simply the name which God applied to the Negro previous to the creation of man. The task of naming the animals devolved upon

Adam. We are taught that, "Adam gave names to all cattle, and to the fowl of the air, and to every beast of the field." [Gen. ii.:20.] Observe the distinction made between the "cattle" and the "beast of the field:" and that, in this statement, the fowl are placed between the "cattle" and the "beast of the field." Theologians pay little or no attention to the "beast of the field," and seem to take it for granted that the "beast of the field" are that class of animals which were designed to be harnessed to the beam and draw the plow. But a careful investigation of this subject reveals the startling truth that this was the creature whom God designed should grasp the handles and direct the team.

When we approach the modern Christian, either priest or layman, with the inquiry, "What is the 'beast of the field?'" he promptly replies: "These are our domestic animals of draught and burthen, the horse, the ox, and the ass, with which we cultivate the fields, and use for other domestic purposes." As is well known, our domestic animals of draught and burthen with which we cultivate the fields, subsist on grass, hay and the cereals; not one of them is a flesh eating animal. But the biblical "beast of the field" is a flesh eating creature; he is the worst form of flesh eating animal; he is a man eater, as shown by the following: "And the Philistine said to David, Come to me and I will give thy flesh unto the fowls of the air, and to the beast of the field." [I. Sam. xvii.:44.] Among the "cattle," or quadrupeds, are numerous carniverous animals that will feed upon the flesh of man; but, as has been shown, the Negro is the only "beast," or ape that will feed upon the flesh of man. Hence, the "beast of the field" to which the Philistine said he would give the flesh of David, and the "beast of the earth" to which David said he wouid give the flesh of the Philistine were identical. This ndicates (1) that when Adam named the animals, he named the Negro the "beast of the field;" (2) that both the Philistines and the Israelites recognized the Negro as a beast. The Negro made his appearance upon the earth as the "beast of the earth" and is sometimes referred to by that name. When Adam named the ani- mals he named the Negro "the beast of the field:" and this name is generally applied to him in scripture, though he is frequently referred to simply as "beast."

Further evidence that the "beast of the field" is a man eater, is furnished by Rizpah's touching exhibition of mother love and devotion in guarding the bodies of her sons who were hanged by David's order. Rizpah "took sackcloth and spread it for her upon the rock from the beginning of harvest until water dropped upon them out of heaven, and suffered neither the birds of the air to rest upon them by day, nor the beasts of the field by night." (II. Sam. xxi.:10.)

Further evidence of the broad distinction which God makes between the "cattle" and the "beast," is shown in the narrative of the plagues with which God afflicted the Egyptians, to compel them to let Israel go. After afflicting them with frogs, lice, flies, etc.,

God said to Moses, "Go unto Pharaoh, and tell him, Behold, the hand of the Lord is upon thy cattle, which is in the field, upon the horses, upon the asses, upon the camels, upon the oxen, and upon the sheep; there shall be a very grievous murrian. And the Lord shall sever between the cattle of Israel and the cattle of Egypt; and there shall nothing die of all that is the children's of Israel. And the Lord did that thing on the morrow, and all the cattle of Egypt died; but of the cattle of the children of Israel died not one. And the heart of Pharoah was hardened, and he did not let the people go. And the Lord said unto Aaron, Take to you handfuls of ashes of the furnace, and let Moses sprinkle it toward the heaven in the sight of Pharoah. And it shall become small dust in all the land of Egypt, and shall be a boil breaking forth with blains upon man and upon beast, throughout all the land of Egypt. And they took the ashes of the furnace, and stood before Pharaoh; and Moses sprinkled it toward heaven; and it became a boil breaking forth with blains upon man and upon beast." (Ex. ix, i, 3, 4, etc.)

We are thus taught (1) that the "cattle" are quadrupeds, horses, camels, etc. And that the "beasts" were a very different class of animals, as shown by the fact that the "cattle" were first afflicted; then afterwards the "beasts" were afflicted. This is signigcant, when we consider that each succeeding plague was more injurious to the Egyptians than its predecessor. This indicates the relative value of the "cattle" and "beasts;" and that the "beasts" were far more valuable than the "cattle." We can readily understand that this would be so, when we realize that the "cattle" were their domestic quadrupeds, and that their "beasts" were negroes. Previous to the late sectional war in the United States, the negroes in the Southern States were far more valuable than the domestic quadrupeds in those States. A sheep was worth say $2.00; a cow or an ox $25.00; a horse $100.00. But an adult negro was worth from $1,000.00 to $1,500.00. Hence, it was far more injurious to the people of the South to be deprived of their negroes than it would have been to deprive them of their domestic quadrupeds. The same was doubtless true of the Egyptians of Pharaoh's day. Profane history and science teach that the Egyptians owned immense numbers of negroes. The negro is figured on the Egyptian monuments of 4,000 years ago. (2) The "cattle" of the Egyptians were afflicted with "a very grievous murrain," while the "beasts" were afflicted with "boils breaking forth into blains," just as the men of Egypt were. This is significant. (3) The Egyptians, who were masters of the country, are accredited with owning both "cattle" and "beasts," while the Israelites, who were in bondage to the Egyptians, are accredited with owning "cattle" but not "beasts." (See Ex. x, 9, 24, 25; Ex. xii, 38.)

The Canaanites, whom the Israelites were commanded to destroy, and possess themselves of their
country, were the owners of great numbers of negroes,
as shown by the following: "And the Lord thy God
will put out those nations before thee by little and by
little; thou mayest not consume them at once, lest the
beasts of the field increase upon thee." (Deut. vii, 22.)
Observe that there was no fear expressed lest the
"cattle" or the "creeping thing" increase upon the
Israelites! But not so with the "beasts of the field"
—the negroes. Let us bear in mind that the country
of the Canaanites was a rich, productive country, "a
goodly land;" and that it was in the highest state of
cultivation—"a land flowing with milk and honey;"
that it abounded with cities, towns, villages, farms,
vineyards, orchards, etc. And that it was occupied
by "seven nations greater and mightier" than Israel.
And it would have been impossible for this comparatively small number of Israelites to have occupied the
numerous fine cities, towns, villages, farms, etc., and
maintain this splendid civilization which had required
ages to develop. It was the expressed desire of God
that the land of Canaan, with its wealth of every
description, should become the property of the Israelites; and if the Canaanites were all destroyed "at
once," much of their civilization would crumble into
ruins for the want of being cared for; and it would
require centuries for the Israelites to increase to such
an extent as would enable them to occupy the entire

land. Hence, it was the part of wisdom for the Israelites to first possess themselves of only so much of the land as they could successfully handle; leaving the remainder with its wealth and civilization in the hands of the Canaanites to care for and preserve. In addition to this, it seems that there was a greater number of negroes in the land of Canaan than the Israelites could at first profitably handle; so if the Canaanites were all destroyed at once, much of the civilization and wealth of these seven nations would fall into the hands of the negroes and be wasted and destroyed. The negro is as prolific as the white, and would increase as rapidly; they would prove very troublesome neighbors; as the freed negro never fails to prove. Besides, it would have been a violation of the law of God to release the negro from the control of their former owners and give them no new ones. Hence, "The Lord thy God will put these nations out before thee by little and by little; thou mayest not consume them at once, lest the beasts of the field increase upon thee."

The evidence that the Israelites possessed negroes is found in the following command: "And six years shalt thou sow thy land, and shalt gather in the fruits thereof. But the seventh year thou shalt let it rest and lie still; that the poor of thy people may eat; and what they leave the beasts of the field shall eat. In like manner thou shalt deal with thy vineyard, and with thy olive yard." (Ex. xxiii, 10, 11.)

Here we have additional and positive proof that the "beast of the field" is not our domestic quadrupeds of draught and burthen; these animals will not eat grapes and olives. Besides, it is not supposable that God would require the Israelites to turn their oxen, horses, etc., into their vineyards and olive yards to browse, trample down, and destroy them every seventh year. The negro would gather the grapes and olives and not injure the vineyard or olive yards. Besides, the negro will eat the products of the fields, gardens, orchards and vineyards, or anything that a man will eat, and then eat the man. God's love and wisdom is displayed in this command restraining the Israelites from abandoning themselves to a mad, ceaseless struggle for the accumulation of wealth. Every seventh year the land was not to be cultivated; it should "rest and lie still;" and any spontaneous crops which it might produce should be for the poor people; and what they left should be for the negroes. The latter were cared for by their masters, so that they could dispose of their part, and thus realize more or less cash for their own use. So it was with the vineyards and olive yards. These would, of course, produce as abundantly as in any other year. The land-owners were allowed to reserve such parts of the crops of these as were necessary for their own use, but the surplus was not to be sold; this should belong to the poor people, and what they left should be for the negroes. Thus, under God's wise, beneficent law, all

were cared for—the land-owners. the poor and the negroes.   Thus, the negroes were not compelled to labor
incessantly, year after year, without compensation;
but in addition to such "tips" as they might receive
from time to time, they were allowed to share in the
products of the land every seventh year.

   The following charge of the Almighty is one of
the many with which the Scriptures abound, which
go to prove that the Israelites violated the law of God
and descended to amalgamation with the negroes and
with the mixed-bloods: "For mine eyes are upon all
their ways. * * * And first I will recompense
their iniquity and their sin double; because they have
defiled my land, they have filled mine inheritance
with the carcasses of their detestable and abominable
things." (Jer. xvi, 17, 18.) Thus, the Israelites,
like the antedeluvians and the Canaanites, defiled the
land.   What is God's "inheritance?"   Israel was God's
inheritance.   (See I. Kings viii, 51; Isaiah xix, 25,
etc.) Then, by their amalgamation, they had defiled
the land and had "filled" Israel—the nation of Israel—
with the "carcasses" of "things" that were "detestable and abominable" in the sight of God. Observe
that in producing those "detestable and abominable
things" they had defiled the land, just as the Canaanites had done.   Observe also that the Creator of the
heaven and the earth, the Maker of man and beast,
He who fashioned the fowl of the air and the fish of
the sea—God, the Author of all language and all
[14]

speech—declined to give a name to this loathsome offspring of Man and the Negro; and the nearest approach that he would make to naming them is found in his declination recorded in our text, when, in the absence of all name (for these monstrosities are nameless) he bestows upon them the descriptive epithet, "detestable and abominable things."

The above text throws a flood of light upon God's command to Jeremiah: "Thou shalt not take thee a wife, neither shalt thou have sons or daughters in this place. For thus saith the Lord concerning the sons and concerning the daughters that are born in this place, and concerning their mothers that bare them, and concerning their fathers that begat them in this land: They shall die grievous deaths; they shall not be lamented, neither shall they be buried; but they shall be as dung upon the face of.the earth; and they shall be consumed by, the sword, and by famine; and their carcasses shall be meat for the fowl of heaven and for the beasts of the earth." (Jer. xvi, 2, 3.)

We are thus taught: (1) That the men of Israel had persisted in amalgamation so long that their male progeny of mixed-bloods were not distinguishable from pure whites; and that in this way many of the women of Israel had been led into amalgamation. Hence, it was dangerous for a man to take a wife from among them, and Jeremiah was forbidden to do so.

(2) That, in the eyes of God, the offspring of Man and the Negro is only fit for dung on the face of the earth.

It will be observed that the Bible describes two offenses which result from illicit intercourse between the sexes. The one is termed "adultery," the other "fornication." The modern world has been taught to believe that "adultery" is "the unfaithfulness of any married person to the marriage bed." (Webster, *Dictionary.*) And that "fornication" is "the incontinence or lewdness of unmarried persons, male or female." [*Ibid.*] This is opposed to the teachings of scripture. Our Saviour said, "It hath been said, whosoever shall put away his wife, saving for the cause of fornication, causes her to commit adultery; and whosoever shall marry her committeth adultery." (Matt. xix, 9.) Here we observe the distinction made between fornication and adultery; and that a married person may commit fornication. But if for any other cause save fornication a man put away his wife, and another man marries her, both the woman and the man whom she marries commit adultery, but not fornication.

As has been shown, Cain, and other antediluvians, and the people of Sodom and Gomorrha, and the Israelites, were all charged by Jude with committing fornication and "going after strange flesh." Adultery is that offense which men and women commit by illicit intercourse with their own kind of flesh. But fornication is that offense which men and women commit when they associate themselves carnally with the negro, or with the mixed-bloods; that is, with strange

flesh. The New Testament abounds with denunciations of fornication and fornicators, which indicates
that fornication was prevalent in the days of the
Savior; and that, like the prophets who preceded him,
his mission was to break up this wicked, destructive
practice, and the social, political and religious equality
with the negro which inevitably leads to it; and to
restore the relation of master and servant which God
established between man and the negro in the creation.

God charges that the people of Jerusalem and
Samaria committed fornication with the Egyptians,
Assyrians, etc., whose "flesh is as the flesh of asses,
and whose issue is as the issue of horses." (Ezek.
xxiii, 20.) When we turn upon this statement the
light of Paul's declaration that "there is one kind of
flesh of men, another flesh of beasts," etc., it becomes
plain that the horse and the ass and the negro all
belong to one kind of flesh—the flesh of beasts; and
that the Egyptians, Assyrians, etc., had descended to
amalgamation. Hence, their flesh was corrupted, and
was strange flesh to that of the people of Jerusalem
and Samaria. Bearing this in mind, the following is
instructive:

"Son of man, set thy face against Pharaoh, king
of Egypt, and prophesy against him, and against all
Egypt. * * * Therefore thus saith the Lord God:
Behold, I will bring a sword upon thee, and cut off
man and beast out of thee. And the land of Egypt
shall be desolate and waste. No foot of man shall

pass through it, nor foot of beast shall pass through it neither shall it be inhabited forty years. And I will make the land of Egypt desolate in the midst of the countries that are desolate, and her cities among the cities that are laid waste, shall be desolate forty years; and I will scatter the Egyptians among the nations, and will disperse them through the countries. Yet thus saith the Lord God: At the end of forty years will I gather the Egyptians whither they were scattered. And I will bring again the captivity of Egypt, and will cause them to return into the land of Pathros, into the land of their habitation; and they shall become a base kingdom. * * * Therefore thus saith the Lord God: Behold, I will give the land of Egypt unto Nebuchadrezzar, king of Babylon; and he shall take her multitude, and take her spoil, and take her prey; and it shall be the wages of his army." [Ezek. xxix, 2, 8, 9, etc.]

Thus, we are plainly taught by the Bible that, acting under Divine influence, Nebuchadrezzar invaded Egypt and took the Egyptians captive, and scattered them through the countries over which Babylon held sway; and that neither foot of man nor foot of beast passed through Egypt for forty years; that the land of Egypt was utterly waste and desolate, and was not inhabited for forty years. In direct conflict with this Bible teaching, profane history, sustained by scientific research, teaches that from the first settlement after the deluge Egypt has always been inhabited in the sense that we understand the term.

Now, if we accept the teachings of atheism and those of the modern church that the whites, blacks, browns, reds and yellows are all "races of men" in different stages of development, how are we to reconcile the teachings of profane history and of science with the Bible, as to this forty years of Egyptian history? Shall we decide that Nebuchadrezzar entered Egypt and carried away every white, black, brown, red and yellow of the so-called "races of men," and that in addition to this he removed every animal, wild and tame, great and small, and thus left Egypt "utterly waste and desolate," and that she remained in this condition forty years? This would be absurd. But when we disabuse our minds of this atheistic theory that man is a "species" which is divisible into "races of men," and accept the teachings of scripture and the sciences that the white is the only man, and that the negro is an ape, and that the reds, browns and yellows are the result of amalgamation between whites and negroes, and are not a part of God's creation, this subject becomes plain. We can understand that Nebuchadrezzar entered Egypt and removed every pure-blooded white and every pure-blooded negro, leaving the lower animals and the mixed-bloods; and that God declined to recognize these base-born products of his violated law as inhabitants. And that neither "the foot of man" nor "the foot" of beast (negro) passed through Egypt for forty years. When the whites were all removed, and the mixed-bloods left, then, in the eyes of God Egypt was "waste and desolate" and was not "inhabited," and so remained for forty years. This shows that a country which is occupied solely by mixed-bloods is in the eyes of God "waste and desolate" and not "inhabited." Yet the modern church is expending millions of dollars annually in the vain, criminal effort to Christianize these degraded creatures which God has declared to be only fit for dung on the face of the earth.

The attitude of the modern clergy toward the negro is in striking contrast to that of David, who, in discussing God's creation of man, says: "Thou madest him to have dominion over the works of thy hands; thou has put all things under his feet. All sheep and oxen, yea, and the beasts of the field." (Ps. viii, 6, 7.) David realized that he had no "brother in black;" on the contrary, he recognized the negro as a beast, "the beast of the field." But then David also realized that man was a distinct creation "in the image of God" and that he was not a highly developed species of ape—the "human species"—of which the White is the highest and the Negro the lowest race. This, of course, would explain the dffference.

Further evidence that our views as to the characters peculiar to man must be materially modified is shown by the narrative of the Fall, as follows:

"Now the serpent was more subtle than any beast of the field which the Lord God had made. And he said to the woman, Yea, hath God said, Ye shall not eat of every tree of the garden? And the woman said unto the serpent, We may eat of the fruit of the trees of the

garden, but of the fruit of the tree which is in the midst
of the garden God hath said, Ye shall not eat of it,
neither shall ye touch it lest ye die. And the serpent
said unto the woman, Ye shall not surely die: For God
doth know that in the day ye eat thereof, then your eyes
shall be opened and ye shall be as gods, knowing good
and evil. And when the woman saw that the tree was
good for food, and that it was pleasant to the eyes, and
a tree to be desired to make one wise, she took of the
fruit thereof, and did eat, and gave also unto her husband with her and he did eat. And the eyes of them
both were opened, and they knew that they were naked,
and they sewed fig leaves together and made themselves
aprons. And they heard the voice of the Lord God walking in the garden in the cool of the day. And Adam and
his wife hid themselves from the presence of the Lord
God amongst the trees of the garden. And the Lord God
called unto Adam and said unto him, Where art thou?
And he said, I heard thy voice in the garden and I was
afraid because I was naked, and I hid myself. And he
said, Who told thee that thou was naked? Hast thou
eaten of the tree whereof I commanded thee thou shouldst
not eat? And the man said, The woman thou gavest to
be with me, she gave me of the tree, and I did eat. And
the Lord God said unto the woman, What is this that
thou hast done? And the woman said, The serpent be-
guiled me and I did eat. And the Lord said unto
the serpent, Because thou hast done this thou art cursed
above all cattle and above every beast of the field;

upon thy belly shalt thou go, and dust shalt thou eat all the days of thy life.'' (Gen. iii.)

We observe (1) that the tempter of Eve was a beast of the field. This would scarcely have been more clearly indicated had the text read, ''Now the serpent was more subtle than any other beast of the field which the Lord God had made.'' (2) It is evident that when Adam gave names ''to every beast of the field'' with which he was to be associated in the garden of Eden, in his efforts ''to dress it and to keep it,'' the characteristics displayed by this individual led Adam to name it the serpent. This was simply a name given it to distinguish it from others of its kind. Hence, the name Serpent no more indicates that it was a snake than does the name of the late Indian chief, Sitting Bull, indicate that he was a bull which habitually assumed the sitting posture. (3) Observe the adroitness with which this beast approached Eve with the inquiry, ''Yea, hath God said, Ye shall not eat of every tree in the garden?'' The language employed clearly indicates that this creature was perfectly familiar with the subject of which, in pretended ignorance, he was seeking information. And when viewed in the light of subsequent events, it becomes plain that this question was a part of a well-conceived and skillfully-executed plan to deceive the woman into violating the law of God. Just here Eve made the mistake of her life; she should have rebuked this creature, and sent him about his business. But instead of doing this the unsuspecting woman in the simplicity of her

nature frankly replied: ''We may'eat of the fruits of the
garden.   But of the fruit of the tree which is in the
midst of the garden, God hath said, Ye shall not eat of
it, neither shall ye touch it lest ye die.''

''And the serpent said unto the woman, Ye shall
not surely die.   For God doth know that in the day ye
eat thereof, then your eyes shall be opened, and ye shall
be as gods, knowing good and evil.''   Then, embold-
ened by his success in gaining the confidence of the
woman, the serpent proceeds (1) to assail the word of
God; (2) to instil into the woman's heart distrust of
God; [3] to engender in her mind discontent with her
lot; [4] to arouse in her the unhallowed ambition that
she and her husband ''be as gods.''   As shown by the
narrative, the serpent accomplished his iniquitous design.
The woman, accompanied by Adam, and perhaps by the
serpent, approached the forbidden tree, and ''took of
the fruit thereof, and did eat and gave also unto her
husband with her, and he did eat.''

The modern clergy teach that the first sin which
Adam and Eve committed was their eating of the forbidden fruit.   This, as shown by the record, is in direct
conflict with the plain teaching of the Bible.   When they
accepted as their councilor this creature over which they
were designed to ''have dominion,'' they violated those
original statutes given man in the creation, and thus
brought sin into the world.   Instead of controlling this
''beast of the field,'' or negro—the serpent—they allowed him to control them, and he led them to

their ruin. Their acceptance of this beast as their councilor necessarily preceded their acting upon his advice. Hence, their eating of the forbidden fruit was a second and later offense. This reveals the startling fact that it was man's social equality with the negro which brought sin into the world; and it is man's social equality with the negro and the evils which inevitably grows out of it that keeps sin in the world.

We observe that the first curses which God visited upon the serpent were directed solely at his posture. Had the tempter of Eve been a snake, God's sentence, "Upon thy belly shalt thou go," would have been of no effect; it would not have wrought the slightest change in the posture of the snake; neither would it have occasioned him the least inconvenience. On the other hand, it would have placed God in the most ridiculous light, since the only way the snake could go was upon his belly. But when we come to understand that the tempter of Eve was a beast—a negro—this whole subject appears in a very different light. The habitual posture of the negro is the erect. Hence, God's sentence, "Upon thy belly shalt thou go," wrought the most radical change in this negro's posture, and was a most terrible punishment. When God cursed him "above every beast of the field," it deprived him of his erect posture. When God cursed him "above all cattle," he was prevented from going upon all fours, like the quadrupeds. "Upon thy belly shalt thou go" degraded him, in point of posture, to the level of the lowest of the "creeping things."

God's other curse upon the serpent, ''I will put enmity between thee and the woman, and between thy seed and her seed; it shall bruise thy head, and thou shalt bruise his heel," shows that the tempter of Eve was a material creature; a creature of flesh and blood: and that he begat offspring. And it is highly probable that he was the parent of Cain's paramour of strange flesh; and that this curse was fulfilled in Cain's ultimate banishment from the Adamic family to become ''a fugitive and a vagabond in the earth," and an outcast in eternity.

It should be unnecessary to state that God's curses upon the tempter of Eve were confined to this offending beast, and did not extend to the rest of the negroes, since they were not parties to his crime.

We also observe that this ''beast of the field" which tempted Eve possessed articulate speech; and that his mental capacity was such as enabled him to fully understand Adam's relations to the Garden of Eden and its plants, and the laws governing his conduct. And that he was sufficiently subtle to deceive man into violating the laws of God.

Thus, the Bible describes (1) a beast whose habitual posture is the erect; this necessitates a well-formed leg and foot; (2) a beast with a hand. God said of the mountain at Sinai, ''There shall not a hand touch it * * * whether it be beast or man." (Ex. xix, 13;) (3) a beast with articulate speech; (4) a beast with mental capacity sufficient to enable him

MAN, AND THE NEGRO.

to understand the laws of God, and to deceive man into violating them; (5) a beast with which man may associate himself carnally and produce offspring which will at once be indefinitely fertile and capable of appreciating and utilizing all the arts of civilization.

It seems plain that in addition to his general plan of salvation God devised a great labor plan for development of the resources of the earth. That the execution of this plan was entrusted to man, who was designed to perform the mental labor. That the beasts or apes should furnish in the negro the creature which, in the capacity of servant, should perform the manual labor. And that the "cattle" or quadrupeds should furnish the animals of draught and burthen; and together with the fish and fowl, would furnish man and the negro their supply of animal food.

The Bible is simply a history of the long conflict which has raged between God and man, as the result of man's criminal relations with the negro. Hence, when we recognize the negro as a man, we can make no more sense out of the Bible than we could make out of the history of the American Revolution and recognize the Tories as a part of Washington's army. But when we accept the teachings of scripture that man is a distinct creation "in the image of God;" and that the negro is an ape; and that man's criminal relations with the negro have been the prolific source of all the trouble between God and man since the Creation, the mystery with which atheism has enveloped the Bible disappears; and that

sublime current of inspired truth—the Sacred Narrative
—from Genesis to Revelations glides as smoothly as a
stream of oil; not the slightest ripple of discord mars
its majestic flow.

Already science has sounded the note of warning.
M. Reclus, and M. L'abbe de Bonbourg, quoted by
Quatrefages, say that ''at the end of a given time, whatever be their origin, all the descendants of whites or of
negroes who have emigrated to America will become redskins.'' (The Human Species.) What is the redskin?
Simply a savage. Then under the leadership of Enlightened Christianity, and modern Materialism, with
their miserable theory that man is a ''species which is
divisible into races,'' we are descending to savagery; to
ruin in time, and to hades in eternity. While we agree
with the distinguished authors above quoted that the
whites and the blacks will disappear from America, we
do not agree with them that their descendants will all
become redskins. We admit that redskins will be found
here and there; but, in tribes where the blood of the
white largely predominates, we shall have our Mandans,
Decotas, Tuscaroras, Zunians, Menominees, etc. In
other tribes, where the blood of the negro largely predominates, we shall have our Kaws, Carabees, Charnas,
Jamassi, etc. When, through the factional strifes of our
mixed-blooded descendants, our government is broken
up into so many hostile tribes, as was that of our ancient
predecessors, the marriage relations of each will be confined to their own tribe. The white and black blood

will be equally distributed to every member of it; their physical and mental characters will in the course of time become fixed. Our descendants will then present every shade of complexion intermediate between that of the pure White and that of the pure Negro.

The negro, like man, made his appearance upon the earth without weapons either offensive or defensive. But soon realizing the necessity for weapons, his mechanical skill, an essential characteristic of the servant, enabled him to fashion for himself rudely chipped implements of stone. These chipped flints are the earliest evidences of art to be found on the globe. They abound in what is termed the Paleolithic, or Age of Rough Stone. Man was created a metalurgist. How could man subdue the earth without a knowledge of metals? The mixed bloods, who had lost their knowledge of metals, were the artisans of the finely-wrought and polished implements of the Molithic or Age of Polished Stone. Quatrefages compares the so-called "Cromagnon Race" of Europe to the Algonquin Indian. (*The Human Species.*)

WILL YOUR NEXT CHILD BE A NEGRO?

Your children are "bone of your bone" and "flesh of your flesh" then who can believe that the negro is an offspring of Adam and Eve, without fearing that their next child may be a negro.

Chapter VIII.

It was not God's Original Plan that His Son Should be Crucified, but Amalgamation and Disobedience of the Human Family made it Imperative.

The Bible teaches that the design of God in creating man, was that he should "have dominion over all the earth" and the animals. And when created he was commanded to "subdue" the earth and "have dominion" over fish and fowl and beast. It also teaches that man disregarded the design of God in creating him; and violated the law of God by descending to social eqality with a beast—a beast of the field—and accepting as his counsellor this creature over which he was commanded to "have dominion." In a previous chapter we have shown the distinction which the Bible makes between "cattle" and "beasts;" that the "cattle" are quadrupeds and the "beasts" are bipeds—apes; we have also shown that the tempter of Eve was a "beast of the field;" that he was fully aware of the law of God forbidding man to eat of the fruit of a certain tree in the Garden of Eden, and that he was possessed of intelligence sufficient to enable him to seduce man into violating the law of God; that he had the erect posture and possessed articulate speech; we have also shown that though the beast of the field is carnivorous, he is a man-eater.

Dr. Adam Clark in commenting on this subject, combats the absurd idea that the tempter of Eve was of the serpent species. He says, "None of them ever did or ever can walk erect. The very name serpent comes from serpo to creep, and therefore to such it could be neither curse nor punishment to go on their bellies. * * * They have no organs for speech, or any kind of articulate sound; they can only hiss." He says the tempter of Eve, "whatever it was," stood at the head of all inferior animals for wisdom and understanding. * * * "That he walked erect" and possessed "articulate speech." He also notes that the woman manifested no surprise that this animal should "walk erect," reason and dispute with her, which indicates that these things were "common," and that it was an "ape." (See Clark's Commentary, vol. I.)

The Bible plainly teaches that there was in the Garden of Eden a beast that could reason, dispute and walk erect. And when we appeal to science to identify this creature, she points us to the Negro, as the highest grade of ape and the only creature among the lower kinds of flesh that possesses these characteristics.

This social equality on the part of the parents with this beast, led to carnal association in their offspring; and Cain, the first child born to the Adamic creation, led off in this evil course. Hence, Jude describes amalgamation as "The Way of Cain." The degrading punishment which God visited upon Cain for his loathsome crime failed to deter others from following his example; and in the course of time this destructive practice became almost universal and led God in His wrath and disgust to regret that He had made man. Enoch, the seventh from Adam, one of the ancient "preachers of righteousness" strove to eradicate this destructive crime, and warned the people that "God would execute judgment upon all" for "their ungodly deeds." (Jude, 15.) And doubtless there were thousands of other "preachers of righteousness" like Enoch and Noah, who labored to induce the people to abandon this wicked course and respect the design of God in creating man, by living in obedience to His laws; but it was all to no purpose. They persisted in their wicked way for ages until the whole earth was populated with mixed-blooded tribes and nations. The presence of this immense, absorbing element threatened the extinction of both man and the negro. In the destruction of these most important factors, God's Plan of Creation would have been destroyed.

The efforts of the good people of the world having failed to avert this impending catastrophe, God Himself was compelled to come to the rescue and devise a plan for the preservation of His Creation and the destruction of the mixed-bloods whose further continuance would have annihilated it.

"And God looked upon the earth and, behold, it was corrupt; for all flesh had corrupted his way on **the** earth. And God said unto Noah, The end of all flesh is come before me; for the earth is filled with violence through them; and behold, I will destroy them with the earth. Make thee an ark of gopher wood; rooms shalt thou make in the ark, and shall pitch it within and with- out with pitch. * * * And, behold, I, even I, do bring a flood of waters upon the earth to destroy all flesh, wherein is the breath of life, from under heaven; and everything that is in the earth shall die. But with thee will I establish my covenant, and thou shalt come into the ark, thou and thy sons, and thy wife, and thy sons' wife with thee. And of every living thing of all flesh two of every sort shalt thou bring into the ark to keep them alive with thee; they shall be male and female. * * * Thus did Noah; according to all that God commanded him, so did he. * * * And they went unto Noah into the ark, two and two of all flesh. * * * And the Lord shut him in. And the flood was forty days upon the earth. * * * And all the high hills, that were under the whole heaven, were covered. Fifteen cubits upward did the waters prevail;

and the mountains were covered. And all flesh died that moved upon the earth, both of fowl, and of cattle, and of beast, and of every creeping thing that creepeth upon the earth, and every man. * * * And Noah only remained alive, and they that were with him in the ark. And the waters prevailed upon the earth an hundred and fifty days." (Gen. vi and vii.)

The Theory of Development could not survive the scriptural teaching as to the universality of the Noachian deluge. This theory "assumes" that the "different races" of "speaking men" evolved out of "speechless man," about two hundred thousand years ago, according to Haeckel; and that it has required all this immense period of time for the various "races" of the "human species" of ape to attain their respective stages of develment. Hence, it is easy to see that the reality of a deluge covering the whole earth for a period of one hundred and fifty days, and dating back only a few thousand years, would sweep their theory out of existence. No sane person could be induced to believe that these so-called "races of men" have developed out of the ape in this brief period of time.

The modern clergy too, seem to have a dim consciousness that the reality of a universal deluge as described in scripture might have a disastrous effect on some of their long-cherished family relationships. But if the language of the Bible as above quoted, does not describe a universal deluge, then language would fail to do so. We have had a great many professed Christians inform us in all seriousness that, the deluge was merely a local flood, which the Lord sent to destroy some rebellious Hebrews, who lived somewhere in Asia. If this be true, the Lord was certainly not running his affairs on schedule time; and that the "local flood" was a trifle premature to say the least of it; for the Bible plainly teaches that the Deluge came and went long before Eber, the father of the Hebrews was born.

Thus, through the agency of a universal deluge, the most terrific catachism the world has ever known, God swept from the earth all its corrupted flesh, and those who at the time were instrumental in corrupting it; and restored the flesh of the earth to its original purity. For a very considerable time after the Deluge, the seed of the Negro was born "after his kind," and the seed of man was born "in the image of God." The conditions which prevailed in the Creation were restored by the Deluge. "And God blessed Noah and his sons, and said unto them, Be fruitful, and multiply, and replenish the earth. And the fear of you and the dread of you shall be upon every beast of the earth, and upon every fowl of the air, upon all that moveth upon the earth, and upon all the fishes of the sea; into your hand are they delivered." (*Gen.*, ix, 1, 2.) God thus placed Noah and his sons in the same relation to the earth and to the animals, as Adam held in the Creation. The mixed-bloods had all been destroyed; and only the white and the black remained.

On one side of an immeasurable gulf stood man, the
"thinker," with his elevated physical and mental
characters; on the other stood the Negro, the
"worker," with his ape-like physical and mental
characters. And such was the striking contrast
between them, that the idea that they were merely
different races of one species, would have seemed
ridiculous. But since that remote period amalgamation has about closed the gulf. The mixed-bloods
now shade on up from black, brown, red, and yellow
to white; thus giving plausibility to the theory that
they are different races of our species.

The Bible teaches that after the Deluge, Noah
and his family settled on one of the continents, and
that their descendants spread to other continents:
"And the sons of Noah that went forth of the ark,
were Shem, Ham and Japheth. * * * These are
three sons of Noah: and of them was the whole earth
overspread." (*Gen.* ix, 18, 19.)

The Negro, being an ape, entered the ark with the
rest of the animals; and as the descendants of Noah
spread out over the earth they carried with them their
negroes and other domestic animals, domestic plants,
metallic implements, etc., and developed those superb
civilizations the remains of which are found on every
continent of the earth. The extent and grandeur of
these old civilizations indicate that for a long period after
the Deluge these people respected the design of God in
creating man, lived in obedience to his law and main-

tained the relation of master and servant between themselves and the Negro, and were happy and prosperous.
But in the course of ages they forgot God, descended to
amalgamation, and this, in its turn, gave birth to idolatry. "Then was war in the gates." God in his wrath
and disgust showered his curses upon them in the form
of war, famine, pestilence and disease, and destroyed
them from the earth, laid their civilizations in ruins, and
transformed their once prosperous country into the
abode of savages; or left them to be absorbed and destroyed, and their civilization to descend to their mixed-
blooded descendants, as in the case of the Mexicans,
Peruvians, Malays, Hindoos, Chinese, Japanese, Kore-
ans, etc., and these barbarous creatures possess them
today. The strength of our position is shown as follows:

1.   When we turn upon these ancient civilizations
the light of the sciences, we find they were the work of
the Whites. "No Negro civilization has ever appeared.
No Mongolian one has ever greatly developed." The
White is pre-eminently the man of civilization. This is
just what God created him to be. The mixed-bloods
may inherit from their Adamic ancestors their knowledge
of the arts and sciences, but they are almost certain to
lose it; and, when lost, it is lost to them forever; they
have no ability to replace it. Many valuable arts which
these ancient whites possessed were inherited by their
mixed-blooded descendants and lost; such as the art of
tempering copper to the hardness of steel, etc.

· 2. In every case we find the remains of these ancient civilizations in the hands of red, brown and yellow populations, which, in the sum of their characters, are identical with the known offspring of Whites and Negroes in our midst. In addition to this our personal observation, sustained by the most intelligent scientific research, teaches that the only way to produce a brown, red or yellow-complexioned individual is to mingle the blood of the White with that of the Negro· Yet it is astonishing that we disregard the teachings of scripture, the sciences and our personal observation, and accept the undemonstrated and undemonstratable theory of atheism, that in the remote past the same class of creatures were produced by development from the ape that we now produce by amalgamation between Whites and Negroes; and that the Malays, Indians, Chinese, etc., are ''lower races of men'' who have descended from the ape, and who in their various stages of barbarism and savagery present so many cases of ''arrested development.''

Monoism, the belief in one God only—the Creator of the heaven and the earth; he who made the animal ''after his kind'' aud who created man in His ''image;'' the rewarder of the good and the punisher of the wicked was the religion of Noah; and was handed down to his descendants. But when they descended to amalgamation with their negroes and persisted in this crime, perhaps for centuries, they became demoralized and degraded. The amalgamationists among them were doubtless often denounced, perhaps punished for their criminal relation with the Negro. It is probable that they were ostracised from the society of decent people who respected God and insisted on the observance of His law.

The amalgamationists of modern times in this country have received just such treatment at the hands of decent people. In this we find another illustration of the truth that history repeats itself. The history of these ancient amalgamationists is repeated in that of the amalgamationists of our day.

More than two hundred and fifty years ago, when the first Negroes were imported into this country, the clergy took their position on the religious level of the Negro, and for centuries their effort has been to drag the American people and the world at large down to the base plane of the "brother in black." They have not only succeeded in this, but they have dragged the people down to the political level of the Negro, and in many sections of the country to the social level of the Negro. But these infamous crimes, and the amalgamation to which they inevitably lead, was only accomplished by centuries of the most persistent effort. The man who would degrade himself so far as to take a negress to wife was looked upon with scorn and contempt. And many of the states enacted laws making amalgamation a punishable offense. And in many of these states these laws are in force to-day, though in the southern states these laws were generally repealed after the late war. In many sections of the country amalgamation through transient amours is tolerated; yet if a man were to openly marry a negress his neighbors would feel themselves outraged, and the community scandalized and the offenders would be compelled to seek safety in flight. Many a degraded wretch who had thus offended has suffered violence at the hands of an indignant populace. Hence, when viewed in the light of these comparatively recent events, it is easy to see that the first amalgamationists in the re- mote past would fare badly at the hands of his neighbors who knew that amalgamation was a violation of the law of God and that its indulgence had led to the deluge.

Under such circumstances it would seem natural that these ancient amalgamationists, who were determined to pursue their wicked course, would desire that some sem- blance of respectability should be given to their acts, and this could only be accomplished by devising some scheme by which the Negro and his amalgamated progeny would be admitted into the family of man; for at that period, and for long afterwards, as shown by the history of Is- rael, the Negro was recognized as a beast—the "beast of the field."

Let us bear in mind that when these people violated the law of God and descended to amalgamation, His blessings, under whtch they had grown rich, powerful and happy, were withdrawn, and his curses visited upon them instead; the blessings of peace, with its elevating, educational advantages and its agricultural, mechanical and commercial vocations, all tending to the building up of happy, prosperous homes, were exchanged for the horrors of war; the men of the land, and especially the

young men, were torn from home and loved ones, and
deprived of the softening, elevating influences of
woman's sweet companionship; the advantages of a fixed
place of abode, the society of the family, and the peace
and safety of the home, were abandoned for the exposure of the camp, the long, tiresome march and the dangers of the battle-field; the vocations of peace were exchanged for the profession of war, and demoralization
was the inevitable result. The burthen and expense of
these wars, with all their train of evils, fell upon the
masses of the people. As a result, the masses gradually
became less prosperous and more illiterate; and as they
became more ignorant and poverty-stricken they became
more demoralized and degraded. This condition of
affairs gave the amalgamationist his opportunity and he
took advantage of it by openly renouncing God and the
doctrine of Creation with God as the Creator. He **took**
advantage of the existence of various tribes and nations
of mixed-bloods and combined them with Man and the
Negro to form the "species—Man." Thus, the Negro
and his amalgamated progeny were thrust into the family
of Man, where they have since remained in utter disregard of God's Plan of Creation and in shameless violation of his law. In the course of time this theory was
broadened out and gradually crystallized into the general
theory of atheism, which teaches that the existence of
the universe is the result of natural causes; that the
whole world is composed of matter and mind; that there
is **no** immortality; that man is merely an animal—a

highly developed species of ape—the human species, and that this human species of ape is composed of races of men, who trace their line of descent through a series of "animal ancestors" to the lowest form of animal, itself the result of spontaneous generation.

The literature of that remote period, like its authors and their civilizations, has long since crumbled into dust. Hence, we have no means of ascertaing the exact date upon which this crime was consummated. However, we have, in the Bible and profane history, reliable records which enable us by comparison to locate the period in which this catastrophe occurred.

1. The Bible teaches that monotheism was the religion of Noah and his family. The Theory of Development may have, and doubtless did exist, together with idolatory among the antediluvians; but if so, the evolutionist, the amalgamationist, and the mixed-bloods were all swept from the earth by the Deluge.

2. As has been shown, the existence of the theory that there are "races" of men, which is an inseparable part of the theory of atheism, was a matter of record in the sacred registers of Ancient Egypt, from which the data for Plato's narrative of Atlantis was obtained. This indicates that this theory had existed from a period so remote, that it is questionable, whether the Egyptians of Solon's day, had any knowledge of the date or place of its origin. However, we are enabled to determine that the Theory of

Development, made its appearance on the earth in post-deluvian times, at some period intervening between the Deluge, and the time when its existence was made a matter of record in the sacred registers of Ancient Egypt.

In the course of time, the spread of this theory, and the demoralizing conditions out of which it originated, again covered the greater part of the earth with mixed-blooded tribes and nations; thus placing it in much the same condition as it was before the Deluge.

Scattered over several continents, with no organized system of religion, with no concert of action, the God-loving, God-serving people of the earth, were powerless to beat back this ever-increasing tide of atheism and amalgamation; and the extinction of Man and the Negro, and the consequent destruction of the Plan of Creation, was again seriously threatened. In this emergency, God again came to the rescue. But he was restrained from the employment of any agency of universal destruction. In his convenant with Noah and his sons, immediately after the Deluge God had said: "I will not again curse the ground any more for man's sake; for the imagination of man's heart is evil from his youth; neither will I destroy everything living as I have done." (*Gen.*, viii, 21.)

Bound by this covenant God decided to make it possible for man to rectify the evils he had engendered and sweep from the earth the products of his own shameless crime. To accomplish this purpose, he selected Abraham from whom he would raise up for himself a "chosen people," whom he desired should be peculiar in that they would not embrace atheism, nor descend to amalgamation and idolatry, but would love and worship God and live in obedience to his laws.

"Now the Lord had said unto Abram, Get thee out of thy country, and from thy kindred, and from thy father's house, unto a land that I will show thee. And I will make of thee a great nation, and I will bless thee, and make thy name great; and thou shalt be a blessing. And I will bless them that bless thee and curse them that curseth thee; and in thee shall all families of the earth be blessed." (Gen. xii, 1, 2, 3.)

"And the Lord said unto Abram, * * * Lift up now thine eyes. * * * For all the land which thou seest, to thee will I give it and to thy seed forever. And I will make thy seed as the dust of the earth: so that if a man can number the dust of the earth, then shall thy seed also be numbered." (Gen. xiii, 14, 15, 16.)

"And he said unto Abram, Know of a surety that thy seed shall be a stranger in a land that is not theirs, and they shall serve them; and they shall afflict them four hundred years; and also that nation, whom they shall serve, will I judge: and afterward shall they come out with great substance." (Gen. xv, 13, 14.)

[16]

"And when Abram was ninety and nine years old the Lord appeared unto Abram and said unto him, I am Almighty God; walk before me and be thou perfect. And I will make my covenant between me and thee, and will multiply thee exceedingly. Neither shall thy name any more be called Abram, but thy name shall be called Abraham; for a father of many nations have I made thee. * * * And kings shall come out of thee. * * * And I will give unto thee, and to thy seed after the, the land wherein thou art a stranger, all the land of Canaan, for an everlasting possession; and I will be their God." (Gen, xvii. 1, etc.)

God kept His covenant with Abraham, and made of them a great nation—the nation of Israel. He gave them an organized system of political government and an organized system of religion. And in order to counteract the teachings of the Theory of Development, which was universally taught in that day, God gave them the Narrative of Creation, together with the history of the most important events which occurred from the Creation to the arrival of Israel in Canaan. God then led Israel to the land of Canaan, and commanded them to destroy its population of mixed–bloods—male and female—"thou shalt save nothing alive that breatheth." [Gen.,xx, 16.] And take possession of their country and its immense wealth of every description, and this, as has been shown, included a great many Negroes.

Previous to the days of Israel there was no organization among the worshippers of God; every man wor-

shipped God according to the dictates of his own conscience; they usually followed the example of Noah,
and erected an altar upon which they offered sacrifices.
But this disorganized condition of religious affairs under-
went the most radical change when God established the
Jewish Church and gave to the world an organized system of religion; and made Jerusalem the center of the
religious world; its doors stood open to all of pure
Adamic stock; every pure-blooded descendant of
Adam could become a member of the Jewish Church and
participate in its benefit by complying with the law on
the subject. It was the desire of God that Israel should
be the leaven that would leaven to God the whole lump
of humanity, as shown by His promise to Abraham:
"In thee shall all the families of the earth be blessed."
It was God's desire that the Plan of Creation as set forth
in the Mosaic Record should be disseminated throughout
the world, in opposition to the theory of atheism; and
that all men should learn from the Israelites that man had
not developed out of "fish-like ancestors," themselves the result of "spontaneous generation;" but
that man was created "in the image of God;" that there
is no kinship between man and the animals, but that the
kinship is between God and man; that man is not a
species of ape, which is divisible into "races of men,"
but that he is a distinct Creation.

But instead of accomplishing this great mission,
and thus fulfilling the just expectations of God the Israelites "were full of the evil doings that were common

among the Canaanites." [Josephus.] They disregarded the teachings of scripture, and lived out in their
daily lives the teachings of atheism; they forgot the
warnings of God and violated His law by descending to
amalgamation with the Negro and with the mixed-
blooded nations by whom they were surrounded and
with whom God forbid them to intermarry; and in the
course of time the mulattoes were as plentiful in Judea
as they are in any of our southern states. They "defiled" "the land" and "filled" Israel, God's "inheritance," "with the carcasses of their detestable and abominable things." Not only this, but captivated by the
obscene rites, and the more or less promiscuous intercourse bstween the sexes, which usually characterises
the worship of idols, they renounced God, abandoned
His worship and embraced idolatry.

God then visited his curses upon them in the form
of war, famine, pestilence and disease, in order to force
them to abandon their criminal course and return to their
duties and to their allegiance to Him. God even devas-
tated their country, laid their magnificent temples in
ruins and sent them captives to a foreign land and enslaved them. He sent prophet after prophet among
them to warn them of their danger and of the terrible
judgments that would be visited upon them; but these
at best only achieved a temporary success, while in
many instances they were maltreated and even killed.
God then determined to make a final effort to redeem man
from the clutches of atheism, amalgamation and idolatry,

that triplet of crimes that has destroyed and damned nations and even continents, and He sent Jesus Christ,
His only begotten son, and he shared the fate of many
of the prophets who preceded him.

Adam and Jesus Christ are two of the most prominent characters in the Bible, and each is described as the
"Son of God." (See Luke, iii, 38, John, iii, 18.) As
has been shown, Adam was merely a combination of
matter and mind until God breathed into his nostrils the
"breath of life"—immortal life—and Adam became "a
living soul." The language of the text will bear no
other construction than that [1] this "breath of life"
was a new element in the material uuiverse. Hence, a
creation. [2] That it was a part of the substance of
God. [3] That this "breath of life"—this "living soul"
—was incorporated with matter and with mind, as presented in Adam's physical and mental organisms, and established between God and Adam the relationship of
father and son. Thus Adam was the created "son of
God." These three creations, matter, mind and soul,
combine to form man; but man himself consists of a
male side or part, and a female side or part; and one
side or part of these three creations exists in the male
man, their corresponding side or part exists in the female
man. Through the sexual act these three creations are
united and perfected in the female, aud the relationship
of father and child, which existed between God and the
parents is transmitted to the offspring.

Immediately before the Savior was conceived one
side or part of these three creations constituting the

female side or part of a child, lay in the womb of the
Virgin Mary; and God, not by the sexual act, but by
the exercise of His creative power, supplied, and united
with it, its male side or part; Mary conceived, and at the
proper time Jesus Christ, whom God designed should
redeem man from atheism, amalgamation and idolatry,
was born. Thus, Jesus Christ, born of a woman, was
the begotten "son of God."

Thus it is shown that the birth of Jesus Christ was
as legitimate as that of any child that was ever born of
a woman; He was not only the son of the author of marriage, but he was the son of the Creator of the heaven
and the earth. Hence, the blasphemy of the oft-repeated
charge that Jesus Christ was a bastard is only equaled
by its absurdity. The product of a cross between different species of plant or animal, is sometimes called a bastard, but properly speaking, it is a hybrid, while the
product of a cross between different races of the same
species of plant or animal is a mongrel. A bastard is
the offspring of pure Adamic parents that is born out of
wedlock.

Rather than abandon their criminal relations with
the Negro, and the mixed-bloods they killed the Savior
as they did the prophets.

Thus it is shown that sin entered the world
through man's sociality with the Negro, and that this
led to amalgamation, atheism and idolatry; and that
God has made every effort even to the sacrifice of his
son, to eradicate these evils. It is also shown that

every prophet of antediluvian, as well as those of
postdiluvian times came to induce man to renounce
these destructive crimes, and return to their allegiance
to God; and that this was the mission of the Savior.
If further evidence of this is necessary the Savior
furnishes it in his parable:

"There was a certain householder, which planted
a vineyard, and hedged it round about, and digged a
winepress in it, and built a tower, and let it out to
husbandmen, and went into a far country: And
when the time of the fruit drew near, he sent his
servants to the husbandmen, that they might receive
the fruits of it. And the husbandmen took his servants, and beat one, and killed another, and stoned
another. Again he sent other servants more than
the first: And they did unto them likewise. But last
of all he sent unto them his son, saying, They will
reverence my son. But when the husbandmen saw
the son, they said among themselves, This is the heir;
come, let us kill him, and let us seize on his inheritance. And they cast him out of the vineyard,
and slew him." (*Matt.*, xxi, 33, 34, 35, etc.)

In this parable, with God as the "householder,"
the earth, the "vineyard," souls, the "fruit," the
prophets, the "servants," Jesus Christ the "son and
heir," we have an exact illustration of Bible history
from the Creation to the Crucifixion. This parable
teaches:

1. That the earth is the Lord's; that "God let it
out" to man whom he desired should be "fruitful and

multiply," and by a life of obedience to God, would fit their souls for the companionship of the blest, and thus increase the population of heaven. But man violated the law of God by descending to social equality with the Negro, and this led to amalgamation; and, as we have shown the amalgamated progeny of Man and the Negro produces no souls. And when God sent his prophets to insist that they abandon their wicked course, and confine their marriage relations to the Adamic family, and thus be able to give the Lord his dues, they "beat," and "stoned," and "killed" them. God then sent other prophets, time and again, "and they did unto them likewise."

2. It teaches, that the second prophet, and each succeeding prophet, came for the same purpose as did the first; and that the mission of the "Son" was identically the same as that of the prophets who preceded him, and that it shared the same fate.

3. It teaches, that if the first prophet had succeeded in his mission, there would have been no necessity for sending a second, nor any subsequent prophet; neither would it have been necessary to send the Son. Had the Lord received his dues he would have been satisfied.

4. It teaches, that the doctrine, that it was a part of a general plan that the Savior should come and be sacrificed, and that everything pointed to his coming and sacrifice, is a mistake, growing out of our failure to understand the nature of His mission; and that of

the prophets who preceded him. On the contrary, every effort was made to do away with the necessity for His coming and sacrifice—it was the last resort. And when he realized that his end was near, he was still unwilling that the powers opposed to him should triumph, and that he should be sacrificed, as shown by his prayer on the Mount of Olives: "Father, if thou be willing, remove this cup from me: Nevertheless, not my will, but thine, be done." He was willing to live on and suffer in his labor of love. He was aware that when God gave the land of Canaan to Israel, that he had enumerated and forbid every form of illicit lust, which man may indulge within the Adamic family, and had also said: "Neither shalt thou lie with any beast to defile thyself therewith. * * * Defile not ye yourselves in any of these things. * * * That the land spue not you out also when ye defile it, as it spued out the nations that were before you." He realized that his death would hasten the hour when the "land," a second time defiled by amalgamation, would, a second time spue out its inhabitants; and that Israel would be scattered to the "four winds of heaven." He loved the Jews, his mother's people; and he loved their country. No purer expression of patriotism ever fell from patriot lips than fell from the Savior's, when he gave utterance to that agonized cry: O Jerusalem, Jerusalem, thou that killest the prophets, and stonest them which are sent unto thee, how often would I have gathered thy children together, even as a hen gathereth her chickens under her wings, and ye would not!" (*Matt.* xxiii, 37.)

When the earth had been transformed into a cess-pool of amalgamation; when idolatry was universally practiced; when the last flickering ray from the torch of Judaism had been extinguished, and the world was enveloped in a night of atheism, the Savior made his appearance with the announcement: "I am the light of the world; he that followeth me shall not walk in darkness but shall have the light of life." He formulated and introduced upon the earth a religious system that stands peerless among the religions of the world for the breadth and purity of its charity, the loftiness of its aims, and the simplicity of its ceremonies. He formed a religious organization and replaced Judaism with Christianity. In opposition to the atheism and negroism and idolatry of the age, he established his Church on the Narrative of Creation. He attempted to restore the relations between man and the animals which God designed. He attempted to rebuild the barriers between Man and the Negro which God established in the Creation, and which man, in his criminal folly, had trampled down. In the Creation, the position of the Negro at the head of the ape family marked the limit of the animals. But man's unhallowed lust prompted him to take the Negro out of the ape family and thrust him into the family of Man as a "lower race" of the "human species," thus making the so-called anthropoids the limit of the animals. Between these opposing lines, and over the question of their legitimacy, the great battle between God and Man has raged with varying success for ages; in this prolonged conflict, of which the Bible is largely a history, every nation of whites of ancient times has been swept from the earth; the greater part of their splendid civilization has been laid in ruins, and their once prosperous, happy homes have been transformed into the abode of the barbarians and savages their crime produced. Between these opposing lines, the one which God established in the Creation and the one that Man has since established, is the ground upon which the great battle of the world.is yet to be fought to a finish, and untold millions will bite the dust on that field of carnage. But we who believe that there is a God; that there was a Creation; that man was created in the "image of God;" that the animal was made "after his kind;" that "all flesh is not the same flesh;" that the Bible is God's revealed will to man, need have no fear of the result. God and the right will triumph. The spurious Christianity of today based, as it is, on the Theory of Development, will be repudiated by man; atheism will be eradicated from the minds of men; the Negro will be thrust out of the family of Man and forced to resume his proper position among the apes; the mixed-bloods will be destroyed from the earth their presence defiles; and Man, in obedience to the laws given him in the Creation, will proceed to develop the resources of the earth and exert that control over the animals which God designed him to have and commanded him to exercise. These grand accomplishments will usher in the Millennium.

In the Savior's day Judea, suffering under the curses of God for her crimes, had become a province of Rome. His blameless life and the purity of His teachings was a constant rebuke to the corruptions of Judaism. This offended the Jewish officials and they heaped every indignity upon Him; He was scorned, persecuted and slandered; a false charge was brought against him and he was arraigned and tried before the Roman governor, who admitted that the charge was not sustained by the evidence. Yet in response to the demand of the Jews, he ordered Him to be crucified. But even while suffering an ignominious death upon the cross, the innocent victim of atheism, negroism and idolatry, yielding up his life for the sins of a lost world, His wondrous love for man found expression in his dying prayer: "Father, forgive them; for they know not what they do."

After the death of the Savior, his disciples did all in their power to preserve the organization He had formed and to disseminate among men the lofty principles which He taught; but one by one they fell; many of them met violent deaths at the hands of the enemies of the Church. With their great leader and his chief apostles gone, discord entered the Church

and His followers became disorganized, and the teachings of atheism gradually crept in and was accepted and taught in the Church, as we find them being taught today.

This acceptance of the teachings of atheism was practically a repudiation of the teachings of Scripture, and the destruction of the Church was the necessary result. Then God, in his wrath and disgust, turned nation upon nation in war; civilizations that had required ages to develop were laid in ruins, and the whole world of mankind was plunged into the dark ages of ignorance, superstition and crime, through which they have thus far blundered without a church, and must ever remain in this deplorable condition so long as they allow atheism to impose the Negro and his amalgamated progeny upon them as "lower races of men," who may be civilized, educated and Christianized.

The Savior was slain; the organization which He formed was disrupted; and the factions into which it divided gradually accepted more or less of the teachings of atheism and confused them with those of scripture, thus corrupting and destroying Christianity; a spurious Christianity in which the teachings of atheism, confused with those of scripture, is now universally accepted by those who express belief in God and the truth of the Bible. Yet in the face of all these disasters we need not despair. If Christianity, as established by our Savior, had any basis, in fact its ultimate basis was the Mosaic

Record. In opposition to the prevailing atheism of the age, He established His church on the Narrative of Creation. It was the Mosaic Record to which He referred when He said: "On this rock I will build my church and the gates of hell shall not prevail against it." He thus fitly describes atheism and negroism as the gates of hell.

We have the Mosaic Record, the basis of Christianity; we have the principles of Christianity clearly set forth in the writings of the apostles; the cleansing blood of Christ, is still sufficient for the remission of sin. These are the essential elements of Christianity. To destroy the religious organization among men, which the Savior formed, and into which he sought to instill the principles of Christianity, is one thing, and atheism accomplished that, but to destroy the Mosaic Record, the basis of Christianity, to destroy the principles of Christianity as set forth in the inspired writings, to destroy the effacacy of Christ's atoning blood, is another, and quite a different thing, and this atheism can never do.

The people of this or any subsequent period, can renounce their atheism and negroism, and take these elements of Christianity and re-establish the Church of Christ in all its original purity; and their worship will be as acceptable to God, as was that of the primitive Christians. A world-wide religious organization is not essential to salvation, neither is a sumptuous and costly church edifice; neither is a rich, fashionable and aristocratic congregation, and a high salaried preacher. The Savior has said: "For where two or three are gathered together in my name, there am I in the midst of them."

We have traced the atheistic theory of development to the sacred registers of ancient Egypt; and have shown that the acceptance of this degrading theory brought the negro and his amalgamated progeny into the Adamic family as "lower races of men," and precipitated that long-continued conflict between God and Man that has swept nation after nation from the face of the earth, laid their civilizations in ruins, denuded continents of its Adamic stock, and transferred them into the abodes of barbarians and savages.

Man's unhallowed lust, to which this theory owes its origin, insured its continued existence; and that it survived, and was universally taught in the centuries immediately preceding the coming of Christ, and at later periods, as it is taught to-day is shown by the utterances of Mr. Haeckel, who says:

"We will here mention only that as early as the seventh century before Christ, the representatives of the Ionian philosophy of nature, Thales, Anaximenes, and Anaximander, of Meletius, and more especially Anaximander, established important principles of our modern monism. Their teaching pointed to a uniform law of nature as the basis of the various phenomena, a unity of all nature and a continual change of forms.

Anaximander considered that the anemalcules in water came into existence through the influence of the warmtn of the sun, and assumed that man had developed out of fish—like ancestors. At a later date also, we find in the natural philosophy of Heraclitus and Empedocles, as well as in the writings of Demo-critus and Aristotle, many allusions to conceptions which we regard as the fundamental supports of our modern theory of development. Empedocles points out that things which appear to have been made for a definite purpose may have arisen out of what had no purpose whatever. Aristotle assumes spontaneous generation as the natural manner in which the lower organisms came into existence." (*Hist. of Creation,* Vol. I, pp. 78, 79.)

This theory which assumes "that man developed out of fish-like ancestors"—themselves the result of "spontaneous generation"—necessarily assumes that all flesh is akin.

This theory which had come surging down through the ages and had become almost irresistable from the strength it had acquired by its universal ac-ceptance, threatened in Paul's day to sweep the Church of Christ from the Mosaic record and land it, a wreck, on the quicksands of atheism, where we find it today. It was in the heat of his great battle with this overwhelming tide of atheism, in which he after-wards lost his life, that Paul was inspired to give ut-terance to that sublime declaration: "All flesh is not the same flesh: but there is one kind of flesh of men, another flesh of beasts, another of fishes, and another of birds." Hence, there is no kinship between man and the animals.

The universal acceptance of this teaching of the inspired apostle would crush atheism into atoms and would eradicate the theory of development with all its degrading influences from the minds of men. It disproves the theory of atheism that the invertebrate developed into the vertebrate; that the skulless developed into the skulled; that the fish has developed into the fowl on the one side and into the land animal on the other; that the quadruped developed into the biped (ape); that the ape developed into speechless man (Homo primigenius); and that speechless man developed into man with articulate speech.

The acceptance of Paul's teaching would crush the theory of development at every point from the monera to man. If the flesh of the birds is a different "kind of flesh" from that of the fish, then the birds never developed out of the fish. If the flesh of the beasts is a different "kind of flesh" from that of the fish, then the beasts never developed out of the fish. If the "flesh of man" is a different "kind of flesh" from that of the beasts, then man never developed out of the beast. God made the flesh of the fish, and that of the fowl, and that of the beast separate and distinct from each other; and he made the flesh of man separate and distinct from that of the animals,

[17]

Hence, man has no animal ancestors. In his teaching as above quoted, that grand old "Hebrew of the Hebrews" struck atheism at its vital points. To accept this teaching necessitates our rejection of the theory that man is a species which is divisible into races, and that the Negro, the Malay, the Indian and the Mongolian are "lower races of men" in different stages of development.

As has been shown, atheism, which teaches that all flesh is akin, and of which the theory that man is a "species," which is divisible into five or more "races of men," is an inseparable part, was not accepted and taught by the church of Christ in Paul's day; on the contrary, this learned apostle assailed it; yet we find the modern church teaching this theory that the Whites, Blacks, Browns, Reds and Yellows are all "races" of the "species—Man," and that they should associate together on terms of social, political and religious equality; and this, as we know, inevitably leads to amalgamation, and has been shown, amalgamation leads to idolatry. When did this radical change in the teachings of the church take place? It evidently occurred at some period between our day and the days of Paul; and the most charitable and correct view is, that it did not occur in modern times, but that it took place in the remote past.

History teaches that very soon after the death of the Savior, His followers split up into a number of opposing sects, each of which maintained a religious organization which termed the "church," and insisted that its church was the true church, and that its creed embodied the teachings of the Savior aud should be universally accepted. In these factional strifes which continued for generations, the teachings of scripture and especially those of the Mosaic Record, were lost sight of and forgotten, and as a result they fell an easy prey to atheism, that most uncompromising foe to God and religious worship. Gradually the teachings of atheism were accepted and taught by the various sects. This event marks the death of Christianity as taught by the Savior, and also marks the birth of the spurious Christianity of modern times. These sects continued to maintain their religious organizations; but their teachings merely consisted of a mixture of the teachings peculiar to atheism with those peculiar to scripture. This was one of the results of that "falling away" of which Paul warned them. The condition of these sects when the teachings of atheism replaced the teachings of scripture and their subsequent history, is clearly foretold by Paul as follows:

"Now we beseech you brethren * * * That ye be not soon shaken in mind, or be troubled, neither by spirit, nor by word, nor by letter as from us, as that the day of Christ is at hand. Let no man deceive you by any means: for that day shall not come except there come a falling away first, and that man of sin be revealed, the son of perdition; who opposeth and exalteth himself above all that is called God, or that is worshipped; so that he as God sitteth in the temple of God, showing himself that he is God. Remember ye not that when I was yet with you I told you of these things? And now ye know what withholdeth that he might be revealed in his time. For the mystery of iniquity doth already work: only he who now letteth will let, until he be taken out of the way. And then shall the wicked be revealed, whom the Lord shall consume with the spirit of His mouth and shall destroy with the brightness of His coming: Even him whose coming is after the working of Satan with all power and signs and lying wonders. And all deceivableness of unrighteousness in them that perish; because they received not the love of the truth, that they might be saved. And for this cause God shall send them strong delusion, that they should believe a lie: That they all might be damned who believed not the truth but had pleasure in unrighteousness.'' II Thes., ii, 1, 2, 3, etc.

Finally, these various sects, with their mixture of the teachings of Scripture with those of atheism, were combined into an organization which is known as the Catholic church. The Catholic church and the Protestant church, which split off from it, have been the vehicles by which this ancient blending of the teachings of atheism with those of Scripture have been handed down to us. The theory that man is a ''species'' which is divisible into ''races of men,'' is to man the most ruinous part of the teachings of atheism. This theory, which thrusts the Negro and his amalgamated progeny into the Adamic family as ''lower races of men,'' has been universally accepted by the modern world because of its antiquity, and the fact that the church gave it to us; no inquiry as to its origin or its nature has ever been made, though its demoralizing, degrading results confront us on every hand. The universal acceptance of this atheism insured it from assault. Hence, no effort has ever been made to eradicate it from the church. On the contrary, it is assiduously taught in every relation in life from the cradle to the grave. Hence, the man who would attempt to prove that this teaching of the church is all wrong would be denounced as a fit subject for the "fool-killer," a traitor to his "species," a disgrace to his "race."

In this work, the theory that man is a "species" which is divisible into "races" is assailed for the first time in ages; its origin is investigated and laid bare; its opposition to the teachings of Scripture is exposed and its destructive results to Christianity clearly shown. While the church has been active in disseminating this theory from generation to generation for ages, Paul's terrific assault upon atheism, of which this theory is an inseparable part, has, as might have been expected, lain as silent in the Bible as the remains of its great author have lain in the grave.

In this work, for the first time in ages, an investigation is made as to the cause of which Paul's teaching was but the effect. He was battling with some opposing teaching, and we find that he was assailing the theory of atheism which threatened in his day to destroy the Church of Christ, as it afterward did. We find that "All flesh is not the same flesh" was an assault on the theory that all flesh is the same flesh, and that from the monera to man all flesh is akin. His teaching that there are four distinct kinds of flesh was an assault upon the theory that from the monera to man there is just one flesh in different stages of development.

The acceptance of this teaching of the great apostle will prove invaluable to man in determining his proper relation to the animals; it places in his hands the most effective weapon in his battle with atheism; it will do much toward enabling him to re-establish Christianity and thus give to the world a religious system whose teachings and worship will at once prove beneficial to man and acceptable to God.

In our day, thousands of the brightest youths are placed in theological institutions, not to be taught the word of God, but to be systematically drilled in the narrow creed of some religious sect; in the course of time, these young men are graduated, as ignorant of the teachings of the Mosaic Record and the drift of Bible history as they were on the day they entered the kindergarten. The consequence is, that if they read any scientific works they accept more or less of the atheism with which they abound, and this finds expression in their sermons and serves to still further corrupt the minds of their hearers. The laity as a class have too many social, financial, political and religious affairs to look after to read the

Bible, and they know little about it. The same causes prevent their reading upon atheism, and they know nothing of its teachings. Hence, they are unable to distinguish between the teachings of atheism and those of scripture.

The fact that many of the most distinguished writers on modern science are atheists has led people to think that atheism and science are synonymous terms. This is a sad mistake. Modern atheism bears no closer relationship to modern science than alchemy bears to chemistry.

The atheist takes the truths which scientific research has discovered the existence of and makes them the basis of his absurd theories. Hence, a superficial reading of the works of modern scientists gives us merely the atheism whtch floats as a scum upon the surface, and leaves the great truths beneath, unnoticed and unappreciated. The stream of literature which flows out from the modern press carries with it the most refined atheism, which permeates and corrupts every circle of society. The demoralizing conditions by which we are surrounded are largely due to the atheism which flows into our homes through the daily and weekly press and the various magazines. Thousands of articles reeking with the most disgusting atheism enter our homes daily and are read and accepted without question; no effort is made by professed Christians to counteract their pernicious influences. From the innumerable articles from which we might quote to sustain our position, we shall select one from the pen of Charles Dudley Warner, which appeared in the "Chicago American" of September 9th. Mr. Warner, in his article, "Failure of Negro Education," says:

"In the United States a great mass of negroes—possibly over nine millions of many shades of colors—is for the first time brought into contact with Christian civilization. This mass is here to make or mar our national life, and the problem of its destiny has to be met with our own. What can we do, what ought we to do for his own good and for our peace and national welfare?

In the first place it is impossible to escape the profound impression that we have made a mistake in our estimate of his evolution as a race, in attempting to apply to him the same treatment for the development of character that we would apply to a race more highly organized. Has he developed the race consciousness, the race soul, a collective soul, which so strongly marks other races more or less civilized according to our standards? * * *" Observe the pure atheism contained in this article! "His evolution as a race." What has the negro "race" evolved from? If the negro is the result of "evolution" he has necessarily "differentiated" from a lower animal. Hence, God never made the negro at all; he has merely evolved through a series of animal ancestors from the lowest form of animal, itself the result of spontaneous generation. And Mr. Warner expresses a doubt as to

whether the negro has evolved sufficiently far from
his "animal ancestors" as to have developed a "soul."
What an idea? Besides, this teaching carried to its
legitimate conclusions necessarily implies that "a
race more highly organized (like the white) has
evolved so far from their "animal ancestors" as to
develop a "soul." What good can result from sending
our children to the Sunday school one hour on the
Sabbath, and feeding their minds on such filth as this
seven days in every week? The acceptance of this
teaching that the negro is the result of "evolution,"
means the rejection of the scriptural teaching that
there is a God—a Creator. How can we allow our
children taught this atheism from infancy to maturity
and expect that they will be anything else than
practical atheists and infidels? We not only place the
political party to which we belong, above our country,
but we place it above the welfare of our families; if
the editor will only teach our children the principles
of our political party, he has our consent to instill
into their minds all the atheism they can absorb. It
is not membership in this or that religious organiza-
tian that makes Christians of us; it is not our failure
to belong to any religious organization that makes
atheists and infidels of us, it is the sentiments we entertain, and live out and teach in our daily lives, that
makes Christians or atheists of us as the case may be.
For ages this atheism has been poured into our
families and into the church, and as a result, modern

Christianity bears no closer relationship to primitive Christianity than astrology bears to astronomy.

What the world wants is primitive Christianity; it wants a religious system based squarely on the narrative of Divine Creation, and not on the atheistic theory of Natural Development; it wants a church or organization that will enable us to recognize and teach us to respect the broad distinction which God made in the Creation between man and the animals; and any religious system which fails to do this, is simply a delusion and a snare.

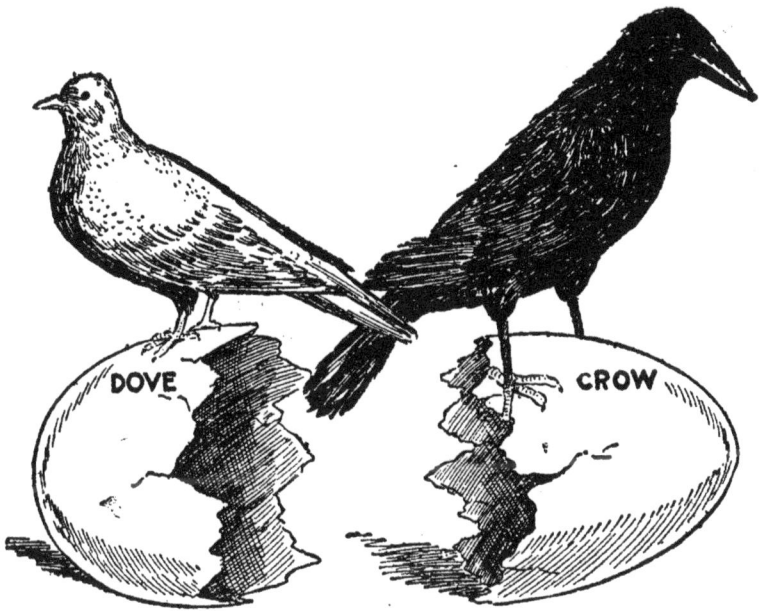

THE EGG OF CREATION.

Were they both hatched from the same egg? If so, are they both in the image of their father? If they are both from the same egg, and both in the image of their father, then "like does not beget like", and it is possible for the Dove to produce an Ostrich.

Chapter IX.

Ignorance of the Bible, and Continued Atheistic Teachings Have Led Astray the Masses, Relative to God's Creation of Man.

The drift of Bible history from the Creation to the birth of the Savior clearly indicates that he came to destroy man's social, political and religious equality with the Negro and mixed-bloods and the amalgamation to which these crimes inevitably lead, and to rebuild the barriers which God erected in the Creation between man and the ape, and to reinstate man in his "dominion over every living thing that moveth upon the earth." The modern church, under the influence of atheism, has torn down the barriers which the Savior re-established between man and the ape, and has again degraded man to social, political and

religious equality with the Negro and the mixed-
bloods; has extinguished the light of the gospel; has
hurled the Adamic family back into the darkness and
gloom and hopelessness of atheism and into the cess-
pool of amalgamation. As a result, Christianity has
long since fled the earth and the gospel of Christ has
been superceded by the gospel of atheism. The relation of the modern church to Christ is fitly described
by Paul as follows:

"But if, while we seek to be justified by Christ,
we ourselves are found sinners, is therefore Christ the
minister of sin? God forbid. For if I build again
the things again which I destroyed, I make myself a
transgressor." (Gal. ii, 17, 18.)

Man's social, political and religious equality with
the Negro and the mixed-bloods, which the Savior
destroyed to a certain extent, and which he desired to
utterly destroy, the modern church, with its clergy
and laity and by every means in its power, proceeded
to "build again." As a result, the gospel of Christ,
which was based upon the scriptural teaching that
man is a distinct creation "in the image of God," is
never heard. And the atheistic gospel that man is a
"species" divisible into "races" is universally taught.
The modern clergy might find it profitable to consider the emphatic declaration of Paul: "But though
we, as an angel from heaven, preach any other gospel
unto you than that which we have preached unto you,
let him be accursed." (Gal. 1, 8.) Though this

curse was pronounced against a certain class of Jews, who desired to mix Judaism with Christianity, it is strictly applicable to the modern Christian who mixes atheism with Christianity. The inspired apostle insisted that the gospel of Christ, based squarely on the Narrative of Divine Creation, should be preached in its purity. This modern gospel, based squarely on the Theory of Natural Development, is certainly another gospel than that of Jesus Christ which Paul preached.

The most unprecedented effort is being made by the professedly Christian world to extend the gospel of Christ to the negroes and mixed-bloods of the earth. Each religious sect wants all of these degraded creatures in its fold. The most openly avowed effort in this direction was made by "Bishop Nelson of the Episcopal diocese of Georgia * * * * * in St. Paul's church (New Orleans) to a very large congregation on the subject: 'Our Relations and Duty to the Colored Race.' * * * Bishop Nelson took as his text Isaiah xliii, 6, 7. * * * Bishop Nelson announced as his first proposition that Christ was the Savior of all races. Although the head of a diocese containing over 1,000,000 whites he would be recreant to his duty if he did not consider himself the bishop of the blacks as well, and to the extent of his power as far as limitations permitted, strive for the welfare of the 900,000 blacks as well as the welfare of the whites in the state of Georgia. The race prob-

lem he considered the greatest that had ever con-
fronted the people of America, and probably the
greatest that ever would be presented to the nation
for solution.   *   *   *   Many absurdities had been advanced as possible solutions of the race problem.
First was that of extermination, an absolutely impossible remedy, and one which none ever seriously advocated, and it deserved only a passing mention."

In antediluvian time, God very seriously advocated
extermination as a possible remedy for the very class of
creatures which, in America, Bishop Nelson is pleased
to term Negroes. And the very effectual manner in
which he applied the remedy—a universal deluge—deserves more than a passing mention. The fact that since
the deluge and at various times, upon every continent of
the earth, God has seriously advocated and applied extermination to this class of creatures, indicates that the
remedy deserves more than a passing mention. Continuing, Bishop Nelson says:

"Miscegenation was utterly abhorrent, unreasonable
and impossible. As a serious remedy it was so absolutely improbable that it deserved little attention."

What an idea! When amalgamation has destroyed
every nationality of Whites of ancient time, and is making the most frightful ravages upon everyone of modern
time, and after "twenty-five years" of study of the
Negro problem, this pious (?) bishop decides that it deserved little attention.

"A third suggestion was deportation.   *   *   *   It
was not feasible,   *   *   *   Finally the bishop spoke of

segregation, which he considered the only proposed solution of the Negro question worth consideration. He believed in giving the Negro equal advantages in the line of schools, churches, lyceums, amusements. He advocated separate churches, not because the Whites objected to the presence of the Negro in the White church. In many churches portions of the church were set apart for the colored communicants. The Negroes themselves wanted their own churches. * * * Bishop Nelson ridiculed the idea of territorial segregation. * * * The solution of the Negro problem seemed to rest upon segregation and Christian education, and the duty of the Episcopal Church was too clear to be denied, too manifest to be shirked. The Episcopal Church or none must solve the question. Education without Christianity and education without true Christian doctrine was worse than ignorance, for it was a source of knavery and the pet instrument of the devil. * * * The time had come for the Episcopal Church to take a firm stand and as a church to provide the educational facilities which, together with the teachings of the church, could and would uplift the Negro as a race. The work was not a hopeless one. Whereas the White race had had 1,500 years of civilization through which to climb to its present position of knowledge and refinement, the Negro had been in contact with civilization but about 150 years, and nearly all of that time as a slave." (See The Times Democrat, Feb. 28, 1898.)

[18]

As has been shown, the negro has been in contact with the modern civilization of America since A. D. 1619. This, in itself is a period nearly double that named by the Bishop, "150 years." In addition to this, the evidence of the negro's contact with ancient Adamic civilizations, is presented by every continent of the earth. The negro was brought in contact with the splendid civilization of the Egyptians. We find him figured, black and colorless, on their monuments of more than 4,000 years ago. In all this immense period of time, he has not lost a single one of his ape-like characters, nor developed the slightest shade of color. The negro of forty centuries ago is the negro of to-day. Dr. Winchell says, "Negro portraits exist which date from the Eleventh Dynasty, B. C. 2006 (Str.) 2400 (Leps.). Hundreds of negro portraits occur from the Eighteenth Dynasty down, B.C. 1492 (Str.), 1550 (Leps.). Monumental evidences of the existence of negroes occur in the Twelfth Dynasty, B. C. 1963 (Str.) 2300 (Leps.). Monumental evidences of the existence of negroes are even found under the Sixth Dynasty, B. C. 2081) (Str.), 2190 (Wilk.), 2967 (Leps.). (*Preadamites*, pp. 209, 10.)

The astonishing ignorance displayed by Bishop Nelson, as to the period of time in which the negro has "been in contact with civilization," presents the most striking contrasts to the utterances of the scholarly Winchell, who, after discussing the great

natural wealth, and almost unlimited resources of
Africa says:

"It is pertinent to inquire if such a continent, so
outfitted with resources for food, clothing, transporta-
tion, intercommunication and commerce, is a situation
suited to cramp the manhood of an indiginous race.
Are these the conditions under which the grade of
humanity would sink from the level of Adam and
Noah to that of a naked black skin, driveling in filth
and wretchedness on the banks of the Congo or the
Zambesi; while under the climatic vicissitudes of
Western Asia and Europe, the same type has risen
perpetually through all grades of advancing civilization? * * * Our wonder at the stationary savage-
ism of virgin Africa is greatly enhanced when we
reflect on the relations of civilized peoples to that
continent. Ever since the dawn of Accadian civilization in western Asia an open highway of communication has existed between the continents—not to speak
of actual communication across the strait of Babel-
Mandeb. More than this, Asiatic civilization entered
Africa and spread itself over the valley of the Nile
and the Mediterranean border, at a period so remote
as to be obscured in the twilight of human history.
It brought with it the cereals and finally the domesticated animals of Asia. It introduced the arts of
industry and the rudiments of the sciences. It established a religious cult which was monotheistic, and
remarkably pure and elevated. It opened commercial

intercourse, not only with Arabia, Palestine, and Babylonia, but with the tribes of the upper Nile and the Libyan region. It engaged in extensive mining operations, not only in the Sinaic peninsula, but in the far southern countries of Nahsi (negroes). It worked quarries of limestone and granite on an enormous scale. It tilled the soil in the presence of the most forbidding obstacles to be found in the habitable Africa. It sent warlike expeditions not only into Asia Minor and Assyro-Babylonia, but into Nubian Ethopia, and even the armies of a civilized people inevitably sow the germs of civilization among barbarians. The negroes have been in contact with these people for 4,000 years, and save through infusion of blood they have not yet learned the first lesson in civilization. Are these the people whom adverse circumstances have crushed from the grade of Adamic civilizability, and forbidden to rise even while the hands of Egypt and Libyia, and Assyria were outstretched to lift them up? The thought is admissible. Constitutional, aboriginal, deep-seated incapacity is the only explanation of the amazing phenomena." (*Preadamites*, pp. 261, 62, 63, 64.)

Bishop Nelson says: "The White race had had 1,500 years of civilization through which to climb to its present position of knowledge and refinement." Let us see! 1,500 years would not take us back to the creation of man by thousands of years. What was "Adam, the Son of God"—a savage? Was a savage, the best speci-

men of man, whom the great Creator of the heavens and
the earth could make? If Adam, whom God honored
in the creation, by the bestowal of His "likeness" and
His "image," and to whom He confided "dominion"
over the works of His hands, was a savage whose descendants have had only "1,500 years of civilization
through which to climb to their present position of
knowledge and refinement," what kind of a God have
we anyway? But perhaps his ecclesiastical position has
led us unwittingly to do violence to the sentiments of
this eminent Divine. His frequent use of the atheistic
terms, "white race" and "negro race" and "racial
problem," indicates that he regards the whites and negroes as so many races of the human species of ape, in
different stages of development. And that, perhaps, like
the late Rev. Henry Ward Beecher, he regards the Biblical story of Adam and Eve in the Garden of Eden as a
myth; "1,500 years" would not take us back to the
antediluvian patriarchs, one of whom, like Elijah, was
translated. Were these all savages? "1,500 years"
would not take us back to the days of Noah, who walked
with God. Was this just man a savage? "1,500
years" would not take us back to those ancient architects, the remains of whose splendid civilizations are to
be found upon every continent of the earth, and which,
even in their ruins command the admiration of the modern
world. Were these peerless architects savages? "1,500
years" would not take us back to the days of Abraham,
the father of God's chosen people. Was this grand old

patriarch a savage? ''1,500 years'' would not take us
back to the days of Moses, the great ''law-giver'' of
Israel; nor to Aaron, the first priest of Israel; nor to
Joshua, the great military captain of Israel. Were these
all savages? ''1,500 years'' would not take us back to
the days of Israel's great king, David. Was the sweet
psalmist, whom God described as, ''A man after my own
heart,'' a savage? ''1,500 years'' would not take us
back to the days of Solomon. Was ''Solomon in all his
glory'' a savage? ''1,500 years'' would not take us back
to the days of the prophets, whom God sent to Israel to
warn them of ''the evil of their way'' and the disastrous
results to which it would lead. Were the prophets all
savages? ''1,500 years'' would not take us back to the
''Golden Age'' of Greece; nor to the time when, amid
one of the most superb civilizations that ever graced the
earth, ''Rome sat upon her seven hills and ruled the
world.'' Were the Greeks and Romans of those days
savages? ''1,500 years'' would not take us back to the
days of our Savior. Was Jesus Christ, the Son of God,
a savage? But we are reminded that in attempting to
discuss his views upon this subject from a scriptural
standpoint, we have again unwillingly placed Bishop
Nelson in apparent conflict with the Theory which he so
warmly advocates, that the Whites and Negroes are
merely different races of the human species. For our
thoughtlessness we humbly crave the indulgence of His
Reverence. According to this Theory, Jesus Christ was
simply an ape, whose ''animal ancestors'' in the remote

past, according to Haeckel, shed their tails, assumed the erect posture, through the differentiation of two pairs of limbs, developed articulate speech through the differentiation of the larynx, and became man, whose ultimate descendants, with the invaluable aids of natural selection, the survival of the fittest, transmutation, etc., have been enabled ''to climb'' to their present position of knowledge and refinement.

What reply could a Bible-believing man, or one versed in ancient profane history, or one at all familiar with monumental evidence make to the combination of ignorance, scripture and atheism presented in this ''sermon'' by Bishop Nelson?

The Times Democrat says: ''The sermon was a very able one and won the manifest approval of the congregation, many of those present seeking an introduction to the bishop after services.''

The press, of which The Times-Democrat is a part, prides itself upon being the moulder of public sentiment. When we pause to reflect upon the demoralizing, degrading conditions which confront us on every hand and which are the direct result of this sentiment, we can but exclaim: What a sentiment is the output of the mold!

The sentiment of the church upon this subject, as expressed by Bishop Nelson, and its indorsement by the press as expressed by The Times-Democrat, lived out in every day life by our ancestors and by ourselves has transformed our country into a cess-pool of amalgamation, and has brought upon us the curse of God.

Ordinarily, as has been shown, amalgamation between Man and the Negro or the mixed-bloods, always begins between the white males and the black or colored females. Woman declines to lower herself so far as to contract a marriage alliance with a Negro or one in whom she is aware of the presence of Negro blood. But two hundred and fifty years of enlightened Christianity is rapidly reducing the women of the north to this base level. Under the pernicious influences of the church and the press, systematic amalgamation has already begun. In the city of Chicago there is an organization known as the "Manasseh Society." Membership in this society requires that each man shall have a negro wife and that each woman shall have a negro husband. Three or four years ago, according to The Chicago Blade, this society had a membership of 480. In addition to this, it is not uncommon for the white females of the northern states to marry those whom they recognize as negroes.

The fine sensibilities of woman prompts her to shrink in horror from the thought of contracting a marriage alliance with such inferior creatures as negroes and mixed-bloods. But, as has been demonstrated in the north, the demoralizing influences of social, political and religious equality with negroes and mixed-bloods, persisted in for centuries, will eventually impair the native instincts of woman and reduce her to the low level of marriage alliances with these degraded creatures. Further evidence of this is found in the marriages which the women of Europe are contracting with these so-called "lower races of men." The women of the northern states and of Europe have been subjected to the degrading influences of social, political and religious equality with the Negro and his amalgamated offspring, whom they recognize as negroes, for a greater length of time than have the women of the southern states. This is shown by the fact that, as long as the Negro in the south was held as a slave, his social ostracism presented another barrier to the southern woman's marriage with him. In discussing this question we should bear in mind that the disposition of woman to be influenced by the social, political and religious education to which she is subjected, is the same the world over. Hence, we have no alternative than to decide that the demoralizing social, political and religious influences which degraded the women of the north and of Europe to the social level of the Negro, will, if persisted in, result as disastrously to the women of the south. It may be argued that the marriages between women and negroes or between the women and the mixed-bloods will be confined to the most ignorant and degraded class of whites. But a moment's reflection must convince us that this position is untenable. It has been demonstrated upon every continent of the earth that this evil practice, like every other which may originate among the lower classes of whites, will ultimately find its way into the highest circles of society. Scientific research will sustain us in the assertion that the mixed-bloods resulting from amalgamation between whites and negroes are to be found in every position in life, from the jungle to the throne.

Prior to the late sectional war between the Northern and the Southern States, a certain amount of religious equality, and such amount of social equality as is inseparable from it, existed between the whites and negroes of the south. To this was added political equality, as one of the results of the war. Consequently the only barrier which separates between the whites and blacks of the south, is that of social caste. The rapidity with which this frail barrier is disappearing· under the combined assaults of the Church and the Press, is absolutely appalling. The effort of the Church to degrade the whites of America to the social, political and religious level of the negro, received its first allies from the American press, in the abolition journals of the north. But since the war, and especially of late years, the press of the south, both religious and secular in its fanatical efforts to pander to the negroized sentiment of the north, is "out-herroding Herod." From the innumerable evidences of this which are furnished us daily, we quote the recent utterances of a leading southern journal, whose editor in an article captioned "Negro Gentlemen," says:

"There is nothing in the color of a man's skin to hinder his being a gentleman, even from the Anglo-

Saxon point of view. If he has self-respect, veracity, and gentle manners, the most necessary ingredients of a gentleman would seem to be in him, and the chances are that expert observers will recognize their presence. * * * There is no incongruity in terms about the expression "a negro gentleman." It conveys an idea of good manners and personal dignity, which is clear and easily understood. The editor of the Sunny South is pleased to note in this connection that we have here in Atlanta a goodly number of colored citizens to each of whom the word "gentlemen" applies with full and correct force." (*The Sunny South*, Oct. 2, 1897.)

Had a southern editor of forty years ago made such a statement through his paper, it would have fired the southern heart from the Atlantic to the Rio Grande, and from the Ohio to the Gulf. From every quarter in the south, the most indignant protests would have been heard. Think how far we have descended toward social equality with the negro, in the brief period of thirty-three years, as indicated by the fact that such sentiments are received with acquiescence. Not a word of protest is heard. Had any comment been made upon this statement of the editor of the Sunny South, he would have been applauded for his broad-minded liberality. His utterances would have been pointed to as an evidence of the disappearance of race prejudice, and the obliteration of color lines in the south. If, under the combined assaults of the Church, the State and the Press, the frail barrier of social caste, which alone intervenes between the whites and negroes of the south has been thus impaired in less than half a century, what basis have we for the hope that, at the end of the next fifty years it will not be utterly annihilated. When this is accomplished, why should not the male descendants of these "negro gentlemen" take wives from among the white ladies of Georgia? It is folly to insist that the female descendants of the former "slave owners" of the south, will never descend to marriage alliances with those whom they recognize as negroes. The weakness of this argument is demonstrated by the fact that, in the north, the female descendants of the northern "slave owners" of less than a century ago, are now intermarrying with those whom they recognize as negroes. However distasteful they may be, it is worse than folly to close our eyes to the fact. This most frightful issue stares us in the face, and it must be squarely met. The women of the north and those of the south are made of the same material; they belong to one family; they are sisters, the progeny of a single pair. Hence, the social, political and religious influences which elevates or degrades the one, must elevate or degrade the other. Like causes produce like results.

From the utterances of this editor, we might be led to suppose that "self-respect, veracity and gentle manners, the most necessary ingredients of a gentleman," were found only in the Negro in his free state. The freed negro in America is certalnly not more free than his wild brother in the jungles of Africa; yet we never heard that "self-respect, veracity and gentle manners" were characteristic of the Negro of Africa. We are opposed to the views of the editor of the Sunny South that these characteristics, especially those of "self-respect and veracity," ever exsted in the Negro at all. But if they did they were engrafted upon the nature of the Negro by his master and mistress of former time. Certainly these "most necessary ingredients of a gentleman" have not been developed by emancipation. The Negro is merely an ape; hence, the more he is relieved by man of the restraints which God imposed upon him in the Creation, the more vicious, unreliable and brutal he becomes.

If it be true, as stated by the editor of the Sunny South, that they are now producing "Negro gentlemen" in Atlanta, Georgia. we feel free to confess that he has clearly demonstrated the correctness of his assertion that "gentleman is a loose and comprehensive word," since it "applies" equally well to man, to the ape, and to his amalgamated progeny," with full and correct force." From this editor's standpoint, "gentleman" is certainly a very latitudinous term, to say the least of it.

When the atheistic theory of natural development has been discarded by man, and the scriptural teaching of Divtne Creation is accepted in its stead, expert observers will promptly decide that "the most necessary ingredients of a gentleman" are that he be born in the "likeness" and "image" of God—that he be a man. And that the absence of these essential characteristics in an individual prevents him from being a "gentleman," without reference to his "self-respect, veracity and gentle manners." Hence, before pronouncing the Negro a "gentleman," the editor ot the Sunny South should have proved him a man.

An article entitled, "Must the Negro," which appeared in the December number of the Globe Review, from the pen of its able editor, Mr. William H. Thorne. presents a pleasing contrasf to the negroism of the great bulk of the American press. Mr. Thorne says:

"During the spring of the year 1895, and after more than thirty years of sincere and old-fashioned abolition sympathy with the Negro race, I made two visits to several of our southern states with results as follows: First—All my old abolition sympathies which had been weakening for over ten years in view of the insufferable self-assertion of our Negroes since the day of their emancipation, vanisned like so many scattered sophistries, for which I had no further use. Second—On returning to New York I published in the next issue of the Globe Review my conviction that, spite of emaneipation and our so-called education of the Negro, and perhaps aided by these absurdities—the Negroes of this country were more than ever a shiftless, unteachable, immoral race, incapable of any true civilization in our land and unworthy of American citizenship. Third—That without mincing matters, or any longer writing or thinking on

the basis of sympathy with the Negro, I was convinced
that inside the next thirty years the South would be
obliged to "re-enslave, kill or export the bulk of its
Negro population." (See The Atlanta Constitution,
Jan. 10, 1898.)

In the midst of the debasing negroism to which the
American people as a class have descended in the last
thirty years, such sentiments from the pen of an original
abolitionist, affords us the most agreeable surprise. Prior
to the late sectional war, we were told by the abolition-
ists of the North and of Europe that if given the opportunity the Negro would demonstrate that he was the full
equal of his "white brother." Our country, already
laboring under the curse of God for its social and religious equality with the Negro, was further cursed for its
amalgamation by being plunged in a civil war, which,
for its expenditure of blood and treasure has no parallel
in modern time. This sanguinary struggle ended in the
emancipation of the Negro and in his elevation to all the
rights, privileges and responsibilities of American citizenship. Since the war the Whites of the South who
contribute the great bulk of the school fund, have yielded
to the popular demand for the education of these so-
called "Negroes" and have shared with these degraded
creatures their educational facilities to the prejudice of
their own children. Now, after all the injury, the demoralization and the degradation to which the people of
the South have been subjected in the last thirty-five
years, one of the ablest of the former admirers of the

Negro, asserts that all his "old abolition sympathies which had been weakening for over ten years in view of the insufferable self-assertion of our Negroes since the day of their emancipation, had vanished like so many scattered sophistries for which he had no further use." And "that without mincing matters or any longer thinking or writing on the basis of sympathy with the Negro, he was convinced that inside the next thirty years the South would be obliged to re-enslave, kill or export the bulk of its Negro population."

Who would have dreamed that in less than thirty-five years after emancipation one of the foremost champions of Negro suffrage would denounce the Negro as "more than ever a shiftless, unteachable, immoral race, incapable of any true civilization and unworthy of American citizenship?" And would speak of "emancipatiou and the so-called education of the Negro" as "absurdities."

It is needless to say that we honor this fearless man, admire his candor and hold in high esteem his lofty patriotism. At the same time we must beg leave to respectfully suggest that his use of the term "re-enslave" in connection with our future relations with the Negro, indicates that he fails to grasp the situation·

As a matter of fact, the Negro was never a slave. To conceive the design of enslaving an individual we must presuppose that he is free; the first act of enslavement is to deprive him of his liberty. This the Negro never had since the creation of man. The

Negro is an ape; hence, his status in the universe, his relation to Man, like that of every other animal, was fixed irrevocably by God in the Creation, and no act upon man's part, whether legislative, executive or judicial, can change it. The will of God upon this most important subject, as expresesd in those original statutes given man in the Creation, "Have dominion over the fish of the sea, and over the fowl of the air, and over every living thing that moveth upon the earth," is the supreme law of the universe; and in the eyes of this great law there is not today, there never was and there can never be on this earth, such a thing as a free Negro. To illustrate: Suppose a man commits a felony and is arraigned, convicted and sentenced to prison for a term of years, but makes his escape, flees to some foreign country, where he lives out his days without being apprehended. Did that man in his exile live out his days and die a free man? No jurist would so decide. From the hour of his conviction that man lived and died the property of the state. So it is in this case; under the law of God the Negro, like every other animal, is the property of man, without reference to whether he is ever brought in contact with him or not. The mere fact that man in his blind, criminal folly, declines to exert that control over the Negro, in common with the rest of the animals, which God designed him to have and commanded him to exercise, does not free the Negro, it can only damn man, for his shameless contempt for

[19]

God's plan of Creation, and for his wanton violation of Divine law.

Man was created free. His personal liberty was implied in his assignment to dominion over all the earth, and over the animals. Hence, man can be enslaved; but since you cannot enslave the horse or the dog, how can you enslave the ape? They all belong to "one kind of flesh," and were placed under man's dominion in the Creation. This absurd idea that is optional with man to enslave, or to emancipate the Negro, is another result of placing man and the ape in the same family.

Had the Negro been imported here as an ape, as God made him, and had we maintained only such relations with him as were legitimate, the combined world would have been powerless to have taken a Negro from the south; God would have stood by the south to defend and maintain the relation of master and servant which he established between man and the negro in Creation. But instead of this, under the influence of the theory of development, combined to a certain extent with the equally anti-scriptural church theory that the Negro is the son of Ham, he was brought here as a "lower race of man"—the Ham race—whom it was legitimate to enslave as a means of civilizing, educating and Christianizing; as might have been expected, an amalgamation at once began; and soon it transformed every farm, and many a home in the southland into a harem; it debauched the youth and manhood of the land; it sent many a fond, devoted wife and mother broken-hearted to the grave; it corrupted the flesh and defiled the earth, and brought our country under the curse of heaven, until God in His wrath and disgust, decreed that the so-called "slavery system," which was conceived in crime, brought forth in iniquity, and was based solely on his violated law, should be blotted from the face of the earth; then "angels wept and devils laughed" at the spectacle presented here by a continent drenched in the blood of its sons, hemispheres in mourning, the civilized world in tears. And just so long as we allow the negro and his amalgamated progeny imposed upon us as "lower races of men," with whom we may associate on terms of social, political and religious equality, just so long will we labor under the curses of God, just so long will these degraded creatures have more or less political dominion over us, just so long will the youth and manhood of the land be debauched by amalgamation, just so long will the chastity of our wives and the virginity of our daughters be subjected to their brutal assaults.

The emancipation of the Negro in the United States was not the work of an anti-slavery party, nor of a pro-slavery party, nor of a Lincoln, nor of a Davis, nor of a Grant, nor of a Lee, nor of "the boys in blue," nor of "the boys in gray." These, one and all, were mere instruments, wielded by our outraged God, to compel us to recognize and respect His plan of Creation, and to live in obedience to His law. Realizing that even the horrors of a four year's war had failed to dissipate our mad dream of forming man, the ape and their amalgamated progeny into "one universal brotherhood," God determined that our depraved lust for social, political and religious equality with the Negro and the mixed-bloods should be fully satisfied. As a result, these degraded creatures were promptly declared free; were at once clothed with the suffrage and reck-lessly thrust into the legislative, executive and judicial departments of our national and State governments. In the last thirty years the Whites of the South have spent about one hundred millions of dollars on the public schools for the education of the so-called Negroes— these mixed-bloods, to say nothing of the millions of dollars that have been spent on colleges, churches, etc. And what is the result? To-day our wives and our daughters are not safe from their brutal assaults beyond the range of our shot-guns. They degrade our religion, demoralize our politics, debauch our youths, plunder our citizens, murder our officials, rape our women, and con-duct themselves generally as the curse they are and will always be so long as they are allowed to defile our land with their presence.

Speaking of the mixed-bloods of South America, Von Tschudi says: "As a general rule, it may be fairly said that they unite in themselves all the faults, without any of the virtues of their progenetors. * * * As members of society they are the worst class of citi-zens."

Dr. Barthold Seeman says: "The character of the half castes is, if possible, worse than that of negroes." (*Preadamites*, pp. 85, 178.)

In the face of such statements from these high authorities, the following from the Vicksburg Daily Herald of April 19th, should afford food for grave reflection:

"In presenting an application to Congress for a larger appropriation for the Washington police, Commissioner Wright, of the District Board, asserted that the 90,000 colored population of that city included a criminal contingent equal in vice and desperate crime to those of any city in the world—that they 'regard life of no value whatever.'" This statement was made with every excusatory exception of its application to the uncriminal mass of the race. But it was resented by an indignation meeting in the Second Baptist church, when, with much Inflammatory circumstance the commissioner's removal was asked in the name of the 90,000.

The resolutions adopted raise no question of the truth of the commissioner's statement—it was in fact the truth resented. Writing of the commissioner's report and the Negro meeting, the Baltimore Sun correspondent thus affirms what is charged by the former:

"There is a class of Washington Negroes dangerous, vicious and obnoxious in the extreme. When these do not commit violations of the law they delight in indulging in all sorts of petty annoyances and exhibitions towards the Whites. Instances of pretentious rudeness and incivility toward white people, he goes on, are of common occurrence in the street cars, in public places and on the sidewalks. More than twice as many Negroes as Whites were arrested for carrying concealed weapons, more than twice as many for disorderly conduct, more than twice as many for assault and battery, more than twice as many for petty larceny, and thirteen more for grand larceny; twice as many for profanity, seven times as many for criminal assault, and more than five times as many for house-breaking at night. Seven murders were committed by Negroes to two by Whites.

"In all the most heinous offenses known to criminology the Negroes were largely in the excess. A very large proportion of all crimes are committed by young Negro toughs under 25 years of age. The discouraging, even appalling, nature of these figures, their profound significance, is only to be rightly measured when joined with the reflection that for years past the District has been a veritable Negro eleemosynary. Here he has been cuddled and courted politically, protected in all his equality of rights by the law—his aspirations and efforts for social elevation encouraged and assisted as nowhere else. And such is the harvest—with a third of the pepulation, more than half of the greater crimes, and a far larger proportion of the lesser, are committed by the Negroes.

"But the worst feature of the incident is the rally of the law-abiding Negroes to the defense of their criminals—sheltering and encouraging color line law-breaking at the woeful sacrifice of reputation. This is a revelation of racial trait that will repel and dishearten every well-wisher of the Negro—cool faith in his ever attaining a reputable social status. The picture has one luminous merit alone—it will serve to dispel delusions. Displayed at Washington, it is like a light set on a hill, imprinting its lessons on every Congressman with more convincing and impressive force than all the speeches and writings in vindication of the South's racial policies.''

We may allow ourselves deceived by religious fanatics, and by designing politicians—we may close our eyes to the truth—but the fact remains; a very considerable proportion of these mixed-bloods have actually descended to a savagery in the midst of a high civilization in which they were born and reared, and this too, despite the most persistent efforts of the Press, the Church and the State, to educate, elevate and Christianize them. And the worst feature is, that what is termed the "better class" are in full sympathy with the criminal class.

For years the misguided philanthropy of the people of the North has prompted them to shower their favors upon the negro with the most lavish hand, and now the base born ingrate turns like a mad dog upon his benefactors and bites the hand that fed him. When the great bulk of these so-called negroes were in the South the crimes of murder and rape which they delight to perpetrate were confined to that section, and when the outraged communities would rise and wreak summary vengeance upon some black murderer or rape fiend, they were denounced by the press of the North as savages. But for some years there has been a steady flow of negroes from the South into the North, and as their numbers increase, the crimes which are common among them in the South are committed here, and we observe that the people of the North have adopted the Southern mode of suppressing them. A few weeks ago the telegraph brought the news that a desperate mulatto after attempting to induce a general uprising against the whites, had murdered the officials sent to arrest him, and that 20,000 indignant whites were hunting and killing the negroes in New Orleans. Scarcely had the public recovered from the shock when the news was flashed to us that for a similar offense 25,000 indignant whites were hunting and killing negros in New York, and almost simultaneously came the news of a "race riot" at Liberty, Ga.

The following from the St. Louis Republic of Sept. 14, is a specimen of the results of social equality with these degraded creatures: "Deleware, Ohio, Sept. 13. A colored barber, who, it is, alleged, has insulted several white girls, is to-night under the protection of about 100 colored men, assembled in South Delaware. About 200 armed white men are scattered in the vicinity of the college grounds, waiting for developments. The negroes have threatened to shoot if any attempt is made to harm Beck. Intense feeling prevails."

Not only the unprotected woman, but the little helpless child, is assaulted and outraged by these brutes. If a correct list was obtained of all the cases which the defenseless women and helpless children had been outraged by the black fiends in the last thirty years, it would recall hundreds of scenes of horror which are not alone sufficient to "give the blush to shame," but would make the "cheek of terror pale."

Think of such creatures as active participants in the social, political and religious affairs of a great nation like ours! Think of the fact that amalgamation, the crime to which these base-born creatures owe their existence, is rapidly on the increase in this country, as shown by the fact that each succeeding generation of them becomes whiter and whiter. Think of the fact that many of our most distinguished clergymen are open advocates of this loathsome crime, and that they have become so demoralized as to attempt to defend it on Bible grounds.

Dr. T. Dewit Talmage, in a recent sermon, addressed more especially to sisters, says of Miriam, the sister of Moses: "She had possessed unlimited influence over Moses, and now he marries, and not only so, but marries a black woman from Ethiopia; and Miriam is so disgusted and outraged at Moses, first, because he had married at all, and next, because he had practiced miscegenation, that she is drawn into a frenzy and then begins to turn white and gets white as a corpse. Her complexion is like chalk; the fact is, she has the Egyptian leprosy.'' (See Weekly Commercial Appeal, Memphis, Tenn., Feb. 8, 1898.)

This blasphemous statement is the most pitable display of that gross ignorance of the teachings of scripture which characterizes the modern clergy, that has ever attracted our observation. And its utterances clearly indicates that Dr. Talmage has no more conception of the Plan of Creation, that he has no more knowledge of man's relation to God and to the earth and to the rest of created things, and that he is as grossly ignorant of the Plan of Redemption, which he proposes to teach, as a Hottentot. At the same time, his intellectual ability, his literary attainments and his eloquence, leads the press to scatter his utterances broadcast throughout the world to demoralize, degrade and damn every man and woman who reads and accepts them.

Who but a thoroughly demoralized pulpit advocate of amalgamation, could conceive the absurd idea that God selected a degraded amalgamationist with a ''black'' wife to lead to the Land of Promise the descendents of Abraham, whom he had chosen for no other purpose than that they should preserve in its purity and increase the Adamic flesh of the earth, execute his designs with reference to the development of the resources of the earth, and the control of the animals and ultimately destroy the mixed-bloods from the globe.

The Egyptians had descended to amalgamation as is shown by the fact that we find depicted on their monuments not only the white and the black, but the so-called "colored races." In addition to this we find them described in scripture as a "mingled people," and the curses of God were showered upon them. The Canaanites were specifically charged with lying with beasts, and thus defiling their land; and God ordered their extermination. Now, if it be true, as Dr. Talmage asserts, that Moses "had practiced miscegenation" by marrying a "black woman," what did God mean when He said to Moses: "Speak unto the children of Israel, and say unto them, I am the Lord your God. After the doings of the land of Egypt wherein ye dwelt shall ye not do; and after the doings of the land of Canaan whither I bring ye shall ye not do: neither shall ye walk in their ordinances." (Levt. xviii, 2, 3.)

God simply meant that Israel should preserve and increase the Adamic flesh in its purity, and live in obedience to His laws; and not descend to amalgamation and its kindred evil, idolatry.

From the language of Dr. Talmage one might reasonably infer that the germ of leprosy lurked in disgust and frenzy, and that he desired to warn the "sisters" of our day that they must not feel "disgusted" and "outraged" and be "drawn into a frenzy" if their brother "practiced miscegenation" by marrying a "black woman," lest, like Miriam, they begin "to turn white" and get "white as a corpse and then whiter than a corpse;" and their "complexion" becomes "like chalk;" in "fact," develop a case of "Egyptian leprosy."

The Bible history of this period clearly demonstrates that, with the exception of the Israelites, amalgamation was prevalent to a greater or less extent among all the nations of the earth. Miriam and Aaron were aware of this, and their complaint against Moses because he had married an Ethiopian woman was the expression of their fear that the wife of Moses was a mixed-blood. But this was a reflection upon God who, as they should have known, would never have selected a degraded amalgamationist with a black wife to lead Israel to the land of promise. And Miriam was afflicted with leprosy as a punishment for their offense.

In some sections of the earth, as among the Canaanites, amalgamation was of long standing and had about absorbed and destroyed the Adamic flesh of these nations. We see that when "Abraham was old and well stricken in age," he said unto his eldest servant of his house that ruled over all that he had: "I will make thee swear by the Lord, the God of heaven, and the God of earth, thou shalt not take a wife unto my son of the daughters of the Canaanites among whom I dwell: But thou shalt go unto my country and to my kindred, and take a wife unto my son Isaac." (Gen. xxiv, 3, 4.)

What was wrong with "the daughters of the Canaanites?" They belonged to a rich, powerful nation, and owned one of the richest, most highly developed countries on the globe—"a land flowing with milk and honey." Why did Abraham decline to recognize them as his kindred?

The mission of Abraham's servant, under Divine guidance, was successful, and Rebekah became the wife of Isaac, and bore him Esau and Jacob. When Jacob reached maturity, "Reebekah said to Isaac, I am weary of my life because of the daughters of Heth: if Jacob take a wife from among the daugnters of Heth, such as be of these of the daughters of the land, what good shall my life do me?" Evidently this fond mother realized that if her son Jacob took a wife from among the Canaanites her life had been lived in vain. Why? "And Isaac," startled at the thought, "called Jacob and blessed him and charged him and said unto him, Thou shalt not take a wife of the daughters of Canaan. Arise, go to Padanarum, to the house of Bethuel, thy mother's father, and take thee a wife from thence of the daughters of Daban, thy mother's brother. And may God Almighty bless thee and make thee fruitful and multiply thee, that thou mayest be "a multitude of people." (Gen. xxvii, 46, and Gen. xxviii, 1, 2, 3.)

If Jacob had taken a wife of the daughters of Canaan, why could not their progeny become "a multitude of people?" Nearly five centuries after this Moses described the attitude which God desired the Israelites to maintain toward the Canaanites, as follows: "And when the Lord the God shall deliver them before thee thou shalt smite them and utterly destroy them; thou shalt make no covenant with them, nor show mercy unto them: neither shalt thou make marriages with them; thy daughter thou shalt not give unto his son, nor his daughter shalt thou take nnto thy son." (Deut. vii, 2, 3.)

The explanation of all this is found in God's charge against the Canaanites that they lay with beasts; and thus "defiled" their "nations" and defiled "the land." Hence, their descendants were amalgamated; they were mixed-bloods—a mingled people.

In other sections of the earth, as in the "cities" described as "very far off" from Canaan, amalgamation was in its incipiency, as shown by the following command: "When thou comest nigh unto a city to fight against it, then proclaim peace unto it. And it shall be, if it make thee answer of peace, and open unto thee, then it shall be that all the people that is found therein shall be tributaries unto thee and they shall serve thee." (Deut. xx, 10, 11.)

The distinction, which was made between the Canaanites and the people of the cities "very far off" was due to the fact that in the latter amalgamation was in its incipiency; that is, it was confined to the white males and black females. The women of these "cities," true to the native instincts of their sex, declined to associate with the black males and were confining their marriage relations to the white males. As a result, their offspring was of pure Adamic stock. This was the material which God designed the earth to be populated with. Hence, if, upon the approach of Israel, the "people" of these "cities" accepted their offer of "peace" and opened their "gates" to them, they were to be made "tributaries" to Israel. That is, they should be made a province, and to this extent a part of the nation of Israel. They had,

perhaps, lost all knowledge of the true God and had
doubtless embraced a corrupted form of religious worship. They would learn of God from the Israelites; they
would abandon their idolatry and accept the religion of
Israel; they would abandon amalgamation and live in
obedience to the law of God. The Israelites might
"make marriages" with them. They were not forbidden
to do this. Thus, in the course of time, these people
would become an inseparable part of the Jewish empire,
and would "serve" Israel in its efforts to increase the
Adamic flesh of the earth, and exterminate the mixed-
bloods. This indicates that the Israelites of that day
were not confined in their marriage alliances to the tribes
of Israel. All that God required of them was that their
marriages be made with pure Adamic stock.

Thus it becomes evident that it was the desire of
God that his "chosen people" should be "peculiar" in
that they would never descend to amalgamation. But
that Israel should be the leaven that should leaven to
God the whole lump of humanity. Under their salutary
influence the Adamic family would be brought to a
knowledge of God. Divine worship would supercede
idolatry. The mixed-bloods would be exterminated
and amalgamation made a capital offense throughout the
world. But instead of doing this, we are taught both by
sacred and profane history that the Israelites not only
violated the law of God by descending to amalgamation,
but renounced His worship and embraced idolatry. In
his confession to Ezra, Shechaniah said, "We have tress-

passed against our God, and have taken strange wives of the people of the land. * * * Now, therefore, let us make a covenant with our God to put away our strange wives and such as are born of them. * * * And they made proclamation throughout Judah and Jerusalem unto all the children of the captivity that they should gather themselves together unto Jerusalem. And that whosoever would not come within three days * * * all his substance should be forfeited, and himself separated from the congregation of those that had been carried away. Then all the men of Judah and Benjamin gathered themselves together unto Jerusalem for three days. * * * And all the people sat in the street of the house of God, trembling because of this matter and for the great rain. And Ezra, the priest, stood up and said unto them, Ye have transgressed and have taken strange wives to increase, the trespass of Israel. Now make confession unto the Lord God of your fathers, and do his pleasure; and separate yourselves from the people of the land and from the strange wives. * * * Let now our rulers of all the congregation stand, and let them which have taken strange wives in our cities come at appointed times, and with them the elders of every city and the judges thereof, until the fierce wrath of our God for this matter be turned from us. * * * And Ezra the priest with certain chiefs of the fathers * * * sat down in the first day of the month to examine the matter. And they made an end with all the men that had taken strange wives by the first day of the month." (Ezra x, **2, 3,** etc.)

Why were these females whom the men of Israel were compelled to "put away," together with their off-spring by them, termed "strange wives?" Evidently it was not because they were not Israelites. The people of the cities "very far off" with whom the Israelites were permitted to marry were not descendants of Abraham. It was because they were not of pure Adamic flesh; they were "strange wives" because they were of strange flesh. They were mixed-bloods, resulting from amalgamation between Man and the Negro. And God could foresee that if the Israelites continued to take these "strange wives" and intermarry with their progeny they would finally absorb and destroy the Adamic flesh of Israel. This disastrous result accomplished, God's promise to Abraham that all the families of the earth shall be blessed in him could never have been fulfilled. Thus, not only was God's Plan of Creation involved in this "matter" but His plighted word was at stake. Hence, God afflicted the men of Israel until they made "confession" of their sin and put away their "strange wives" and such as "were born of them." It will be observed that this crime was confined to the men of Israel. The women of Israel, be it said to their honor, had not disgraced their sex by taking strange husbands. We desire to call special attention to this, as evidence that the teachings of Scripture upon this subject harmonize with the teachings of science that amalgamation

[20]

always begins between the white males and the black or colored females.

Continuing, with reference to the "cities afar off," the inspired writer says: "And if it will make no peace with thee, but will make war with thee, then shalt thou besiege it: And when the Lord thy God hath delivered it into thy hands, thou shalt smite every male thereof with the edge of the sword: But the women and the little ones, and the cattle, and all that is in the city, even all the spoil thereof shalt thou take unto thyself; thou shalt eat the spoil of thine enemies which the Lord thy God hath given thee." (Deut. xx, 12, 13, 14.)

Why was this distinction made between the men and the women and children of these cities? Was it because the men were idolaters? If so, the women were also idolaters, and it is characteristic of women to be more devoted to any system of religion which they embrace than are the men. Why did God make such a distinction between these women and their children who were to be preserved and taken into Israel, and those of the Canaanites and their children, which were to be "utterly destroyed?" These distinctions were made by God. Hence, they were based upon the highest intelligence, and were actuated by the purest motives and sustained by reasons which were absolutely just. The distinction which God commanded to be made between the men and the women and children, should they decline their offer of peace, is a further evidence that in these "cities afar off" amalgamation was in its incipiency. It was confined to the men and the negresses and the colored females. The women of these "cities," like the women of Israel in the days of Ezra, declined to lower themselves by forming marriage alliances with the Negro or the mixed-blooded males.

Hence, if upon the approach of Israel the men of these cities declared for war rather than abandon amalgamation. and accept the law of God and become "tributaries" to Israel and ultimately a part of the Jewish nation, through their social, political and religious relations with them and their intermarriages, which were not forbidden, then they were to be put to the sword. "But the women and the little ones" were not involved in this crime. Hence the command to Israel: "Take them to thyself.". They were to be taken into the fold of Israel, where they would learn of God and His law and be taught to love and obey Him. And through their marriages with the Israelites their descendants would ultimately become an inseparable part of the Jewish nation. Thus, their preservation would increase the Adamic flesh of the earth. This command of God furnishes another illustration of the harmony of scripture with the teachings of science that amalgamation always begins between the men and the black or the mixed-blooded females.

God's commands with reference to the destruction of these mixed-blooded nations have been seized upon by infidels and used as evidence to disprove the inspiration of the Scriptures. Mr. Thomas Paine says:

"When we read in the books ascribed to Moses, Joshua, etc., that they (the Israelites) came by stealth

upon whole nations of people who, as the history itself
shows, had given them no offense, that they put all those
nations to the sword; that they spared neither age nor
infancy; that they utterly destroyed men, women and
children; that they left not a soul to breathe; expressions
that are repeated over and over again in those books and
that, too, with exulting ferocity; are we sure that these
are facts? Are we sure that the Creator of man commis-
sioned these things to be done; are we sure that the
books that tell us so were written by His authority?
* * * The Bible tells us that those assassinations
were done by the express command of God. To believe,
therefore, the Bible to be true, we must unbelieve all our
belief in the moral justice of God; for wherein could
smiling infants offend? And to read the Bible without
horror, we must undo everything that is tender, sympa-
thizing and benevolent in the heart of man." (*The Age
of Reason*, p. 62.)

In his denunciations of God and His commands to
Israel to utterly destroy these mixed-blooded nations,
Col. R. G. Ingersoll says:

"Is it possible for man to conceive of anything more
perfectly infamous? Can you believe that such direc-
tions were given by any except an infinite fiend? · Remember that the army receiving these instructions was
one of invasion. Peace was offered upon condition that
the people submitting should be the slaves of the invad-
ers; but if any should have the courage to defend their
homes, to fight for the love of wife and child, then the

sword was to spare none—not even the prattling, dimpled babe. And we are called upon to worship such a God; to get upon our knees and tell Him that He is good, that He is merciful, that He is just, that He is love. We are asked to stifle every noble sentiment of the soul and to trample under foot all the sweet charities of the heart. Because we refuse to stultify ourselves—refuse to become liars—we are denounced, hated, traduced and ostracised here, and this same God threatens to torment us in eternal fire the moment death allows him to fiercely clutch our naked, helpless souls. Let the people hate, let the God threaten—we will educate them and we will despise and defy him." (*Forty-four Lectures Complete, Lecture "God,"* p. 2.)

It must be admitted, to the shame of modern Christianity, that these unblushing denunciations of God and these unjust criticisms on his word, have never been squarely met and refuted by the modern clergy. They have ridiculed and denounced the infidel, but have never met his assaults with anything worthy of being termed arguments. A moment's reflection should convince us that, under existing conditions, this was impossible. The theory of atheism and that of the church is that man is merely a highly developed species of animal, of which the White is the highest and the Negro the lowest race, with the browns, reds and yellows as intermediate races of men. When we accept this atheistic theory, no amount of reasoning, no amount of sophistry can reconcile the extermination of these nations; the butchery of fathers, mothers and even the "prattling, dimpled babe," with our conception of a wise, just, merciful and loving God. The whole transaction is repulsive to every sentiment of our being. To ask us to pronounce it good is an affront to our intelligence. But is this atheistic theory true? Is Man simply a highly developed species of ape—the human species—and is this human species divisible into five or more races of men, dependent upon the whim of the infidel who makes the classification? Is it true that all these so-called races of men have descended from one pair by gradual divergence? As has been shown, the atheists deny this. Is it true that the differences which we observe in the physical and mental characters of these so-called races of men are due to natural selection, the survival of the fittest, etc.? If not, then our premise is wrong; and arguing from a wrong premise, our conclusions must necessarily be erroneous. Is it true that these so-called white, black, brown, red and yellow races of men are the progeny of a primitive pair? Are they the descendants of Adam, the son of God? Away with this modern church doctrine that man is a species, divisible into races. Let us bear in mind that this wretched doctrine that man is a species of ape, divisible into races of men, is an inseparable part of the Theory of Development, which denies the existence of God, repudiates his word and attributes the phenomena of the universe to natural causes. A glance at the facts should enable us to see that we can never harmonize the word of God with this theory which denies the existence of God; and that it is not the proper medium through which to view the acts of God. If we desire to form a rational conception of the teachings of Scripture and of the motives which influence God in his dealings with men, we should not disturb the harmony which exists between the Mosaic record and all subsequent Bible history. We must repudiate this atheistic theory that man is a highly developed species of ape and accept the Scriptural teaching that man is a distinct creation in the image of. God. We must also accept the teachings of Scripture and of science that the Negro is an ape, and that the so-called brown, red and yellow races of men of other portions of the earth, like these in our midst, are the offspring of Man and the Negro. Hence, they are merely the products of God's violated law and are not a part of His creation. When viewed from this standpoint, the extermination of these nations is seen in a very different light.

If, from time to time, God in His wisdom had not destroyed the mixed-bloods or the great bulk of them, this dangerous, aborbing element would long since have destroyed man. This disastrous result accomplished, ro creature under heaven would have been clothed with Divine authority to subdue the earth and have dominion over fish and fowl and beast. And God's whole plan of the physical creation would have been nullified. And not only this, for in the destruction of man, the central figure in creation, all religion worthy of the name, and all fear and love and worship of God would have been destroyed from off the earth and God's sublime plan of the spiritual creation would have been utterly annihilated.   Hence, we must recognize His destruction of the mixed-bloods as an act of mercy of such magnitude as only the mind of Deity could conceive, and God's wondrous love for man inspire.

Mr. Paine is in his grave. He has long since learned that the Bible is the product of inspiration and that God's will to man is revealed in the scripture.   When he lived he proudly asserted: "I have annihilated the scriptures."   But subsequent events have demonstrated the emptiness of his boast.   So far from raising a tempest of infidelity that would sweep the Bible into oblivion, his purile assaults upon the word of God have never caused the slightest ripple on the surface of revealed religion.

Mr. Ingersoll has also died.   In point of blasphemy his denunciations of God and His acts in destroying the Canaanites, etc., are only equaled by the statement of Dr. Talmage that Moses practiced miscegenation and married a black woman from Ethiopia.   The several statements of these gentlemen upon these subjects indicate that they are about the same grade of thinkers, while their sentiments on the Negro question indicates that as teachers they naturally belong in the same class.   The sentiments of these distinguished advocates of man's social equality with the Negro, lived out in the past, has transformed the descendants of highly civilized, cultivated people into barbarians and savages; has laid in ruins civilizations which required ages to develop; has desolated and destroyed continents and has brought the world under the curse of God.

We have long since been convinced that just on the principle that the most dangerous wolf, consequently the worst wolf, is the wolf in sheep's clothing; so, the dangerous infidel, consequently the worst infidel, is the pulpit infidel. The attempt of Dr. Talmage to hold up to the world the marriage of Moses to a woman of Ethiopia, as evidence of God's approval of amalgamation, is simply infamous. How the fathers and mothers of our country, especially those of the South, can expect to raise their children up to a decent life, and can entertain the hope that they will not descend to amalgamation, and yet allow the demoralizing utterances of this pulpit amalgamationist to enter their homes weekly through the press in the guise of sermons, is beyond our comprehension.

This declaration by Dr. Talmage that Moses practiced miscegenation and married a black woman from Ethiopia is false, and is at once opposed to the teachings of Scripture, of science and of profane history. 1. As has been shown, it was the desire of God that miscegenation should not be practiced. Hence, He would never have selected as the leader of Israel a degraded amalgamationist with a black wife.

2. The punishment which God visited upon Miriam for her complaint against Moses because he had married an Ethiopian woman proves that the wife of Moses was of pure Adamic stock—that she was white. 3. The Ethiopians were not Africans, but Asiatics. Ethiopia was located "in the province of Oman, in southern Arabia." (See *Preadamites*, p. 17. Note the long list of high and recent authorities cited by Dr. Winchell.) 4. The Ethiopians developed one of the great civilizations of ancient time. This in itself demonstrates that they were whites, for scientific research has shown that "no Negro civilization has ever appeared; no Mongolian one has ever greatly developed." 5. The Ethiopians were one of the richest, most enterprising and most powerful nations of their time. They developed a commerce which extended to two and perhaps more of the continents of the earth. This furnishes further proof that they were whites, not blacks. Scientific research demonstrates that "no wooly-haired nation has ever had an important history." Mr. Bancroft says: "The Semites early peopled the Arabian peninsula and established a state in Ethiopia, as some believe, before Egypt had attained its full development. The Ethiopians established a flourishing commerce on the Red sea with the eastern coasts of Africa and with India, and contributed greatly to the resources of ancient Egypt." (See *Footprints of Time*, p. 33.) Thus, according to Bancroft and other high authorities, the Ethiopians were

not even the sons of Ham. But, like the Israelites, they were the descendants of Shem. Perhaps Dr. Talmage will kindly explain how it happened that one branch of the descendants of Shem—the Israelites—were white, while the Ethiopians, another branch of the same family, were black. 6. While amalgamation existed among the Ethiopians in the days of Moses to a greater or less extent, they were originally of pure Adamic stock; and that more or less of this stock remained is demonstrated by the fact that the marriage of Moses with an Ethiopian woman received the sanction of God. Further evidence that they were never negroes, but were originally pure whites who were finally absorbed by amalgamation, is found in the fact that nearly nine hundred years after the time of Moses we find them described as a "mingled people," and included among the nations of that class that were destroyed by Divine edict. (See Ezek. xxx, 5.)

The following language of Jeremiah has been seized upon as evidence that the Ethiopians were black: "Can the Ethiopian change his skin or the leopard his spots?" But this certainly is an arbitrary proceeding. There is absolutely nothing in this text that would enable us to determine the complexion of the Ethiopian in the days of Jeremiah. A moment's reflection should convince us that it would be just as impossible for the pure-blooded White to change his "skin" (complexion) as it would for the pure-blooded Negro to change his. The same is true of the so-

called brown, red or yellow races of men. Crossing—
the introduction of different blood, either white or
black, or that of a mixed-blood in which the white and
the black blood exists in different proportions—alone
can change the complexion of a tribe or nation.
The ancients owned negroes and with their labor developed the splendid civilizations, the remains of
which, though often in ruins, are found on every continent of the earth. Having grown rich and powerful, they forgot God, descended to amalgamation and
were destroyed by Divine edict, and their civilizations
laid in ruins, as in the case of the Babylonians,
Assyrians, Ethiopians, etc., or they were absorbed by
amalgamation and their civilizations descended to
their mixed-blooded progeny, as in the case of the
Mexicans, Chinese, Turks, etc. When amalgamation
absorbs the whites and negroes of a nation, the physical and mental characters of the White are blended
with those of the Negro in different proportions among
their mixed-blooded progeny. Hence, as in the case
of our mixed-bloods, they present every shade of complexion. But, through their marriages among themselves, continued for many centuries, the proportion
of white and black blood in the tribe or nation becomes
equally distributed to every member of it. When this
occurs, their physical and mental characters become
fixed. These fixed characters are then transmitted to
their offspring, through the influence of the law of
heredity. Their progeny would then be nearly white

as the Mandans, or black as the Kaws, or red or yellow
as were many of the Indian tribes. We see the influence of the law of heredity in fixing characters
demonstrated in the different breeds of our domestic
fowls, cattle, etc. And, as in the case of the latter,
crossing will at once break up these fixed characters.
Hence, though the Ethiopians were originally pure
whites, they were finally absorbed by amalgamation
and their descendants were mixed-bloods. But it
would be impossible to ascertain what their complexion was in the days of Jeremiah, who lived eight
hundred years after Moses. They may have been
relatively light or they may have been relatively dark,
dependent upon whether the blood of the White or
that of the Negro predominated in them; or they may
have been some shade of brown, red or yellow. Be
this as it may, we may confidently assert on the
authority of the Bible that the Ethiopians in the days
of Jeremiah were neither pure whites nor negroes;
they were mixed-bloods.

Not only our religious and political, but our social
and charitable organizations are steeped in negroism.
We have our negro Free Masons, Odd Fellows, etc.

The Woman's Christian Temperance Union embraces the flower of American and European womanhood. The brightest intellects, the highest culture,
and the most spotless purity of that lovely sex adorn
its ranks. Its lofty aims, the protection of the home
and the advancement of personal purity, harmonize

with the inspired teachings of that highest of all authorities—the Bible. The personal purity, which they so eloquently advocate on the rostrum and through the press, and in every relation of life, is most beautifully, forcibly expressed in their own unimpeachable integrity. But alas! alas! The demoralizing influence of the atheism which envelopes the age in which we live, has drawn this matchless organization into the contaminating stream of social, political and religious equality with the negro and mixed-bloods, and, if adhered to, must ultimately discharge its precious burthen of Adamic intellect, refinement, virtue and beauty, into the loathsome cesspool of amalgamation. Negroes and mixed-bloods are not only admitted to membership in the W. C. T. U. but they are frequently assigned to posts of honor. A notable instance of this, occurred at the Twenty-fourth Annual Convention of the National W. C. T. U. held at Buffalo, New York, in October, 1897. On this occasion the mixed-blooded wife of the mixed-blooded orator, Booker T. Washington, received at the hands of this convention the banner, "on behalf of both the white and colored girls" of Alabama. (See the Union Signal, Nov. 18, 1897.) Never, in all the vicissitudes through which this great commonwealth has passed was she so degraded, as when this base born product of God's violated law was selected to receive the banner "on behalf" of the white girls of Alabama.

The White Ribboners have been themselves taught, and they teach others that, intemperance is the great crime of the age. This is a sad mistake. Amalgamation is the crime of the age. Intemperance, with all the crimes which grow out of it—and their name is legion—shrinks into utter insignificance compared to this all enveloping, all-absorbing, all-destroying crime—amalgamation. Intemperance (and we mean by this the drink habit), affects but a comparatively small percentage of the men, women and children of the earth. Amalgamation either directly or indirectly, affects every man, woman and child on the globe. Intemperance corrupts the morals of the individual or the home. Amalgamation corrupts the flesh of the nation or the continent. Intemperance renders the individual temporarily a savage. Amalgamation renders its ultimate offspring permanent savages. Intemperance destroys the social, financial, political and religious standing of the individual and his family, lays his home in ruins, and consigns those who are dependent upon him to penury and want. Amalgamation destroys the standing of the nation or continent in the eyes of God, lays its civilization in ruins, and transforms its population into barbarians, idolaters and savages. The destructive results of amalgamation are written on the face of every continent of the earth. While advocating personal purity in the individual and the home, the W. C. T. U., by admitting negros and mixed-bloods to membership in their organization on terms of social, political and religious equality, are pursuing in violation of God's law, a course which leads directly to amalgamàtion, and to the further corruption of the flesh of the nation, and of the world at large. In view of these facts, sustained by scriptural and scientific research, would it not be well for the men and women of this order to call a halt?

The great woman who graces the presidency of World's Woman's Christian Temperence Union, and her Adàmic followers, should pause and give this all-important subject their most careful consideration. They should investigate it in the great lights of Revelation and the Sciences. A moment's reflection should convince them that what they desire to first know is not what the Savior did when He came on the earth but what the ancients did, which so demoralized, degraded and damned man and removed him so far from his God as to necessitate the sacrifice of the Son of God to redeem him. In the absence of this essential knowledge, is it surprising that they should go blindly on in the wicked course which the ancients pursued, to reach the frightful doom which God in His wrath and disgust meted out to them? Like causes produce like results. If they wish to know what the Savior said and did when He came on the earth, let them study the New Testament. If they wish to know what the Savior desired to accomplish— what His mission was—what demoralizing, degrading, damning sin He came to purge the earth of, let them obey His command: "Search the scriptures. * * *. They are they which testify of me." (John, v, 39.)

The only scripture which existed in our Savior's time was the Old Testament. Hence, it was to this which He referred. The New Testament was not compiled for centuries after the death of the Savior. If they wish to know what the Savior did, the New Scripture will enlighten them. If they desire to familiarize themselves with the causes which led to His coming let them "search" the "Old Scripture;" "they are they which testify" of Him. They should familiarize themselves with God's plan of Creation. This will enable them to distinguish man from the ape. They should then respect the broad distinction which God made in the Creation between man and the ape, and take' cognizance of the destruction which He visited upon the corrupted flesh or the mingled people, as the mixed-bloods are termed in scripture. They should also familiarize themselves with the teachings of atheism, as set forth by the advocates of The Theory of Natural Development. They should compare the degrading teachings of this atheistic theory with the elevating teachings of the school of Divine Creation.

The men and women of the W. C. T. U. should vigorously apply the pruning knife to their organization until it is shorn of its membership of Negroes and mixed-bloods. These parasites sap its strength, degrade it in the eyes of heaven, bring it in conflict with Divine law, turn its noble efforts in behalf of personal and home purity into weapons with which to assail God's plan of Creation by further corrupting the flesh of the nation and

[21]

the world at large. They should make the white ribbon the emblem, not only of personal and home purity but of Adamic purity—the purity of Adamic flesh. This purifying process will harmonize their efforts with Divine law, wfll reconcile them with God; will give them a standing in the high court of heaven and an influence in the home, the · nation and in the world at large that they have never known and can-not otherwise obtain. Then, with their banner proudly unfurled and conscious that while caressed by the zephyrs of earth it merits the approving smiles of heaven, this noble band, with decimated ranks, but with strength borrowed from on high, may press gallantly forward, con-fidently relying for the ultimate triumph of their labors, their prayers and their hopes on the promises of Him who has said: ''Ask and ye shall receive * * * And no good thing will He withhold from those who walk uprightly.''

Throughout the government departments at Wash-ington, mixed-bloods, the so-called ''Negroes,'' occupy positions in which they are paid handsome salaries, upon which they are enabled to live sumptuously and array themselves in ''purple and fine linen,'' while in many in-stances throughout the land the wives, daughters and sons of the men who, during the late war, suffered the privations of the camp, endured the fatigues of the march and braved the dangers of the battlefield, in defense of the Union, are toiling all the day long and often far into the night for a bare subsistence. Throughout the south·

ern states the government offices are filled with these base-born products of God's violated law, to the exclusion of those who bear His likeness and image. The labor of the white working-man with and without trades, is forced to compete with that of these mixed-blooded apes at starvation prices. Even in the South, a certain class of degraded merchants, actuated by the most sordid motives, are employing "Negro clerks" in their places of business. In the South, the great bulk of the taxes levied for educational purposes are paid by the Whites; the mixed-bloods pay but a small percentage. Yet they have the same educational advantages as the Whites, and in many sections, owing to their small numbers, the Whites have no public schools. Since they have not yet become so negroized as to send their children to the "colored schools" they must either employ a tutor for them or allow them to grow up in ignorance. In the rural districts of Mississippi (and we suppose that like conditions prevail in the other southern states where both White and "colored schools" are supported by the state), the White children get only four months' schooling in the year instead of eight months, which their parents are taxed to pay for, in order that these mixed-blooded apes shall have four months' schooling. What opportunity for acquiring an education have these little White children who are allowed only four out of eight months' schooling for which their parents, relatives and friends have paid? These unfortunate little victims of the misguided philanthrophy, which has grown out of the atheism of the age, will grow up practically ignorant and with little or no appreciation of the advantages of education. Thus, in this, as in every other respect, the sins of the fathers are visited upon the children. These failures to educate the successive generations of the Whites of the South, are so many steps towards barbarism. Instead of each generation being better educated, more prosperous, more refined and more virtuous and happy, they will become more ignoran,t more poverty-stricken, more degraded and more debauched and miserable.

Long after the criminal effort to educate, elevate and Christianize the Negro by social, political and religious equality with him has destroyed the Negro by amalgamation, the demand for the "higher education of the Negro" is increasing. In response to this demand, everything is being done to advance the interest of his mixed-blooded descendants to the utter neglect of the poorer class of whites in our country and throughout the world. This vain, criminal effort to elevate the Negro and mixed-bloods to the lofty plane of man and womanhood, in contempt of God's Plan of Creation and in violation of His law is what its modern advocates term an experiment. Experiment, indeed! This so-called experiment is very nearly as old as man. Its destructive results are demonstrated by continents shattered and torn from their foundations and hurled beneath the waves, under the curse of God; nations blotted from the face of the earth; civilizations laid in ruins; vast areas, once teeming with an intelligent, industrious, happy and prosperous population, transformed into barren wastes or made the abode of the barbarian or the savage. Aside from its criminality, the folly of this attempt is easily seen, when we pause to consider the inferiority of the material upon which it is proposed to make the experiment. Mr. Haeckel, in discussing this question, says:

"Nothing, however, is perhaps more remarkable * * * than that some of the wildest tribes in Southern Asia and Eastern Africa have no trace whatever of the first foundations of all human civilization, of family life and marriage. They live together in herds and their whole mode of life shows much more resemblance to that of wild hordes of apes than to any civilized human community. All attempts to introduce civilization among these, and many of the other tribes of the lowest human species, have hitherto been of no avail; it is impossible to implant human culture where the requisite soil, namely, the perfecting of the brain, is wanting. Not one of these tribes has ever been ennobled by civilization; it rather accelerates their extinction. * * * Even many Christian missionaries who, after long years of fruitless endeavors to civilize these lowest races have abandoned the attempt, express the same harsh judgment, and maintain that it would be easier to train the most intelligent domestic animals to a moral nd c ril-

ized life than these unreasoning, brute-like men. For
instance, the able Austrian missionary, Morlang, who
tried for many years, without the slightest success, to
civilize the ape-like negro tribes on the Upper Nile,
expressly says, 'that any mission to such savages is
absolutely useless. They stand far below unreasoning
animals; the latter at least show signs of affection
toward those who are kind toward them, whereas
these brutal natives are utterly incapable of any feeling of gratitude.' Now, it clearly follows, from these
and other testimony, that the mental differences between the lowest men and the animals are less than
those between the lowest and the highest men."
(*The Hist. of Creation*, pp. 490, 493.)

The great American scientist, Dr. Winchell, while
disclaiming any "special occasion for unfriendliness
to the Negro," says:

"It would be proper to raise the question whether
the negro is capable of appreciating, desiring and
conserving the benefits of civilization. The inertia
of the negro in a state of servitude, his scarcely
improved condition and certain diminution in numbers
since enfranchisement in the United States, his
political and social career in Hayti, his massacre of
the agents and destruction of the agencies of civilization in St. Thomas, his helplessly subordinate station
in the northern States of our Union and in Canada,
his indifference to the benefits of civilization in
Liberia, the persistent vitality of the voudoism

among American negroes, in the close environment of a high civilization, and the negro's facile relapses, as in the Congo nation, into a state of abject barbarism, as soon as the props of foreign aid are removed, constitute a set of facts for grave reflection. If he is constitutionally incapable of availing himself of Caucasian civilization, how many lives shall we sacrifice, and how many millions shall we lavish in attempts to foist it upon him? * * * The world would be better if he were an efficient factor in enlightened humanity. The country would be better if he were an elevating and progressive influence instead of a depressing and barbarizing one. * * * I am not responsible for the inferiority which I discover existing. * * * I am responsible if I ignore the facts and their teaching, and act toward the negro as if he were capable of all the responsibilities of the white race. I am responsible if I grant him privileges which can only pervert to his detriment and mind, or impose upon him the duties which he is incompetent to perform or even to understand." (*Preadamites*, pp. 265, 66.)

Mr. M'Causland says: "The stagnant condition of the West Indian colonies since the emancipation of the negro and the commercial descent of Hayti since it became an independent negro State, evidence the tendency of that race not merely to suspend progress, but also to relapse into the barbarous habits of apathy and idolence." (*Adam and the Adamite*, pp. 73, 74.)

Thc two most powerful agencies to enlighten and
elevate a people or to demoralize and degrade them,
are the Church and the Press. At the present time
each of these is turned against God and His law.
When we trace to its fountain source this stream of
negro corruption which permeates every portion of
our country and the world at large, it leads us to the
Church, not merely to the vestibule, but to the pulpit.
One of the most demoralizing, degrading institutions
which our present degenerate religious system has
developed, and one which accomplishes more perhaps
than any other to degrade man to social, political and
religious equality with the negro and mixed-bloods and
to amalgamation is the Foreign Missionary Society.
This wretched organization with the sanction
and aid of the clergy, deceives our people into
contributing hundreds of thousands of dollars
annually to "carry the Gospel" to the negroes
and to the mixed-bloods of this and other continents in shameless violation of God's law. Every
means which human ingenuity can suggest is
employed to raise money for this iniquitous purpose.
The most recent device is the annuity plan. Under
this "plan" any individual may deposit with the Board
of Foreign Missions an amount of money upon which
the Board pays them during life a certain amount
of interest. At the death of the depositor the amount
goes to the missionary fund. Many a deluded man
and woman becomes the victim of this iniquitous

scheme.   Even the little innocents are not allowed to escape, of whom our Savior said: "Suffer little children to come unto me and forbid them not, for of such is the kingdom of heaven" These have what is known as "children's days." "Children's day" is a Sabbath set apart in the spring of the year, when flowers are abundant.   Systematically trained all the preceding year to walk in forbidden paths which lead to ruin in time and eternity, God's holy Sabbath is debased, and his beautiful flowers degraded, as the Church gathers the little children into the various Sunday. schools and Churches, to receive from them their contributions to the missionary fund to be used in carrying the Bible and the gospel to the negroes and mixed breeds in violation of that Divine law: "Give not that which is holy unto dogs, neither cast ye your pearls before swine, lest they trample them under their feet, and turn again and rend you."

While immense sums of money are being collected to support foreign missions among the negroes of Africa and the mixed-bloods of that and other continents, the men and women in many villages and in many portions of the rural districts of our country are left practically without the gospel.   It must be plain to any unprejudiced observer that the old adage, "Charity should begin at home" is strictly applicable to this case.   Even if the negroes of Africa and the mixed-bloods of other continents were included in the plan of redemption, this kind of charity, which ignores the needs of its home people, and expresses itself on distant continents so far from covering "a multitude of sins" can never cast the slightest shadow upon the most trivial offense.

From the Southern Presbyterian of Feb. 12th, 1898, we learn that in the previous year (1897), "The total income of British foreign missionary and kindred societies was $8,054,196. In the United States, a total of $4,333,611. And the contributions of Canada, $283,706. Making a grand total of $12,671,513. Thus, by the authority of these so-called Evangelical churches, the people of Europe and America are begged, cajoled and bullied out of more than twelve and a half millions of dollars annually for foreign missions, while in many sections of our country the people for whom the gospel was intended are left without it. And what does it all amount to? It does these miserable products of God's violated law no good and brings down upon us the curses of God. Millions have been wasted in Africa and elsewhere, and many misguided men and women have been killed and eaten by these degraded creatures.

China presents a fair specimen; for centuries the Chinese have been associated with the people of Europe and America, and today they are as treacherous and savage as the Indian. They have recently violated every principle of national honor by assailing the foreign legations and murdering the representatives of friendly powers; they tortured the soldiers who were wounded and captured in battle; such was the fear of outrage at the hands of these wretches that the ladies of the legations prepared to take their own lives rather than fall into the hands of the Chinese. They burned the churches and destroyed millions of dollars' worth of property; they tortured to death the male missionaries and outraged the females. From the St. Louis Republic of Sept. 5th, we quote as follows:

"The associated press representative learns from official sources the facts of the killing of several American women missionaries. At the request of the Mission Board the details were withheld, out of regard to the feelings of the relatives of the murdered women, but other prominent Americans, who have long antagonized the policy of sending women to isolated inland posts, think it important that the facts should be known. The names of the women are withheld by request. Two of these women captured while attempting to leave the station where they were located, were led about the country naked, repeatedly outraged, and finally killed by a method too revolting to be described. Two other American women, were coming to the coast with a party, which a number of Chinamen followed and stoned. The women fell exhausted and were taken by the Chinamen into the presence of the local officials. They were prostrated upon the execution block and a feint was made of beheading them. One of them became hysterical and laughed, and thinking her insane the Chinese escorted her to the coast, because of their superstition regarding the insane. On the journey, however, the woman was repeatedly criminally assaulted by her escorts. The other woman, after being exhibited naked for some days and suffering assault by several men, was tortured to death by the same shameful methods as were practiced in the other cases. Two Swedish missionary women arrived at Shanghai after similar experiences, except that their lives were spared. The foregoing are matters of official record.''

''Give not that which is holy unto the dogs, neither cast ye your pearls before swine, lest they trample them under their feet, and turn again and rend you.''

Bishop Fantosati was taken out of his church at Hu-Nan, "and after torturing him in a horrible manner, decapitated him. . They cut out his liver and heart * * * and actually devoured them." (The St. Louis Republic, August 5th.)

The Chinese inherited their cannibalism from their Negro ancestors. In a letter to a relative, a missionary woman says: ''The strain is awful. * * * If they would cut people's heads off or shoot them down decently it would not be so bad, but to be sliced and pitch-forked and quartered alive is another thing. It is awful now, but when it is over China will be new, will be awake and just think of the joy of working there.'' (*Ibid,* July 27th.) Such a display of fanaticism as this seems incredible!

There was not a soul to save in China when the first misguided missionary went there. Now, the

missionaries have been driven out of the country, and
in many instances they have been outraged and tortured to death. The millions of dollars that have
been spent in erecting schools, churches, etc., have
been destroyed and the civilized world plunged into
war with these worthless monstrosities. But while it
was impossible for us to Christianize these creatures,
we have allowed them to defile our country with their
idols.

The very liberal-minded Christians of this country
should read God's law to Israel on the subject of
idolatry. Taken in connection with the distressing conditions which confront us on every hand, it might
serve to remind us of the fallacy of our attempts to
successfully conduct the affairs of our country without
God or the Bible.

Bloodshed and the other curses which God is shower-
ing upon us, marks this era of enlightened Christianity. With these mixed-bloods rioting at home and
warring with us abroad, it may well be said, "The
earth is filled with violence through them!" A careful
investigation of the history of Israel during their
occupancy of Canaan, will show that when they were
in favor with God they were at peace with the world,
and that when they violated the law of God, war was
one of the many punishments with which He afflicted
them. And what is our condition to-day? While
industriously carrying our superabundance of piety
to other lands we have two wars on our hands at one

time.   We present all the evidences of a people laboring under the curses of God.   Corruption in high
places and in low places, marks this reign of atheism,
negroism and the train of demoralizing, degrading,
damning isms that follow in its wake.   In our legislative .bodies, city, county, State and national, the
dearest rights and the most valuable franchises of the
people are bartered away by designing politicians
whom the corrupt condition of affairs have placed in
power.   In our legislatures, supposed to be composed
of the brain, the culture, the integrity of the land,.
American senatorships are sold to the highest bidder
for cash.   And even the American presidency has
become an article of trade.

We should remember that there was a time in the
history of the Egypt when God looked down upon
Egypt and said: "I will teach Pharoah to know that
I am the Lord!"   And that there was a time in the
history of the Israelites when God looked out upon
the twelve tribes and said, "Ephraham is joined to
his idol, let him alone!"   And a glance at our surroundings should convince us that God has long since
said of us: "I will teach the Americans to know that
I am the Lord!"   But the frequent protests which we
hear against the disgusting negroism of the Press,
the State and the Church, should be accepted as so
many happy assurances that God has not yet said of
us, The Americans are joined to their idol, let them
alone.   We are still on fighting ground, we may yet

realize the sweet experience of Israel's poet king: "I was young, but now I am old, yet have I not seen the righteous forsaken, nor his seed begging bread." This inspiring declaration of the aged psalmist, should touch a responsive chord in every parental heart, it should prompt us to call a halt in our reckless careers of folly and of crime, and in our mad struggles for the possession of this world's goods, and should enable us to realize that the richest, most enduring legacy a parent may bequeath his child is the heritage of a righteous life.

NATURAL RESULTS.

The screams of the ravished daughters of the "Sunny South" have placed the Negro in the lowest rank of the Beast Kingdom.

Chapter X.

The Bible and Divine Revelation, as well as Reason, all Teach that the Negro is not Human.

In A. D. 1867, there appeared in the United States a work entitled, "The Negro, What is His Ethnological Status?" By the Rev. B. H. Payne, who wrote under the nom de plume of "Ariel." He asserted that the negro is "not the son of Ham," that he was "not a descendant of Adam and Eve," that he is simply "a beast," and that he has "no soul."

The work produced a marked sensation, especially in "Church circles," and as might have been expected, it subjected its able author to the unmerited abuse of the negroized clergy of the day. Bereft of all argument (a something which these reverened gentlemen seldom condescend to imply in meeting an opponent), they assailed "Ariel" with their favorite, and in this case their only weapons—ridicule and denunciation. And nothing could more clearly demonstrate the correctness of his views, than the fact that in every case the clergy, in their frantic efforts to shield their "brother in black," were compelled to abandon all scriptural ground, and conduct their defense from the atheistic theory that the "negro is a lower race of the human species."

Acting upon a suggestion from our father, we never read "Ariel" until our own views were thought out and reduced to writing, lest we be mislead into accepting any mistakes which "Ariel" might have made.

History will yet accord to "Ariel" the proud distinction of being the first man of modern times to openly and fearlessly declare the negro "a beast," and support his declaration with scriptural proof. And while refraining from any criticism of his book and disclaiming any desire to pluck a single leaflet from the laurels that adorn his brow—laurels that will grow brighter as "the years roll on"—we feel assured that a careful comparison of our respective works will show that while agreeing with him in his conclusions as above set forth, we differ with him on many points in his line of argument. Sufficient for us is the honor of being "A worker for the Lord" and humanity in that great cause, which, sooner or later will culminate in the expulsion of the negro from his present unnatural position in the family of man, and the resumption of his proper place among the apes.

Prominent among the assailants of "Ariel" was the Rev. Robert T. Young, of Nashville, Tenn., who published a pamphlet entitled, "The Negro," a reply to "Ariel." Like every other effort of the kind, Dr.

Young's pamphlet was anything else but "a reply to Ariel." As a matter of fact no "reply to Ariel" can be made on Bible grounds. About all that Dr. Young's "reply to Ariel" proved was that it emanated from a little narrow-minded bigot, who was as ignorant of the teachings of scripture, or of science, or of atheism, in their purity, as a Hottentot, and that he was utterly incapable of distinguishing between the teachings of scripture and those of atheism, is shown by the fact that throughout his "reply" he confuses the teachings peculiar to scripture with those peculiar to atheism. He tells us that the Negro is a man and belongs in the "class" with the fish and beasts, and that he belongs in the "order" with the apes and has "an immortal soul" and may be "converted to Christianity." He accepts the atheist's division of the human species of ape into five races of men, of which the Negro is one of the "varieties." But what specific offense these highly-developed but wicked and fallen apes committed, which so demoralized and degraded them and removed them so far from God—their father—as to necessitate the sacrifice of the Savior to redeem them, seems to have never occurred to Dr. Young to inquire.

After arraigning "Ariel" on the charge of ignorance and advising him "never to write another paper," Dr. Young proceeds to give us some valuable (?) information as to his descent from two European stocks, and the geographical location of his ancestors in the United States, together with the assurance that the Negro is akin to both the Whites and animals, as follows:

"We are from English and German stock. No ancestor of ours ever lived north of Mason and Dixon's line. We have no relative on that part of the planet. We do not believe in the social equality of the Negro.

We do not believe he knows how to handle a vote. * * * Still we believe that the Negro is a descendant of Adam and Eve; that he is the progeny of Ham; that he is a human being and has an immortal soul."

Dr. Young's reference to Adam and Eve and Ham and the "soul" would naturally lead one to suppose that he believed in the Narrative of Creation and also in the Narrative of the Deluge. But how is this? After declaring the Negro to be the progeny of Ham, a descendant of Adam, and consequently a man with "an immortal soul," he says:

"The Negro belongs to the class—Mamalia; to the order—Bimana; to the genus—Homo; to the species—Man. He is one of the varieties." (The Negro, pp. 4, 5.)

Dr. Young might have informed us as to which of the two schools of learning, Divine Creation or Natural Development, he obtained this idea, but he did not. He might also have explained what these classes, orders, etc., embrace, but he did not, and the most charitable view to take of the matter is, that he never knew. One of the duties of an author is to make himself understood; if he knows anything he should convey to his readers, in plain language, such knowledge as he desires to impart. Since Dr. Young has seen fit not to do so, we feel it a duty that we owe our readers to take up his statement as above quoted in the mystifying condition in which he was pleased to leave it and finish the job for him.

We fail to discover in the scriptures the slightest reference to such things as "the class—Mammalia;" "the order—Bimana;" "the genus—Homo;" "the species—Man," or "the varieties" of men. And inasmuch as these things are unknown to the scriptural school, we have no alternative than to seek their origin and an explanation of their meaning in the school of atheism, and here we find them an inseparable part of the theory of Evolution which teaches, in direct opposition to the scriptures, that man, that most complex organism, is merely a development from the most simple. (See Haeckel's "History of Creation;" also his "Evolution of Man.")

As has been shown, the Bible teaches that there are four different "kinds of flesh," that "there is one kind of flesh of man, another flesh of beast, another of fishes and another of birds." In disregard of this scriptural teaching, the atheist takes these four "kinds of flesh," and masses them into what he is pleased to term, "The Zoological System." He then divides, and sub-divides this Zoological System into Classes, Orders, Genera, Species, Races, Sub-races and Varieties. Having declared man to be a mere animal, he insists that man must take his position in the "Zoological System" with the rest of the animals, that man belongs to the class—Mammalia (Haeckel) to the order Bimana (Linnæus), that he belongs to the species—Man, etc. (Atheism and Enlightened Christianity.)

Having traced Dr. Young's statement as above quoted, to the school of atheism, in which it originated, let us dissect and analyze it in the light which atheism alone can throw upon it, with the view of ascertaining its full import.

After informing us that "the negro is a descendant of Adam and Eve, that he is the progeny of Ham, that he is a human being, and consequently a man," Dr. Young says: "The negro" (and of course all the other "varieties" of men) "belongs to the class—Mammalia." What does the class of Mammalia embrace? All creatures that suckle their young, it not only embraces man, but also the apes and quadrupeds of the land animals, and the whale family of the fish. (See Haeckel's History of Creation, pp. 344, 345.) Thus placing representatives of three different kinds of flesh in one 'class.' If man is a mere animal and must take his position in the Zoological System with the rest of the animals, what goes with the Narrative of Creation, which teaches that man is a Creation 'in the image of God,' and that the animals were all made after their kind?" If the flesh of man is to be massed with the flesh of beasts and that of fishes and birds in one universal Zoological System, what goes with the teaching of Paul that "All flesh is not the same flesh, but there is one kind of flesh of men, another flesh of beasts, another of fishes and another of birds?"

Dr. Young says: "The Negro" (and of course all the other "varieties" of men) "belongs to the order—Bimana." What does "the order—Bimana" embrace? All two-handed creatures; it not only embraces man, but also embraces the whole ape species from the Lemur on up to and including the negro. Thus placing representatives of two different kinds of flesh in one "order." If it be true as Dr. Young teaches that man "belongs" in the same "order" with the apes, what goes with the Mosaic Record which teaches that man was created "in the image of God," and that the apes or "beasts" were made after their kind—the ape or "beast" kind? If the flesh of man and the flesh of the apes or "beasts" "belongs" in one "order" what goes with the teaching of Paul that, the flesh of men, is a different kind of flesh from that of beasts or apes?

Dr. Young says: "The Negro" (and of course all the other "varieties" of men), "belong to the genus—Homo." What does "the genus—Homo" embrace? It not only embraces all of the so-called "races" of speaking men, but also embraces "primeval man (Protanthropus—Homo primigenius.")

. In a previous chapter we have given Mr. Haeckel's description of this much-talked of gentleman, not the least vestige of whom has ever been found. But since Dr. Young assures us that he belongs in our genera, it should be interesting to learn something of his origin, etc.

Mr. Haeckel says: "These ape-like men, or Pithe-canthropi, very probably existed toward the end of the tertiary period. They originated out of man-like apes, or anthropoids, by becoming completely habituated to

an upright walk, and by the corresponding stronger differentiation of both pairs of legs. The fore hand of the
anthropoids became the human hand; their hinder hand
became a foot for walking. * * * 'This differentiation of the fore and hinder extremities was, however,
not merely most advantageous for their own development
and perfecting, but it was followed at the same time by a
whole series of very important changes in other parts of
the body. The whole vertebral column, and more especially the chest, the girdle of the pelvis and shoulders, as
also the muscles belonging to them, thereby experienced
those changes which distinguish the human body from
that of the most man-like apes. These transmutations
were probably accomplished long before the origin of
articulate speech, and the human race thus existed for long
time with an upright walk and the characteristic human
body connected with it, before the actual development of human language, which would have completed
the second and the more important part of human development.' * * * 'The origin of articulate language
and the higher differentiation and perfecting of the larynx
connected with it, must be looked upon as a later and the
most important stage in the process of the development
of man. It was, doubtless, this process which above
all others helped to create the deep chasm between man

and animals and which also caused the most important progress in the mental activity and the perfecting of the brain connected with it." (*Ibid*, vol. ii, pp. 398, 406, 408.)

Thus, according to this atheism which Dr. Young is compelled to accept and teach in his attempt to prove the Negro a man and defend him from "Ariel's" charge that he is a "beast," man (the White), the so-called "Caucasian race," or "Mediterranean man" (Homo Mediterraneus), traces his line of descent back through the "Mongol" (Homo Mongolus), and through the Mongol to the "American Indian" (Homo Americanus), and through the Indian to the "Malay" (Homo Malayus), and through the Malay to the "Negro" (Homo Niger), and through the Negro to "Primæval man (Homo primigenius). These and their "varieties" constitute "the genus—Homo." But, from Homo-primigenius on up to and including Homo Mediterraneus, they are all apes in different stages of "development." Through his various "differentiations" and "transmutations," aided by "natural selection and the survival of the fittest," the genus—Homo, has "progressively developed" and "far outstripped his animal ancestors." (Haeckel.)

If man is a mere animal, and must take his position in the zoological system with the rest of the animals, and if, as Dr. Young asserts, man "belongs to the class—Mammalia; to the order—Bimana; to the genus—Homo," etc., and traces his ancestry to a "speechless" ape, the Old Testament teaching that man was created in the "image of God," and that the animals were made after their kind, is disproven and should be repudiated. And if the Mosaic Record which Moses wrote was false, we could not with propriety accept anything else that he wrote as true. Hence, consistency would require that all the writings of Moses be repudiated. These include not only the Narrative of Creation, but those of the Fall and the Deluge, the raising up of the Israelites as God's "chosen people" and their history up to the time of their entry into Canaan; the laws which God gave them for their government, together with the establishment of the Jewish Church, and the observance of the Sabbath. With these all disproven and repudiated, the Old Testament would be practically destroyed. Besides, all the Old Testament writers accepted and endorsed the writings of Moses. Hence, consistency would require that their writings should also be repudiated. We would then have no Old Testament at all.

We have traced the Theory of Development to the sacred registers of ancient Egypt, and have shown that it was taught in the centuries preceding the coming of Christ. This theory which assumes that man "developed out of fish-like ancestors," themselves the result of "spontaneous generation" necessarily assumes that "all flesh" is akin. Hence, the flesh of man may with propriety be massed in one universal zoological system, which is divisible into Classes, Orders, Genera, Species, Races, Sub-races and Varieties.

As has been shown it was in his battle with this demoralizing theory, which degrades man to the level of the brute, that Paul gave utterance to that sublime declaration: "All flesh is not the same flesh; but there is one kind of flesh of men, another flesh of beasts, another of fishes and another of birds." "Hence there is no kinship, no "blood relationship" as Haeckel would have us believe, between man and the animals. This being true it follows that the flesh of man can not be massed in a zoological system with that of the beasts, the fishes and the birds. There is no "class—Mammalia," in which the flesh of man "belongs" with that of the apes, quadrupeds and whales. There is no "order—Bimana" in which the flesh of man "belongs" with that of the apes. There is no "genus—Homo," embracing Homo Mediterraneus Homo Mongolus," "Homo Indian," "Homo Malayus"

"Homo Niger," and "Homo primigenius." Man was created in the "image of God," and does not trace his line of descent back through a series of animal ancestors to the lowest form of animal life," the form value of which "was not even equal to that of a cell, but merely that of a cytod" itself the result of "spontaneous generation."

If the teaching of Paul as above quoted is disproven by the opposing teachings of Prof. Haeckel, Dr. Young and every other atheist and infidel, in the pulpit and out of it, it should be repudiated. And if this teaching of Paul's is false, we cannot accept as true, anything else that he wrote. Hence, consistency demands that all the writings of Paul be repudiated, and inasmuch as the teachings of all the authors of the New Testament are in absolute harmony with those of Paul, consistency demands that their writings should also be repudiated and we would have no New Testament. Hence, with the Old Testament disproven and repudiated, and the New Testament disproven and repudiated, we would have no Bible left, no authority upon which to base our belief in the existence of a God, the rewarder of the good and the punisher of the wicked, no authority upon which to base our belief in a Creation with God as its Creator, nothing upon which to base a religious system or the observance of the Sabbath.

In the destruction of the Bible—God's revealed will to man—the last ray of Divine inspiration is extinguished, and the world enveloped in the gloom and darkness and hopelessness of atheism, and the dream of the atheist is realized in the existence of a universe without a God, a Creation without a Creator, man without Religion and the world without a Sabbath or a Bible.

In view of all that our ancestors and our ancient kinsmen upon the various continents have suffered under the judgments of God for their criminal relations with the negro, and in view of all that we are suffering to-day under the curses of God for our criminal relations with the negro and his amalgamated progeny, is not this additional sacrifice of the Bible, with all its elevating, ennobling soul-inspiring teachings, too much for us to endure for the sole privilege of further revelling in the disgusting odor of a "brother in black?"

Had any open, avowed atheist been called upon to write Dr. Young's views as above set forth, he would have pursued precisely the same line of argument used practically the same language and employed identically the same terms. No utterance more unadulterated with the least tinge of scripture ever flowed from the pen of Haeckel, it is atheism pure and simple.

We have contended that Christianity has fled the earth, and the Church of Christ has been absorbed and destroyed by atheism, and nothing could more fully sustain our contention than the very fact that, in a professedly Christian age and in a professedly Cnristian land, the shameless utterances of this Doctor of Divinity has stood unassailed for more than thirty years, to demoralize, negroize, degrade and damn every man and woman whose misfortune it may have been to read and accept it.

Dr. Young says: "The Negro (and of course all the other varieties of men), belongs to the species—man; he is one of the varieties."

In order to disprove this statement of Dr. Young's and disabuse Bible-believing people of the absurd idea that there is such a thing as a "species—man," it is only necessary to ascertain what constitutes a "species."

The French naturalist, M. de Quatrefages, in discussing the relationship between species and races, says: "Species is the unit and the races are the factions of this unit." (The Human Species, p. 40.)

To illustrate: There is a species of animal known as the ape species; this species is composed of a number of races and embraces every ape from the lemur on up to and including the Negro—the genuine Negro. The lemur is one "race" of the ape species; the baboon is another race of the ape species; the gorilla is another race of the ape species; the Negro is another race of the ape species, and so on throughout the series. This enables us to understand that a species must necessarily be composed of a greater or less number of races, and that a race must necessarily be a fractional part of a species. Hence, there can be no species that is not composed of a greater or less number of races; neither can there be a race that is not a fractional part of a species. This being true it follows that a single individual or even two individuals—a male and a female—differing from all other creatures and bearing no relationship to them, is not a species, since races, the combination of which is necessary to the formation of a species, is wanting.

The Bible teaches that the fish and fowl and beast were all made of different kinds of flesh; and that no kinship exists between these different kinds of flesh; and that no kinship exists between them and God; it also teaches that the animals belonging to these different kinds of flesh were all made after their kind. And investigation has shown that the various animals belonging to these different kinds of flesh are divided into families or species, and that these families or species are divisible into races.

The Bible also teaches (1) that man was not made after any kind, but was created in the image of God. (2.) That even the flesh of man is a different kind of flesh from that of the fish, or fowl, or beast. Hence, there is no kinship between man and the animals. (3.) That the Creator combined in man the Matter Creation, the Mind Creation, and the Soul Creation; the latter a part of the substance of God, thus establishing between God and man the close relationship of father and son. Hence, man is a creation, as distinct from the animal in which only the matter and the mind creations are represented, as he is from the plant or the planet in which the matter creation is alone represented. (4.) That the male side or part of the man creation made its appearance on the earth prior to that of the female, and that the Adamic creation remained in this imperfect condition for a considerable period. Surely this lone man, representing only one side or part of his creation and utterly incapable of reproducing his kind, for the want of a female, was not a species, for races, the essential characteristics, were wanting in him. And when God decided to perfect the Adamic Creation by making a "helpmeet" for Adam, he made the female man out of the male man; thus making this primitive pair of "one flesh," with characteristics identical. Surely this one pair of individuals was not a species, since races, the essential characteristics of a species, were wanting in them. Hence, the most positive evidence that God had no desire that there should be "species" and "races of men" is found in the fact that He made no such thing as a "species—man."

That Adam fully realized that he was not an animal but an immortal being, is shown by his explanation as to why he called his wife's name Eve: "Because she was the mother of all living." (Gen. iii, 20.)

This explanation was given prior to the time when Eve conceived by Adam, and when, as a matter of fact, she was not the mother of anybody; yet, paradoxical as it may seem, she was "the mother of all living." From the moment the female animal conceives, its offspring begins to die, in the sense that each moment of its life brings it nearer to the period of its final dissolution. Hence, the female animals whose progeny are mere creatures of time may properly be described as the mothers of all dying. But not so with woman. Adam realized that in the ovary of

Eve there was one side or part of "a living soul," which, when perfected, by being united with its corresponding side or part which existed in him, would produce an immortal being, which, when its physical life was ended would take its flight from the scenes of earth to an endless existence in the realms of eternity. Hence, in contra-distinction to the female animals— the mothers of all dying. Eve, this immortal being, was the mother of all living.

After endorsing Blumenbach's division of the human species into "five races of men"—"the Caucasian, or European; the Mongolian, or Asiatic; the Indian, or American; the Negro, or African, and the Malay," and giving their various complexions, etc., Dr. Young says:

Thus we see the Caucasians are white, the Mongolians are yellow, the Indians are copper-colored, the Malayans are dark-brown and the Negroes black—a pleasing variety of colors. These all belong to the one great family of man, proving that unity in diversity and diversity in unity is the law of Nature." (*Ibid*, p. 8.)

Did it never occur to Dr. Young that if God had wanted a "species—man," composed of different "races of men," and presenting "a pleasing variety of colors," that it is a trifle strange He never made it in the Creation.   To our mind the very fact that God never made a ''species—man,'' is the best evidence that He never wanted anything of the kind.   If additional proof of this was necessary, it could be found in the fact that throughout the scriptures no mention is made of such a thing as a ''species—man.''

Dr. Young says: "It never entered our mind to read 'Ariel's' book until we were requested to answer it. * * * On reading the book carefully a second time, we must confess that we were at a loss for language to express our astonishment at any sane man who would write it or could believe it. Ethnological Status of the Negro, indeed! What does he know of zoology or ethnology, or any branch of natural science? If he had read any work in hybridity it would have saved him many a blunder. He writes along in total ignorance of the fact that a hybrid is organically incapable of propagating his race or his kind." (*Ibid*, p. 11.)

In opposition to the statement of this learned (?) D. D., that "a hybrid is organically incapable of propagating his race or his kind," we present the testimony of those eminent anthropologists, Drs. Topinard and Quatrefages.

Dr. Topinard says: "Between species the crosses are common and fertile * * * as the progeny of the hare and the rabbit, the dog and the wolf, the jackal and the fox, the camel and the dromedary, the alpaca and the llama or vecuna, the horse and the zebra or wild mule, the bison and the European ox, etc. There is, therefore, no reason to suppose that we have been deceived as to the reality of certain species, and that such were only varieties. * * * It is now certain that the limit of species is not an absolute obstacle to fertility, and consequently that its circumscription has nothing decided about it." (*Anthropology*, p. 368.)

Dr. Quatrefages says: Sexual unions in plants, as in animals, can take place between individuals of the same species and the same race; further, between different races of the same species, and finally, between different species. In the two latter cases we have what is called a cross. This crossing itself is differently named according to whether it takes place between different races or different species. In the first case it produces a mongrel, in the second a hybrid. When the cross unions are fertile the product of the union of mongrels is called a mongrel, the product of the union of hybrids a hybrid." (*The Human Species*, p. 63.)

According to the atheists' division of the so-called "Zoological System," animals belonging to different Genera are further removed from each other than are animals belonging to different Species, and again, animals belonging to different Orders are further removed from each other than are animals belonging to different Genera.

Dr. Topinard says: "It is stated that individuals of different Orders have given birth to offspring, as between the bull and the mare, whose progeny or jumarts, inhabited the Atlas mountains and the mountains of Piedmont. It is a bitter, authenticated fact that the phenomena takes place between different Genera. M. de Bouelle, in 1873, described the offspring of the cross between the ibex of the Pyrenees and the domestic goat. The Pehuelhas in the Chillian Alps crossed the latter with the sheep, and obtained a very vigorous breed called chábins (buck-sheep), whose descendants, fertile through an indefinite number of generations, are of considerable commercial value on account of their skins and fleeces, known by the name of Pellons." (*Ibid*, p. 368.)

Thus it is shown that the mere fact that the product resulting from unions between Whites and

Negroes is fertile, is no evidence that they belong to the same Species or that they belong to the same Genera, or even to the same Order, while the Bible plainly teaches that the product resulting from unions between different kinds of flesh—that of man and beast—is indefinitely fertile, as in the case of Cain and his wife who were not of the same flesh.

Dr. Young might have profited by the warning and advice of Pope:

"A little learning is a dangerous thing:
    Drink deep, or taste not the Pierian spring:
    There shallow draughts intoxicate the brain,
    And drinking deeply sobers us again."

Dr. Young gives us his conception of Matter, Mind and Soul as they exist in the Universe as follows:

"The whole world is made up of Mind or Soul and Matter. The term Matter is a name which we apply to a certain combination of properties, or to certain substances which are solid, extended and divisible, and which are known to us only by these properties. The term Mind, in the same manner, is a name which we apply to a certain combination of functions or to a certain power which we feel within us, and is known to us only by these functions. Matter we know only by our senses. Mind or soul only by our consciousness. [Dr. Abercombie.] The profoundest philosophers write concerning the negro's mind as they do concerning that of the white man. The negro has all the intellectual faculties—consciousness, perception, memory, association, imagination, comparison and pure reason. He has all the sensibilities, animal feelings, rational feelings, aesthetic emotions and moral emotions. He has a free will and is governed by motives. He dreams, walks in his sleep and may become insane. [*Ibid.*] His immortality is found in those principles of his nature by which he feels upon his soul the awe of a God, and looks forward to the future with anxiety or with hope, by which he knows to distinguish truth from falsehood, and evil from good, and has forced upon him the conviction that he is a moral and responsible being. This is the power of conscience—that monitor within which raises its voice in the breast of every man—a witness for his Creator. There is thus in the consciousness of every dark son of Ham, a deep impression of continued existence." [*Ibid*, pp. 28, 29.]

In the above statement we observe that Dr. Young teaches that "the whole world is made up" of "a certain combination of properties," which is termed Matter and "a certain combination of functions," which is termed "Mind or Soul." Dr. Young thus employs the terms Mind and Soul to describe the mental organism, and thus blends and confuses these two Creations, which God made separate and distinct. He thus eliminates the Soul creation, the possession of which distinguishes Man from the animal, makes him akin to God and endows him with immortality.

This teaching of Dr. Young's degrades man to the level of the brute and attributes his superiority over the animal to his more highly developed physical and mental organisms. Hence, the difference between man and the animal is simply one of degree, not of kind. This is the teaching of atheism, as shown by the utterances of Mr. Haeckel as follows:

"With regard to the human 'soul organ,' the brain, the application of the fundamental law of biography has been finally established by the most careful empiric observations. The same may be said of its functions, the 'activity of the soul.' For the development of a function goes hand in hand with the gradual development of every organ. The morphological differentiation of the various parts of the brain corresponds with the physiological separation or 'division of labor.' Hence, what is commonly termed the 'soul' or 'mind' of man [consciousness included] is merely the sum-total of the activities of a large number of nerve-cells, the ganglia-cells, of which the brain is composed. Where the normal arrangement and function of these latter does not exist, it is impossible to conceive of a 'healthy soul.' This idea, which is one of the most important principles of our modern exact physiology, is certainly not compatible with the widespread belief in the 'personal immortality' of man.'" [*History of Creation*, Vol. II, p. 494.]

What a pitiable spectacle Dr. Young and the clergy as a whole and their deluded followers present in thus assailing God's Plan of Creation and tearing from it one of its three Creations, and accepting the teaching of atheism that the mind and soul are identical! It is easy to prove that the animal has a mind, and that in this respect the only différence between man and the animal is one of degree, and if the mind and soul are identical why should not the "mind or soul" of the animal be as immortal as the "mind or soul" of the man? This leaves us no alternative than to base our claims to im-immortality, solely on the superiority of our mind over that of the animal. Based upon a claim quite as flimsy as this, the immortality of man is made to appear absolutely ridiculous, and its utter annihilation as an easy task for the atheist, as shown by the utterances of Mr. Haeckel, who says:

"We know for certain and can demonstrate the fact at any moment under the microscope that the wonderful process of fertilization is nothing more than the commingling of two different cells, the copulation of their kernels. In this process the kernel of the male sperm-cell transmits the individual peculiarities of the father; the kernel of the female egg-cell transmits those of the mother; the inheritance from parents is determined by the commingling of both kernels, and with it likewise begins the existence of the new individual, the child. It is against all reason to suppose that this new individual should have 'an eternal life' without end, when we can minutely determine the finite beginning of its exist-ence by direct observation." (*Ibid*, pp. 494, 495.)

Thus it is easy for the naturalist to prove that the mental organism of man is composed of identically the same elements as that of the animal; that it is brought into existence in the same way and serves the same purpose; that it is alike liable to accident, disease and final dissolution; that it is not immortal. And the scriptures teach nothing to the contrary; on the other hand it teaches that consciousness, one of the attributes of the mind, a character which prominently distinguishes the animal from the plant, made its first appearance in the fish on the "fifth day."

As we have shown, the Mosaic Record teaches that there were three—and only three—Creations; that these are Matter, Mind and Soul. The existence of these three creations was known to the ancients, and the broad distinction between the matter creation as it exists in the physical organism of a man, and the mind creation, as It exists in his mental organism, and his soul creation, is clearly recognized in the Savior's command: "Thou shalt love the Lord, thy God, with all thy heart, and with all thy soul, and with all thy miud." (Mat. xxii, 37.)

The three Creations, Matter, Mind and Soul, as they exist in man, must each express its love for God. Hence, "Thou shalt love the Lord, thy God, with all thy heart (the physical organ), and with all thy soul (the immortal organ), and with all thy mind (the mental organ)."

As has been shown, the followers of the Savior split up into a number of religious sects after His death; and in their factional strifes, which were carried on for generations, the teachings of scripture, and especially those of the Mosaic Record, were lost sight of and forgotten; and the teachings of atheism crept in and have been

handed down to us by the church. We must bear in
mind that though the church people of that remote period
were grossly ignorant and were thoroughly demoralized
by the teachings of atheism, they believed in the immortality of man, as taught by the Bible, in opposition to
the teachings of atheism that man is not an immortal
being. But we must also bear in mind that these people
had been taught that man had developed out of "fish-like
ancestors," and that this is an inseparable part of the
theory of atheism that "the whole world is made up" of
matter and mind. Hence, in their attempts to harmonize
this theory with the scriptural teaching that man is an
immortal being, they were led to believe that mind is the
immortal part of man; hence, that mind is peculiar to
man, and that the animals have mere instinct. And this
is the teaching of the church to-day. This affords the
only rational explanation of how the term "soul," which
the Bible employs to describe the immortal organ in
man, became confused with the term "mind," to describe the mental organ as the "mind or soul." As a
result, when we take up any work or mental science, it
makes no difference whether its author is an open,
avowed atheist or whether he is a professor of theology,
we find the mental organ described as the "mind or
soul."

The characteristics of the Negro, as above described by Dr. Young, clearly demonstrates his possession of mind. Hence, when these ancient religious sects decided that mind was peculiar to man, they were compelled to recognize the Negro as a man—"a lower race of man," and inasmuch as the mind, in their opinion, was the immortal part of man, the Negro's possession of mind was accepted as conclusive evidence that he is an immortal being. Of course the same line of argument applied to the mixed-bloods. Hence, the presence of the Negro and his amalgamated progeny in the family of man, and in the church, is largely due to this anti-scriptural and erroneous theory that mind and soul are identical.

We are constantly compelled to combat this erroneous theory in our discussion of the Negro question; nothing is more common than to hear the defenders of the Negro exclaim: "The Negro has a mind; he reasons, forms ideas and expresses them; he can distinguish between right and wrong, and this proves that he is a man with an immortal soul and may be civilized, enlightened and Christianized!" This is absolutely no evidence at all! Mind is common to all animals; they all reason, form ideas and convey them by certain sounds and signs to their fellows, and they all possess the moral faculty, though in less degree than man or even the Negro, and they can distinguish between right and wrong, otherwise we could not teach them that it is right to obey and wrong to disobey their master. Hence, they would be unfit for domestic purposes.

It is evident that at some period in the remote past some shrewd atheist conceived the design of purloining the scriptural term "soul" and confusing it with the term "mind" to describe the mental organ, in order to render the theory that "the whole world is made up" of matter and mind, more acceptable to those who were inclined to believe the Bible as true, as they understood it. Hence, we find that the modern atheist, like the modern theologian, describes the mental organ as the "mind or soul."

Atheism can furnish no rational explanation of the origin of mind. It simply teaches that, like everything else, it is the result of development. This is absurd! We know (1) that matter preceded mind. Hence, if mind developed out of anything, it must have developed out of matter. Now we know that matter and mind are distinct elements and that the one could not have developed out of the other. (2.) We know that the elements of animal life and those of plant life are identical, and that they exist in the animal and in the plant in the same proportions. Hence, if the elements of life developed mind out of matter in the animal, it is strange that they did not do so in the plant under precisely the same conditions of climate, etc. The whole proposition is at once irrational, unscientific and anti-scriptural.

The modern church, like atheism, can give no explanation of the origin of mind. Ages ago all knowledge of the origin of mind was lost to the world. During all this period, and long before, it has been known that matter was the material out of which all bodies were formed. The belief that the soul of man is immortal dates back to the Creation; it is questionable whether there has ever been a time since the days of Adam that this belief was not entertained to a greater or less extent. But, as we have shown, it was confused with mind a few centuries after the death of Christ, and no very clearly defined idea of it was possible under such conditions. At a remote period in the past, the world lost all knowledge of the fact that the Mosaic Record teaches the existence of three—and only three—distinct Creations. It remained for the author of this work to discover that the Mosaic Record fully explains the origin of mind; that it was one of three distinct creations and made its first appearance in the material universe, in combination with matter as presented in the physical organism of the lowest order of animal, the fish; that this

(24)

combination of matter and mind is common to man and the animals, but that the soul is a Creation distinct from mind; that it made its first appearance in the material universe in combination with matter and with mind in Adam; that it is a part of the substance of God, and forms the relationship of father and son between God and man, as shown by the fact that the Savior traces His line of descent to His most remote ancestor, "Adam, the Son of God."

Thus the long-lost knowledge of the three Creations, Matter, Mind and Soul, are restored to us, and the beautiful unfolding of God's Plan of Creation as set forth in the Mosaic Record, is clearly revealed:

1. Matter, created "in the beginning," the basis of all formation—the material out of which all bodies are formed.

2. Mind, a new element, which made its first appearance in the material universe on the "fifth day," in combination with matter as presented in the physical organism of the fish.

3. Soul, a new element, which made its first appearance in the material universe on the "sixth day," in combination with matter and with mind as presented in the physical and mental organisms of Man.

MAN, AND THE NEGRO.

With this knowledge regained, the Plan of Creation may be fully understood, and the Plan of Redemption so easily comprehended that "the wayfaring men, though fools, may not err therein."

In his attempt to ridicule the argument of "Ariel" that the Negro is a beast, Dr. Young says:

"But suppose 'Ariel's' doctrine be true? What a spectacle does the venerable Church of God present! Instructing young 'beasts' in the Sunday School! Baptizing 'cattle' into the Christian Church! Administering the Lord's supper to a species of 'monkey,' and teaching a 'noble animal' to worship the Lord on the Christian Sabbath, etc., etc." (*Ibid*, p. 28.)

In the above statement Dr. Young furnishes further evidence that his ignorance of the teachings of modern science, is only equaled by his ignorance of the teachings of scripture. It is evident that he has never discovered the broad distinction which the Bible makes between "cattle" and "beasts," consequently he could not be expected to understand that the "cattle" are quadrupeds, and that the "beasts" are bipeds (apes). His whole work shows that in his ignorance of the teachings of atheism and of scripture he is incapable of distinguishing between the two, he don't know a man from a monkey. Hence, he can't distinguish between the

Church of God and a menagerie. He don't seem to realize that the very moment the Church began instructing "young beasts in the Sunday School," it would cease to be the Church of God; he don't seem to realize that the very moment the "Christian Church" began "baptizing cattle" it would cease to be the Church of Christ. And though the Church may administer the "Lord's Supper" to a "species of monkey," the penalty attached to this offense shows that they cannot do it with impunity: "Wherefore whosoever shall eat this bread, and drink this cup of the Lord unworthily shall be guilty of the body and blood of the Lord. But let a man examine himself and so let him eat of that bread and drink of that cup. For he that eateth and drinketh unworthily, eateth and drinketh damnation to himself, not discerning the Lord's body." (I. *Cor.* xi, 27, 28, 29.)

Dr. Young says: "Our Tennessee savant, 'Ariel' says, a white man is a human being, and has a soul, that the negro is a beast and has no soul. Suppose a white man marries a negress—will their daughter have a soul? 'Ariel' says 'No.' Suppose this half-breed marries a white man—will their daughter have a soul? 'Ariel' is in Carlyle's 'center of indifference.' Suppose this quadroon marries another white man—will their son have a soul? Alexander Dumas writes very much like he had a soul. 'Ariel' will be forced into the 'everlasting yea' after awhile." (*Ibid*, p. 14.)

Dr. Young has informed us that "The whole world is made up of mind or soul and matter." This as we have shown is in direct contradiction of the plain teaching of the Mosaic Record, that there were three distinct Creations—Matter, Mind and Soul, and that these are combined in man. Hence they can only be reproduced in the offspring by associating a pure-blooded man with a pure-blooded woman. The mere fact that Alexander Dumas possessed a fine mind, is no evidence that he possessed a soul. His intellectual traits were transmitted to him by his white ancestors, through the influence of the law of heredity. If Dr. Young will examine the genealogical table of Cain's descendants he will find that Cain's progeny by his wife of "strange flesh" possessed mental characters of a high order, yet they were not of pure Adamic flesh and were thrust out of the line of descent from Adam to Jesus Christ.

Dr. Young, who describes the mental organ as the "mind or soul," is a minister, and according to his theory is laboring to save the minds or souls of his congregation. Have these people lost their minds? Are they all crazy?

Well might Dr. Young have voiced the plea of Burns:

"Oh wad some power the giftie gie us,
To see oursels as others see us!
It wad from mony a blunder free us,
And foolish notion."

The manner in which our views upon the important subjects discussed in this book will be received in certain quarters is perhaps indicated by the correspondence which we quote from the Christian Standard (Cincinnati, Ohio), of Feb. 27, 1897. This correspondence appeared in the department of the Standard which is devoted to "Biblical Criticism," and conducted by Dr. J. W. McGarvey, president of the College of the Bible, Lexington, Ky.

A lady in Garden City was very much shocked at our views of the Negro question, etc., and wrote to Dr. McGarvey on the subject. We give the correspondence in full as it appeared in the Standard, as follows:

"A CALL FOR THE FOOL-KILLER.

It is a part of the business of this department of the Standard to notice books of a critical character. We vary our practice this week by announcing one before its publication:

'Garden City, Miss., Feb. 1, 1897.

"Dear Bro. McGarvey:—There is a gentleman in our viliage writing a book (do not know the name), who says he could not conscientiously belong to any church now extant, for we are breaking God's express command. He says the serpent in the Garden was a Negro—beast. That God made only one man to have dominion over all the earth. There is no such thing as 'race.' Says that's why Cain's offering was not accepted. He cites us to Jude. Says the Negro is not a human being, and we are all sinning in trying to convert them. Now please explain what Jude means when he speaks of Cain, and you will oblige an earnest   INQUIRER.' "

"As to the question, 'What Jude means when he speaks of Cain,' I think there is no difficulty. He says of certain bad men that they follow in the way of Cain, which means that they follow in the way of a murderer. But as for the notion that the serpent in the Garden was a Negro, somebody should ask the man who says he was why the descendants of that Negro do not crawl on their bellies and eat dust? It might be well to ask him some other questions also, if he could answer them; but I think it would be no use; for it is quite evident that the fool-killer for the State of Mississippi has been lately neglecting that part of his bailiwick. Send somebody after him.''

Dr. McGarvey's explanation of what Jude means when he speaks of Cain would be highly amusing, if his failure to handle the subject which he is called upon to explain was less pitiable. Dr. McGarvey's position on the Standard is a sufficient guarantee of his ardent love for the Negro. Hence, the contents of this lady's letter at once wounded his feelings and aroused his wrath. Realizing this, we refrain from commenting on his act in denouncing as a fool a man whom he had never met, and of whose mental capacity and literary attainments he was as ignorant as he is of the teachings of scripture. The value of his criticisms of our views in advance of their publication, we shall leave to an intelligent public to determine. However, we might suggest to this very pious (?) ''disciple'' a careful perusal of the latter part of verse 22, Matt. v.; or we might remind him that the intelligence of the world has long since decided that neither ridicule nor denunciation is argument. "But I think it would be no use."

In addition to his book, "Jesus and Jonah," Dr. McGarvey has written various articles on the book of Jonah. In all of these he confines himself to a discussion of the results of Jonah's disobedience in not going

direct to Nineveh as God commanded him; and fails to
give us the least explanation of the nature of the trouble
between God and the people of Nineveh. A moment's
reflection should convince us that this is the main issue;
and had Jonah gone direct to Nineveh as he was commanded to do, the incidents related of his proposed visit
to Tarshish, which Dr. McGarvey delights to discuss,
would never have occurred. Still the question would remain, What was the trouble between God and the Nine-
vites? So long as we remain in ignorance upon this
subject, it follows that we can never understand and
appreciate the meaning of the Savior's utterances concerning the mission of Jonah to the people of Nineveh.
Supposing, of course, that Dr. McGarvey's failure to
enlighten us upon this most important subject was an
oversight, we respectfully call his attention to it in the
hope that he will kindly furnish the desired information.
His repeated failures to do this lead us to call his special
attention to the incidents recorded in the narrative of
Jonah's visit to Nineveh, which are as follows:

"And the word of the Lord came unto Jonah the
second time, saying, Arise, go unto Nineveh, that great
city, and preach unto it the preaching that I bid thee.
So Jonah arose and went unto Nineveh, according to
the word of the Lord. And Jonah began to enter into

the third day's journey, and he cried and said, Yet forty days and Nineveh shall be overthrown. So the people of Nineveh believed God and proclaimed a fast, and put on sackcloth, from the greatest of them even to the least of them. For word came unto the King of Ninevah, and he arose from his throne and he laid his robe from him, and covered him with sackcloth and sat in ashes. And he caused it to be proclaimed and published through Nineveh by the decree of the king and his Nobles, saying, Let neither man nor beast, herd nor flock, taste anything; let them not feed nor drink water. But let man and beast be covered with sackcloth, and cry mightily unto God; yea, let them turn every one from his evil way, and from the violence that is in their hands. Who can tell if God will turn and repent, and turn away from his fierce anger, that we perish not?" (Jonah iii, 1, 2, 3, etc.)

We observe (1) the broad distinction made between the "herds and flocks" (cattle) and the "beast." (2) That Jonah never charged the people of Nineveh with any offense whatever. He simply proclaimed the judgment of God, that "in forty days Nineveh should be overthrown." (3) The King never questioned the authority of Jonah; neither did he doubt the power of God who sent him. (4) The King expressed no surprise at this threatened visitation of God's wrath; made no inquiry as to the cause of the trouble, nor offered any protest against the judgment of God. On the contrary, he fully realized the nature of the trouble, and the justice of God's judgment, by proceeding to rectify the evil. Hence, he issued his edict that all business should be suspended, even to the feeding and watering of the herds and flocks; and that all the energies of "man and beast" should be concentrated in an effort to appease Divine wrath, and thus save the city. (5) The King fully realized that it was the criminal relations existing between the men of Nineveh and their beasts that had brought the city to the verge of destruction under Divine judgment. This is demonstrated by the fact that he laid identically the same penalty upon man and beast. Each was required to observe a fast; each was to be covered with sackcloth; each must "cry mightily unto God," each must "turn from his evil way, and from the violence that is in their hands." Thus, it is shown that the beasts were compelled to do identically the same things which the men of Nineveh did in their efforts to appease the wrath of God, and save the city. "And God saw their works, that they turned from their evil way; and God repented of the evil that he had said he would do unto them; and he did it not." [Jonah iii, 10.]

This act of God's clearly demonstrates that it was the criminal relations existing between the men of Nineveh and their beasts which led him to issue his judgment against the city; but when "man and beast turned from their evil way, and from the violence that was in their hands, God repented of the evil that he had said he would do unto them; and he did it not."

We are thus taught (1) that there were beasts at Nineveh with which the men of Nineveh held such criminal relations as brought that great city to the verge of destruction under the judgment of God. (2) That these beasts, like the men of Nineveh, could understand the nature of the Divine judgment. (3) That these beasts, like the men of Nineveh, understood and appreciated the full import of the King's edict, and obeyed it. [4] That these beasts, like the men of Nineveh, covered themselves with sackcloth as an evidence of their grief for the crime to which they were parties. [5] That these beasts, like the men Nineveh, cried mightily unto God, thus demonstrating their possession of articulate speech. [6] That these beasts like the men of Nineveh, turned "every one from their evil way," and from the violence that was "in their hands." [7] These beasts, like the men of Nineveh, had hands.

It is possible that Dr. McGarvey may consider ours a book of a "critical character." And we shall indulge the hope that in his "notice" of it he will kindly explain what manner of beast this was with which the men of Nineveh held such criminal relations as brought that great city to the verge of destruction under the judgment of God. Tell us, what manner of beast was this which could understand the Divine judgment as proclaimed by Jonah? What manner of beast was this which appreciated the full import of the King's edict and obeyed it? What manner of beast was this which, in obedience to the King's edict, was covered with sackcloth as an evidence of his grief for the crime to which he was a party. What manner of beast was this which cried mightily unto God, and turned every "one from his evil way" and from "the violence that was in their hands?" Tell us, what manner of beast was this with a hand?

Three of the oldest books of the contents of which we have any definite knowledge are the Blble, the Rig Veda of the ancient Aryans, and the Popol Vuh of the ancient Americans. Perhaps Dr. McGarvey will kindly explain the significant fact that the Bible, in two places describes a beast with a hand; that the Rig Veda, in two places, describes a beast with a hand, while the

Popol Vuh describes a period of "great peace" in the remote past, when the Whites and the Blacks were alone represented in the population of the world; no Browns, Reds or Yellows are mentioned, as they certainly would have been had they then existed. Was the death-knell of this period of "great peace" sounded by the first infant cry of the first mulatto whose presence defiled the earth in God's eye, after the deluge? But to return to Nineveh! We observe that when the words of Jonah were brought to the King, he arose from his throne, laid his robe from him, covered him with sackcloth and sat in ashes; and that in obedience to the royal edict, man and beast were covered with sackcloth throughout Nineveh. Did the beast, like the King, lay aside his customary attire and cover himself with sackcloth? Be this as it may, tell us, what manner of beast was this which at Nineveh was dressed like a man and a king?

THE END.

www.ingramcontent.com/pod-product-compliance
Lightning Source LLC
Chambersburg PA
CBHW041926260326
41914CB00009B/1177